HEARTS OF THE MOUNTAIN

HEARTS
OF THE
MOUNTAIN

*Adolescents, a Teacher,
and a Living School*

TAL BIRDSEY

GREEN WRITERS PRESS | *Brattleboro, Vermont*

Printed in the United States

10 9 8 7 6 5 4 3 2 1

Green Writers Press is a Vermont-based publisher whose mission is to spread a message of hope and renewal through the words and images we publish. Throughout we will adhere to our commitment to preserving and protecting the natural resources of the earth. To that end, a percentage of our proceeds will be donated to environmental activist groups and The Southern Poverty Law Foundation. Green Writers Press gratefully acknowledges support from individual donors, friends, and readers to help support the environment and our publishing initiative.

Giving Voice to Writers & Artists Who Will Make the World a Better Place
Green Writers Press | Brattleboro, Vermont
www.greenwriterspress.com

ISBN: 978-1-7328540-1-7

Cover Design by Dede Cummings
COVER PHOTO COURTESY OF NORTH BRANCH SCHOOL
WWW.NORTHBRANCHSCHOOL.ORG

THE PAPER USED IN THIS PUBLICATION IS PRODUCED BY MILLS COMMITTED
TO RESPONSIBLE AND SUSTAINABLE FORESTRY PRACTICES

CONTENTS

Introduction by Deborah Meier ix

Preface xv

FIRST DAYS 1

FALL 71

WINTER 153

SPRING 255

Epilogue 317

Works Cited or Referenced 329

Permissions 333

Acknowledgments 337

For my father

INTRODUCTION

by Deborah Meier

I SOMETIMES THINK I'VE FALLEN DOWN the hole with Alice into a world where all words have changed meaning. Where words don't mean what they say. "Personalized learning" is the latest example in education; it means that one can be schooled without ever having to make contact with any real, live persons. Between the invention of new meanings for old words and the invention of new words, I've given up reading about school reform.

And then Tal sent me the manuscript to this book and I couldn't put it down. Some will complain that the school he writes about isn't a "real" school, but that's exactly what it is—a place where real people meet daily with other real people and tackle real issues in their lives.

At the North Branch School, a group of youngsters of varying ages sit together—or sometimes by themselves—and work on making sense of the world they live in. They do this with each other's assistance, the help of a few interesting adults, and all the resources they can get their hands on inside and outside of the classroom. These lucky children are in that rare place where everything we know about how humans learn always has, and always will be, taken seriously. Imagine: a place created for the purpose of maximizing human learning, designed with that purpose in mind!

We are born theorists—a fact I discovered as a parent and Head Start teacher. Each and every one of us. And out of some innate and never-stopping curiosity, we go to great lengths to make sense of things: the connections between x and y. We do this even when we are asleep (so sleep experts claim). I've been obsessed with our innate passion for theory ever since my own children started school, and I saw it again when I began working as a teacher inside of Chicago public schools.

Tal Birdsey's tale of his life as a teacher is confirmation of how "easy" creating life-long learners might be if we could school ourselves to forget everything we've learned about what schools should be. He even reminds us that learning efficiently requires being loved and respected by the adults who teach us. Our teachers represent our modes of humanness. We are, cats and dogs and humans, apprentices to the more mature members of our species—elders, parents, shamans, teachers. We need settings that take for granted that we will become adults roughly like those older wise ones. In those settings some will learn faster than others, and some with greater enthusiasm. So what?

I began thinking about this in the 60s when people mistakenly were trying to convince me that some children ("those ones," and "them") were failing because they weren't born with capacities to learn quickly. This was said in many schools of education, not to mention the daily media, and has been taken for granted in Western civilization as far back as I can tell. But if that were true, I thought, how could we possibly hope to build the kind of robust democracy that was, we were also told, the "American genius?" In fact: It could not be true.

Teaching without learning, of course, is another absurd idea, but as I used to remind those who criticized our small secondary schools in NYC, what they saw as our inefficient use of time and space produced more successful children in less time, not more. In the district where I previously worked, over half the students never graduated, and even more probably shouldn't have—they weren't well-prepared for the tasks of an adulthood, especially one aspiring to be democratic.

The kind of loving respect that Tal demonstrates for each of his students may seem utopian, but it's "easy." In fact, under the right circumstances, it's hard not to feel and do for our students. Tal shows us what the right circumstances look like.

Can this sort of learning and teaching be scaled up? Of course, many will dismiss this book because the numbers at North Branch are so small. Would it work in a school of a thousand? Probably not. But why would anyone imagine creating schools for hundreds and thousands? The "it-wouldn't-scale-up" critique was made of the schools I started in East Harlem, which helped many people begin to question why we thought it was more efficient to design schools that made it harder for humans to learn.

So thanks, Tal. Thanks for doing what you did, and thanks for writing about it for us. These are the stories about remarkable classrooms and schools that we need in order to restore our appreciation for living things of all sorts, and especially humans. Every last one.

One must remember the quivering thing, the living thing.

—Virginia Woolf, *To the Lighthouse*

PREFACE

IN 2001, in a rural town in the mountains of Vermont, we started a small school. It was for grades seven, eight, and nine.

We had neither money nor expertise. We were one teacher, four parents, and one town citizen. We started with ten students in a rented house with a dirt driveway in the village of Ripton in the Breadloaf Wilderness, a mile from Robert Frost's summer farm.

What few books and materials we had were kept on shelves made from plywood we scavenged from construction sites. Our school had one bathroom, one wood stove, and numerous red squirrels that made frequent appearances during morning algebra class. Our science teacher had never taught science before, our math teacher had never taught math, and I, the head teacher, had never before run a school.

It wasn't much of a school in the beginning. Often we wondered if it would survive.

But the little school in the mountains of Vermont did survive. There is a story in a book about it—the book is called *A Room For Learning: The Making of a School in Vermont*—which recounts how we made the school out of a dream of what a school could be. We believed, contrary to prevailing theory and practice, that if we gave the students responsibility and freedom, they would make a school that was an expression of their most vivid dreams and highest ideals.

We wanted a school that the students felt was theirs, where they could learn from each other, the outside world, and from what they created together. We sought to develop their capacity for love, wonder, and openness—to help them grow to their brightest, biggest, most full versions of themselves, no matter their abilities or backgrounds. We wanted to find the balance teaching the knowledge and skills of the various disciplines, while never losing sight of our primary concern: each student's growth toward becoming an ever more loving, caring, compassionate, courageous person.

The central pedagogy, if there was one, was simply this: the voices, energies, and aspirations of the students would be more than enough to create a vibrant, living school.

Over time, the school grew to twenty-seven students. We wanted to keep it small, intimate, close. A modern-day one-room schoolhouse, all of us learning together as best we could.

We moved out of our rented house and built a new schoolhouse up the road from the Ripton village, near the end of the paved road. The Green Mountains surround the school. A trapezoidal-shaped soccer field stretches towards the woods. A stone wall, overgrown with ferns and blackberry brambles, runs along the length of the field. There is a stone patio, a small herb garden, plantings of perennials, and an iron school bell on a post. Behind the school is a unicursal labyrinth, a bread oven, and a nature trail, all constructed by students over the years.

It is a remote and bucolic setting for learning. The woods are filled with maples and beech trees. When the wind blows, or when rains pound on the metal roof, or when crows call over the field, we hear all of it.

This book is about our little school in the wooded mountains, about school as a place where learning is an experience of high adventure and growing and living is wild and joyful, deep and transformational, where we never know exactly what might transpire on a given day because we create it as we go. A school of mystery and possibility, where old ideas about learning and what school should be are decimated by the colossal tenderness and fierceness of children reckoning with and discovering and reckoning with what matters most; where children come to school thrilled with what is happening to their minds and hearts, each of them learning to believe that something great, something as big as their lives, is reachable.

TAL BIRDSEY
Ripton, Vermont

FIRST DAYS

Don't listen to anything I say.
I must enter the center of the fire.

—RUMI

THE HUGE WOODEN FRONT DOOR HUNG OPEN. Carpools arrived and departed. A handful of parents chatted in the gravel driveway. September sun warmed the dew-soaked soccer field.

Twenty-seven students, our whole school, shambled in, hung their bags in their cubbies, and gathered in the Big Room around a long wooden, oval table. They were nervous and unsure, loud or quiet, talking and joking, looking at the ceiling or wrapping their arms across their chests, fidgeting or sitting stone still. They were enclosed in the shells of themselves, prepared only with new folders, mechanical pencils, and reams of lined paper, every sheet blank.

I stood in the door watching them. Above us, posts and beams, tamarack rafters, and wide sheathing boards of a reclaimed 1850 Vermont farmhouse rose over the classroom. The central beam stretching over our heads had been a sapling during the Revolutionary War and still showed rough bark and the hatch marks of the adze that squared it, wooden pegs shaved to rough points protruding from the posts. Morning light streamed in through a large triangular dormer window. Sky, treetops, and passing clouds were visible as the morning light illuminated cobwebs and dust motes drifting in the open space. Every wall was a high bookshelf packed with thousands of volumes: great novels, paperbacks, atlases, art histories, and philosophical treatises, mostly donated or scavenged from yard sales and dumpsters. High above the shelves, posters on our Wall of Fame: Martin Luther King and Mother Teresa, Jimi Hendrix and Eleanor Roosevelt.

In contradistinction to the typical spare, monochrome, cinderblock school, we wanted every particle of our learning process around us, hanging from the rafters or pinned to the wall, all of it a record of our encounters. Duct tape, plywood, accumulated glue and glitter, maps, dioramas, papier-mâché, string, words we found to speak to each other—the true detritus and blood platelets of a living school.

Every vertical surface was cluttered with newspaper clippings, postcards, quotes, and photographs. There was Rosa Parks gazing at us, the number "4091" hanging around her neck; a post-card of Langston Hughes gazing out, with his smooth, black hair combed back; a rusted gallon maple syrup can on a shelf. Hanging below, a carved wooden mask from Ghana, a gift from a student purchased at the local TJ Maxx. On shelf tops, stacks of papers, a soap sculpture of a mockingbird, Buddhist singing bowls, protractors, drawing pads, a screwdriver, empty coffee mugs, a small box of cut fragments of stained glass, a yogurt container filled with colored pencils, and three small plaster busts: Churchill, Marx, and Socrates, drawing pads, a bird's nest, empty coffee mugs ... A dog-eared poster counseled, "Keep Calm and Carry On." Another poster, Matisse's "Icarus," hung by the whiteboard alongside the work of students—doodles conceived in literature class, scraps of paper, quotes painted onto trash cans, and a photocopy of a poem by Whitman we'd read the year before: *We also ascend dazzling and tremendous as the sun, / We found our own O my soul in the calm and cool of the daybreak.*

I looked ahead to the year before us. I sought the first words I would offer my students; I didn't want to fill the year or their minds with what I knew, or what I thought they should know.

Of course I would start with names. But from there, I wanted to ask big questions, ones that called them out and burrowed in, worked their hearts and beckoned their souls.

My aim was not to deliver something to them—that would be too passive, predictable, controlled. The aim was free creation—a higher domain where students would feel the currents of life, where true conversation and community would be made. The dream was school as a thriving, boundless organism, brimming with the richness of life. After all, shouldn't school be wondrous and alive, a place of infinite possibility? That was the only standard worth aiming for.

I wanted them to fill the school with themselves here, where, as Wallace Stevens wrote, *the voice of one / Meets nakedly another's naked voice.* But to do that, I had to know them. What was the biggest question I could devise to start the conversation? Something of great magnitude announcing our embarkation. A question to shatter, disrupt, inspire, and pry open. Questions to disturb the universe—so how to disturb the universe of children who were tentatively taking their first steps toward adulthood?

As August had given way to September, I had rolled possible questions around in my mind. *Who are you? Why do you breathe? What is your most true desire? Why do you live? What is a good life? What is your holy grail? How do you want or need to grow? What are you doing here? What do you need to do in this, your one wild and precious life?*

I recalled Wislawa Szymborska's poem, "The Century's Decline," the end of which asks:

"How should we live?"
someone asked me in a letter.
I had meant to ask him the same question.
Again, as ever,
as may be seen from above,
the most pressing questions
are naïve ones.

Then, at eight thirty in the morning, as the sun tipped over the tree line and spilled across the field, I had a most naive and pressing question with which to begin. I shelved the Lesson Plan, the Unit, and the Final Exam. I closed the door on Rubrics, Standardized Tests, Evaluative Norms. I forgot about Content, Curriculum, Information. I boxed up Rules, Schedules, Pacing, and Syllabi. I held onto a single thought: the students before me, and who they were, and who they wanted to become.

The exam is the history of mankind, wrote Szymborska. But they could not know mankind until they knew themselves.

I looked at the tightly-packed chairs and all of them looked at me. Katelyn, an eighth grader, glanced rapidly around the room. Her eyes were shining, her hair, still wet from her morning shower, twisted and resting on her shoulder. Nadia, a ninth grader, sat to the right. Her long blond hair was wound into a loose French braid. Three Uniball pens were lined up side by side, exactly parallel to a sketch pad. She sat upright, hands clasped on the pad, looking at me, ready to begin.

I leaned against the doorjamb as they scooted chairs up to the table. The nervous talking quieted. *What's making them shut up? What do they expect to happen?*

The most pressing questions are naïve ones. "Okay, uh . . ." I paused.

I stared down at a Nalgene water bottle and a vase of Queen Anne's lace at the center of the table.

"So . . . what happened to summer? What are you guys doing here?"

They looked at me and no one spoke.

"How come you're all so quiet?"

Nobody answered.

"Pretend like I'm not here. I have to get some things. You can keep chatting."

A few of them picked up feeble threads of small talk. Hannah, a pixie-sized seventh grader, looked around in a state of mild terror. I walked into my office, picked up a collection of

Wislawa Szymborska's poems, and walked back into the room. I stepped through the kids, around the table, and squeezed to my creaking wooden chair.

"Stand up, you guys, " I said. They pushed back from the table and rose, chair-legs clanking as they jumped to move—anything to release tension, to do *something*.

"Everyone open your eyes. Wider. Make them pop out of your heads. Stretch it! Wrinkle your forehead. Make the whites show all around. Wider!"

They faced each other, awakening, smiling and laughing, contorting their faces, eyebrows pushing up their scalps. Brody, who could have passed for a fourth grader, looked as though he was in great pain. Nolan, a tall ninth-grade boy, smiled as his eyebrows stretched towards his scalp.

"Now, keep them open," I said. "Do not close them, not ever, not even for one second. Keep them open so you can see and be alive to *everything*, so everything can come in. You have to keep them open all year long! You can't close them, EVER!" Laughter filled the room. "Okay, sit down. Let's get this show on the road. Who wants to start?"

They looked at me and at each other. No one raised a hand.

"Someone want to go first? Name: first, middle, and last. Who wants to start?"

They still looked around, hands tight in their laps, waiting. When I'd first started teaching, such silence would have paralyzed me. Now I was confident enough to wait. I knew they had worlds inside them. I knew their hearts were as big as the mountains.

At the back wall of the room, up against a bookshelf, sat an eighth-grade boy with his hand half-up, his legs apart. He wore the black-striped jersey of the Italian soccer club Juventus and orange lacrosse shorts. Greasy bangs hung in front of his eyes. He'd come from the Ripton Elementary School across the road. He looked exhausted, nearly defeated, but he was willing to begin.

"What's your name, Callum?"

A few of the students smiled.

"Callum."

"Can you tell us your full name?"

"Callum Thorburn Auerbach." He blushed as he said it.

"Are you blushing because you told us your middle name is Thorburn, or because you're nervous?"

He shrugged.

"You shouldn't ever be embarrassed by that name. It's a beautiful name. Who are you named after?"

"My grandfather." He looked down at the floor. He appeared about to cry and I didn't know why.

"Is Callum Scottish?"

He nodded without looking up.

"Hey, that means maybe you could participate in the Scottish Highland games. You know, where the guys heave huge trees in muddy fields and carry three-hundred-pound rocks while wearing kilts and going commando."

A few of the students giggled. Callum looked up and shrugged again. No smile played across his lips. He had wanted to talk, but now he was closing.

Callum's sister, Nora, had graduated from the North Branch School two years before. Nora no longer lived with him at his father's house. She'd moved in with his mother in Rochester. Callum hadn't seen Nora or his mother for six months. All of this I knew. The facts of his life were inescapable, but to teach him, I had to let him know it was safe for the facts to come out of hiding. To teach him, for him to be alive, I needed him to know he would be safe—here, today, now—that he was held in the embrace of his teachers and his classmates and his school, no matter the terms of his life.

"Callum," I asked gently, "do you miss Nora?"

"My sister?" He looked up. I nodded.

"Uh . . ." There was a pause as he leaned forward. His hair still hung in front of his face, a tangled brown screen, his last defense. Tears began to fall to the floor.

"You miss her a lot," I said.

He nodded, but his face was hidden.

"Let the tears come. It's okay." We sat in silence, an immense silence.

"Have you talked to her recently?" I asked quietly.

His chest convulsed. He could barely choke out the word "No."

"Why not?"

He shrugged.

"Are you mad at her?"

He shook his head. His elbows were on his knees and he knotted his hands together, squeezing them until the knuckles were white.

"Is she mad at you?"

Again he shook his head.

"Are you mad at your mom or dad?"

He gave a barely perceptible shrug.

"Do you understand that when you cry it might be a gigantic feeling of love that you have inside of you that wants to come out? That these tears might be tears of love? Or confusion. Or loss."

He nodded.

"But you just feel sad? Because you miss her?"

He nodded.

Other teachers, locked into schedules, bound by the exigencies of curriculum, fearful of repercussions, would bypass such a moment. But everything that mattered lived inside such a moment. We could dwell in it as long as we needed.

The room was silent. Light and the blue morning sky were illuminated in the window above us. A door to the outside was open to the warm September morning. The table shone golden in the light and every eye was on Callum hunched over against the bookshelf with all his words caught in his throat.

"Callum?" I said, as quietly as I could.

"Yeah."

"Take a big breath, take it in deep." We waited for a few seconds more. "Callum, take your time—when you're going for the big stuff, you get to take as much time as you need. How should we live? What is a good life? How should you live?"

"A good life?" His words croaked out of some tangled, inchoate place.

"How would you define it?"

He lifted his head. Tears streamed down his face. "Freedom to—" his voice choked.

"Slow, man, slow. Relax. A simple definition, a sentence. It doesn't even have to be a sentence. Another word. Take your time. We have a whole year. We have three years. I'm not teaching to a test, so we have time. There is no test. Just us here. We're right here with you."

He shook his head. There was another long period of silence.

"Go easy. Take a deep breath. See what comes." I looked around the room. Everyone was looking up, hands on the table, looking at Callum, looking at me, expectant.

Callum's head still hung as he said it, but his voice was clear. "Freedom is words flowing. A good life is words flowing." Then he looked up.

"A good life is freedom, and freedom is words flowing?"

He nodded.

"That's great, Callum. That's great. We can learn from that."

He nodded, his hair falling across his wet face. A constellation of teardrops arrayed on the concrete floor between his unlaced basketball shoes.

"Somebody get Callum some tissues."

Katelyn slipped out of the room and came back with a wad of toilet paper. Callum took it without looking and held it to his nose.

"Words flowing. Callum, your words are flowing. That's freedom and that's a good life."

No one moved. Every face was turned toward him.

"Callum?"

He looked up.

"Is that what you're here for? To find out what you have to say?"

He shrugged. A shrug was potentially a barrier, one that perhaps protected him. To continue to pursue it, to challenge him, was to go at a place in him that was vulnerable or raw. I could draw back, or I could keep on. Though I was hesitant, I wanted to push. I wanted something to happen that would make the room come alive.

"Maybe to find words to tell your sister you miss her? To find out where those tears come from? To find out what love is? To find your own words? To see where freedom takes you? To find out how to live a good life? To get words flowing."

He shrugged again, and nodded.

"Maybe all those feelings of sadness and missing her are mixed up with immense love. It's good to feel the love you have for her. It's okay to feel the sadness. Let all those feelings out or the good feelings will never see the light of day and she'll never know and you'll never know, and then where will you be? If you keep the feelings of love trapped inside, the world will have less love."

He nodded.

"Okay, Callum," I said. "Everyone stand up again and open your eyes wider than you did before. Here's your first assignment. You have to give everything, just like Callum did. And you have to write a speech about what you're feeling. Callum just told us 'A good life is freedom, and freedom is words flowing.' You have to write about the idea of freedom that you want here. About a good life. Not Callum's, not mine—your idea. You have to make your words flow about *your* idea. Callum wants words flowing. We want words flowing. But that also might mean we want other things flowing. Tears, laughter, courage, learning, questioning, craziness, curiosity, doubt, fear, divinity, holiness. Your speech is where you're going to try to describe your idea of how to live and how we will live. All I'm asking is for everything, for you to give everything you have, and go all the way."

Some of them nodded, all of them still straining forward with eyes wide open.

"I'll help you. I'm a trained professional and I'm here to help. Okay?"

A few more nods.

"Now, who wants to go next?"

I lied to them. I'm not a trained professional. I do not have a degree in education or a license from the state of Vermont. But I have taught for nearly thirty years, and I have learned to question and listen.

That night I sat at home on the screen porch listening to the green frogs sounding from the edge of the pond and questioned myself. Did I push Callum too far? Did I expect too much? Should I have let him off and hewed closer to less personal matters? It would have been easy to avoid the emotional currents which, after all, is something most teachers did in order to retain control and order. And yet, I sought a kind of divine and vivid disorder. How was he to become himself or know himself if we bypassed what made his heart ache or sing?

Callum was no different than any other student who entered school, any school. Like him, they came in vulnerable, tender, angry, confused, hopeful, meek, posturing, blind to themselves, voiceless, without a vision. No matter what social, academic, athletic, or artistic strengths they possessed, they were also relentlessly gifted at hiding their deep and most fragile selves. Because they were afraid, unsure, and untested. Silently, they asked: *Who will want to know me or my particular life? Who will accept me as I am? Who will love the person I dream to become?* If my students stayed hidden, we and they would never get to see or enact the glorious powers inside them. I believed, as teachers must, that children possessed fierceness and beauty. My own great teachers had not simply been masterful deliverers of information or knowledge, they began with the assumption that I had a greater self inside, lurking, waiting, hungering. My best teachers had demanded that I find that self and that I live those powers out.

My work was to make it safe for my students to come out of hiding. I had to push them and lead them, or follow when they led. *You'll be safe,* I told them, *no matter where you go.*

Yes, adhering to core standards would be easier, I thought, sitting in the still night. But Callum's words—*freedom is words flowing*—would never be found on any rubric or standardized test. No core curriculum or test would likely elicit that phrase from the depths of a human heart. Those words were born from a conversation that neither he, nor I, nor any school system could have predicted or planned. I simply allowed school to be a place where he was liberated to think and feel, to go to the dark, hard, uncharted places and begin to make something from them. I would give them my belief, and they would find theirs.

The next morning, I listened as they scratched their way to ideas of a good life, towards a vision that might make a compelling speech. As they talked, I willed myself to make their thoughts my own, to let their lives inhabit my mind.

They moved slowly: glacially, it seemed. It took time for them to find their feelings, and it took time for me to find the right questions. It took more time to turn feelings into words that could be transformed into a beginning-of-the-year speech, which was no more or less than an introduction of themselves to each other. These speeches did not have to follow a strict expository form; the words simply had to be true. They could employ scenes from real life, sometimes sad or painful, sometimes joyous or triumphant; moments from long ago or from that morning in carpool; childhood memories; experiences in school and at play; references to films, songs, and plays; quotes of famous people; dialogues with parents, grandparents, siblings, and friends. I gave them absolute freedom to fill their speeches with images of themselves.

"How should we live?" I asked them. "What is a good life?" In my own mind, I was thinking about the summer that had just ended. I was missing my children, my two teenage sons and my four-year-old daughter, and the time spent with them. I was thinking about the long days of summer when I could think my own thoughts with beginnings and ends. I listened to my students, yes. But as they talked, I could imagine myself sitting on the screened porch, sipping coffee with the smell of the woodpile drifting in with the breeze. I remembered the summer days when the sun was hot, and the sounds of our children playing badminton and soccer, or bounding on the trampoline and running up and down the hill, or splashing in the pond. I remembered our dog, Jasper, barking at whatever moved in the woods. I remembered evenings, the voices of legions of frogs camouflaged in the tall grasses at the edge of the water, bats circling at dusk against the black trees and dark blue sky, the crickets and owls sounding at night through open windows.

I thought of Shakespeare's sonnet: *how shall summer's honey breath hold out / Against the wrackful siege of battering days?* I was thinking of summer and my own grown children, even as I sat at a table surrounded by twenty-seven beautiful students.

"When you write," I said, "when you begin, you must include your life. It's where your thoughts were born. Last night I sat on the porch and listened to the frogs and owls and the smells of the woodpile. I thought about you guys and what we're doing. I thought about my children. I thought about Callum, and I thought about what each of you has inside of you."

They looked at me silently, still waiting.

I asked them to begin telling stories, all of which would be fodder for their speeches. They spoke of older siblings leaving for college. They recalled playing innocently and free as small children in gardens and sandboxes and ditches and closets. They remembered the first time being left by their parents at preschool, or feeling lonely or left-out in elementary school, or the terror of finding out they could not do what their classmates could. They talked about their fears of coming into school on their first day. Or that they were different than their classmates. They spoke of missing their friends from the previous year who'd graduated. They tentatively wondered if they would have friends in the coming year, if they were smart enough, if they had *something* that made them special, if they could become someone important. They looked at the year ahead, just like I did, and they worried about how they could create something big, worthy, or meaningful. They wondered if they could carry the school themselves.

"When I think of last year, I just think of everything being gone," said Nolan. "At the end of last year I was as sad as Callum was yesterday."

"Were you sad last year because of the great thing that was ending?" I asked.

"Yeah, but now I'm thinking that it's impossible to make something like that again," he said. His head, perched high on his thin neck, swiveled. He looked around the table to his classmates from the previous year.

"Things have to die in order for something else to live," said Nadia. Her voice was serene and gentle. She was looking down at the table, but then straight at Nolan.

"Death is all around us," I said. "Summer is gone. Last year is gone. We're all growing and changing, and time doesn't stop. *You're* growing and changing. The frogs were singing their last songs of the summer last night."

Yes, I was talking about the older students from the year before who had left. I was talking about the pond and summer, and my own children growing up and away. I was talking about my sons, who had once been my students, who had been a part of my teaching every day, who now were growing up. I was talking about life, the sweetness of it, the way it breathed and lingered and vanished.

"But we have each other, and this school, this day, and this year."

There was not a single movement or shift in the room. Jasper lay sleeping on the rug behind me, mud on his paws from his tromping in the woods. They were listening, because it was real, because their stories and feelings were real. Callum's feelings were real, and Nolan's feelings were real. When I said last year was dead, that was real too. They were captivated—maybe a little scared—and so was I.

Our school, and life, were not, could not be, utopia. It was not the golden age. It was not always going to be freedom or beauty. The rivers were not flowing with honey. But we had to believe: better to wade in deep, better to be aware of what was here and what was not, of what was lasting and what was fragile, of what was glorious and what would eventually disappear. I waded in too, bringing myself to the table-edge with them, to figure out how to turn the wrackful siege of battering days into days of building and creation.

It took days to do introductions and set them on their courses for their speeches. Light and attention needed to be brought to each child.

Bennett raised his hand for his turn.

"What's your name, Bennett?" Bennett was muscular, built as solidly as a fire-plug, and a fierce lacrosse player.

"Bennett Hanson."

"Okay, Bennett," I said. "What is freedom, and how does it lead to a good life?"

"Uh. A good life is—is like Gandhi or Martin Luther King?" His voice, unsure and unclear, hung quietly in a room full of peers who barely knew him, who wanted to see if he could find an answer.

"That's an okay place to start, Bennett, but is there anything more personal? I mean, did you know Gandhi?"

"No. But he did, like, a lot for people. Like for freedom . . ."

"But what did he do? How did he *live*? How did he find freedom? What gave him those powers? He had to look at his life and know his life to know what freedom was. He felt that stick of racism on his back and lived the consequences of it. You have to tell us about what you know, in the heart of your heart, from what *you* have lived."

"I guess I'm not sure." Now he was off-balance, nervous, slipping toward something he'd never consciously considered.

"Is there anyone a little closer who might be an example for you?"

"Uh, like . . ."

"Someone you actually know?"

"I don't know."

"How about your maw and paw. From Arkansaw."

"Huh?" He looked at me like I was crazy.

"Your mom and dad."

"What about them?"

"What about them? You know them better than MLK. Have *they* given you freedom or a good life?"

His eyes turned watery, and his cheeks burned red. He looked down at the table.

"They give me everything," he said with a shaking whisper.

Two weeks later, Bennett read to the class his speech about his gratitude. About how thankful he was for his father for driving to get doughnuts on cold mornings in their dirty old truck they called Blue-y; for his mother, who made him peanut butter sandwiches and cut them into strange triangles when he was little; for the way his mother and father always woke him up in the morning with the simple words "Hey there, hey sweet one."

His speech was his thank you for the childhood and the good life they had given him.

Yes, Bennett appeared tough, athletic, nonchalant. But when he read his speech about his mother and father, his voice was tremulous and tender.

Who will not secretly rejoice when the hero puts his armor off... who will blame him if he does homage to the beauty of the world? wrote Virginia Woolf.

Bennett was doing homage to the beauty of his world and we could rejoice in that. His armor was off. From there, everything could happen.

Katelyn had come to us midway through the previous school year. Her mother was in and out of jail. Her father cut firewood and drove trucks on the back roads of rural Vermont and was virtually invisible in her life. She and her little sister lived with their grandmother in a trailer park in East Middlebury. Katelyn had an angelic face, huge eyes, and long brown hair.

When she entered the school, we had been mid-way through a yearlong study of historic revolutions around the world. On her first day she elected to do her project on the French Revolution and Marie Antoinette. "Oh my god! I'm so excited!" she exclaimed. "I've *always* wanted to learn about her. This is the most fun thing I've *ever* done in school!" She fell in love with young Marie, and it was easy to see why: Marie was a sweet girl who had everything—Katelyn's own dream.

Katelyn's speech reached back in time to when her family was still together. She recalled how she and her little sister slept in their bottom bunk, with sheets hanging over the bed so that they were enclosed in a womb-like cave. She described her sister snuggling up to her, pressing against her body as though Katelyn were her mother.

Was this proper subject matter for an expository speech in middle school? I had encountered such doubts uncountable times from parents and other teachers. *What do their personal lives have to do with school?* My answer was simple: if we took time to listen, we'd find that these kids overflowed with virtue, wisdom, love, and artistic power. American schools rarely asked students to delve into the topic about which they had the most interest and knew most intimately—themselves. They were asked to write about great books, but they were discouraged from using a personal perspective. The lived experience and the lessons of life were treated as alien, or even disruptive, to the curricular subjects at hand. Students were asked to write about Huck Finn's journey, but their own miraculous journeys—harrowing, triumphant, serpentine, tentatively beginning, or yet undiscovered—were somehow not considered valid subject matter. It transpired, incredibly, that raising school-wide test scores, preparation for SATs, or learning how to locate the subjunctive clause was more important than attentiveness to the developing soul of a child.

Yet I had seen it again and again: when students talked about their own experiential understanding of love or loss, they understood profoundly, say, the innocence of Scout Finch, or the existential despair of Holden Caulfield. When they read about Maya Angelou's silence, they understood their own propensity to sublimate their deepest feelings. When they saw how many questions Wislawa Szymborska asked in her poems, they comprehended the power of confronting doubt or existential confusion; and their questions made them understand Szymborska's. When they talked about their love for their siblings, they understood George's love for Lennie. When they spoke about their own loneliness and fumbling attempts for human contact, they understood the Chief's allegiance to McMurphy. When they articulated their own feelings of alienation in rampant consumer culture, or when they felt the emptiness of living life through a computer screen or phone, they understood Winston

Smith's resistance to the powers of Big Brother. When they understood or had contact with their deepest feelings, they became more alive to worlds and ideas beyond them.

But it wasn't always as easy as saying, "On your marks, get set, go!" Once, a student, Alycia, had written about a fight with her mother at home. Alycia had transcribed the fight as best she could, trying to convey the complexity of her feelings. I received a phone call one day from her mother, saying she needed to meet me after school that afternoon. She had read a scene from the story.

"Our life at home is not your fucking business," she told me.

"Alycia is my business," I said. "And at this school she, like all the kids here, has freedom to write what she feels is important to her in the best way she can."

Alycia's mother stared at me, her face red in anger.

"So long as she's at this school, she has that freedom. She's writing about her life as she understands it. If you demand that she not have that freedom, then her being at this school will not work."

I was mindful of her mother's feelings, and I understood her feelings of vulnerability and her sense of exposure. However, my first allegiance was to Alycia. My allegiance was to helping unleash the expressive powers living inside my students. It was one thing for me to fend off bureaucratic interference, but having parents dictate what was or was not proper subject matter was an existential threat both to the school and to the artistic and emotional freedom of the students. I was not going to let parents determine the curriculum, say what could or could not be said or written in our school, impinge on the sacred space we were working to create, or limit the reach of the voices developing in the room. If I ceded that, the school was no longer mine, and it was no longer the students'.

On a weekly basis, I wrote to the school community about what happened during our days. I constantly put it into context. *This happened at school this week. This is what adolescents do. This is their process of growth and development. What is happening here is complex and beautiful.*

The Sunday after the first week, I wrote to the school community. *In Stephen Dunn's poem 'Homage to the Divers,' he imagines us all as bold underwater explorers, seeking the great treasure of the depths. . . . First, though, he asserts that there is a key for which we must dive. A key to existence? Happiness? He only tells us that, above all, we must believe, all of us, that the treasure is reachable.*

> A love poem at the bottom
> of the sea, in a treasure ship,
> reachable, yes,
> we must believe reachable.
> In an air-tight container
> somewhere in the captain's quarters,
> somewhere off Hatteras,
> written by . . .
> a key in a skeleton's hand,
> and the whole world up above
> diving for it,
> some with all the equipment
> some holding their breath.

I always conceive of my students as those bold divers, I continued. *I believe in them as ones who believe in somewhere, who will go with full heart and faith into the difficult thing. Our dream is to see them break the surface and emerge having done that difficult thing, bringing up meaning where otherwise there would be little; exploring and mapping landscapes of experience, inner questions, and personal texts; opening up to a community of different minds; and defining value where otherwise there would be none.*

When parents read what was happening at school for their children, they were sometimes perplexed, often ecstatic, and universally grateful. School for their children was not predictable or boring. It was alive.

Haley, a ninth grader, wrote about her father, Bud, whose heart functioned at ten percent capacity. Once a psychologist, like Haley's mother, Bud had been forced to retire. The chamber walls of his heart were tissue-thin, and he was awaiting a heart transplant. The simplest tasks—climbing a set of stairs, getting up from a chair—left him exhausted. When his strength was up, he was able to work in his garden with Haley.

So Haley lived with her father's condition, and when asked to think, talk, or write about what was most important to her, he inevitably came up. We learned the stories over time. If he had been rushed to a Boston hospital, then she'd been awake in the night helping her mother load him into the car. When doctors told him he could no longer garden or build stone walls, Haley wept as she gazed over the untended beds. When the wait for a new heart was extended yet again, she came to school and cried, pushing her hair behind her ears, spitting out her rage in morning meeting. "How much fucking longer is he going to have to wait?" Tears mixed with her schoolwork practically every day. And yet she laughed. She cursed the equations in algebra. She got anxious if I had not yet read her writing. She sang songs from *Wicked*. She copied lyrics from *The Rocky Horror Picture Show* all over her binder. She turned in her lit assignments with sketches of morning glories weaving around her name.

On a hot September afternoon, the doors were swung open. The distant sound of a chainsaw somewhere in the Ripton woods mingled with the movements of the students around the table and the trees outside the door rustling in a light breeze. The flickerings of birds and butterflies outside passed in the light around us. Through the copse of trees behind the school, the neighbor's rooster crowed. We were raggedly circled around our big table, which was mostly covered with binders and papers, math assignments, empty chip bags, laptops, a tray of watercolors. I sat at the middle of the long side, my chest to the table edge.

Haley stood before us at the head of the big table, her hands on the sides of the lectern, reading her speech about freedom. Winn, an eighth grader, carefully folded a collection of tiny origami cranes out of tinfoil, each one the size of a blueberry. Nils sat away from the table with his legs resting on another chair, pulling on the threads of his jeans.

The class was pressed up close to the table, which was covered, as always, with a profusion of notebooks, computers, tupperware, scissors and glue-sticks. The room was quiet. Haley's speech did not debate a point, ask for a vote, or support a thesis. It was, simply, a revelation of her heart.

A stained white tank top and darker sports bra underneath stood off against my pale skin as I stood in front of my full-length mirror. I held out a hand and looked at my uneven nails and slightly longer fingers. I wore black soccer shorts and as I stared at my hair, it seemed to curl out into blonde frizz above my head as the air became more humid. My face was pale and dotted with some freckles and my eyebrows seemed too blonde to see. I didn't like this image of myself and I didn't want to be me anymore. I turned away and opened the door, so I wouldn't have to pick out my imperfections. I walked down the smooth wooden stairs, walking slowly and biding my time. I reached the bottom, turned to grab my sneakers and left the house. I tied the shoelaces in place and stuck my earphones in my ears blocking out the sounds of everything except the pounding of my heart. I scrolled down the music list to podcasts and then to "This American Life." I turned down the driveway and started to run, trying to forget everything and just listened to the voice of Ira Glass. "This American Life" is a radio show that has different themes every week and there are always different stories about people in America, their stories, stories that fit the theme. I loved listening to these. I had listened to at least thirty podcasts during the summer. It always made me stop thinking about how I felt about myself and whether I could change. Instead it put me in a place where I could think about other people's stories and problems and what they went through. The sound of my sneakers was a kind of rhythm to keep me moving forward away from what I was always thinking about and what I never wanted to think about. A line of sweat slid down my forehead and I wiped it away with the back of my hand, just listening, trying to forget. I saw the long dirt road ahead just stretching on what seemed like forever and I just kept going because that's what I had to do, it was the only thing to do. The trees were so perfectly green and true around me and the details that were easy to miss when I wasn't looking were so clear to me and so amazing and beautiful. The veins in a glossy, wet leaf stood out against the smooth, rough gravel under my feet. A pale yellow and black butterfly perched on a leaf, lightly fluttering its fragile, beautiful wings. Wild flowers of the most breathtaking pinks and maroons stood planted in the ground, but swaying in the breeze so they didn't seem grounded after all. I looked down at my thighs, they were bright red and wet with sweat. I looked straight ahead again, Stop thinking, *I told myself,* just let go. *I turned the volume up higher and the voice of someone else filled my head, all meaningless noise, and I sprinted across the dirt road, my feet thudding on the warm ground, the wind and stones flying with me.*

*And I felt like I never wanted to stop, just my soul running
free, my body left in the dust as the rest of me raced ahead,
completely free. But not just free, but happy to be who I was
and happy that I was sprinting down a dirt road, in the
middle of the woods at the foot of a mountain.*

Her speech contained no standard format, "thesis," conventional topic sentences, footnotes, or formal structure. It was a speech about how to live a good life. No boundaries on expression were imposed. Something more essential appeared before us: a girl who, despite all, had a soul that ran free with the wind and stones.

My students—like all adolescents—were in a continual, sometimes frantic search to see themselves as powerful, beautiful and complete. Rarely did they find moments of absolute clarity. Haley's speech about a run in the summer mountains became rare inner seeing—a fleeting glimpse of her growing awareness of her self, a pale and freckled Narcissus, gazing into her depths. The external beauty and internal powers of her soul she was able to apprehend was no more or less than an analogue for what she wanted to see and believe about herself. As we listened to her story, she led us through her vision of veined leaves to a vision of her.

When I was in first grade, I caught a baby rabbit in my yard. My mother and I put him in an empty fish tank with leaves, lettuce, and a metal lid filled with water. Never in my school life had I been so excited to go to school. I had a gift, something that made my heart race. I wanted my class and teachers to see what I had found. My teacher met me at the door to the classroom and instructed me to place the glass tank on a shelf at the front of the room. Our daily routine commenced. We sat in rows of desks and took out our handwriting books. I tried to make a perfect "a." I gazed at my bunny, spinning in its wheel. We colored. We spelled. We did not talk about rabbits, nor draw rabbits, nor learn anything about the science of rabbits. No questions were asked about the bunny. We did not gather around the glass to laugh at the bunny's nose, or to touch its fur, or wonder about its siblings or its large ears, or discuss the ethics of releasing or keeping it.

I watched it hopping about in its glass enclosure on the counter all day. The distance between the glass and where I sat was vast and uncrossable. It was one of the longest, most disappointing days I ever spent in school. Whatever excitement I felt about the bunny was of little importance to the school system entrusted with my education. That afternoon, as I knelt in a patch of ivy to release my rabbit, I wept.

I knew that my students needed to believe that school was about and for them, a mirror for them, a place they could hold and be held in, a place for their particular, evolving selves. They could bring their passions and hopes, their struggles and their stories, their treasures, dogs, and old photos, their balls and games.

Levi, who was more than a reluctant student, once asked if he could bring into school the glass orbs he had made in his glass-blowing class.

"Absolutely, please," I said. The next day at lunch he dragged in the school ladder from the shed and climbed up to the dormer window. Perched high above the big-room table, he hammered nails into the window frames and carefully hung the translucent, apple-sized spheres so the sunlight would pass through them during the day. We marveled at their grace and lightness, and thanked him for what he gave. He himself glowed, filled with light to be seen and recognized. Those glass orbs still hang in the windows, reminding me of the imperative of welcoming whatever a child can bring into our school—and of the importance of holding those gifts aloft.

If students knew that the school's center was their lives and concerns, they would give devotion to their work, compassion to their classmates, and respect and love to each other and their teachers. This did not require the planning, skills, or educational degrees of a veteran teacher. Most certainly it did not require lesson plans, syllabi, or phalanxes of administrators. It only required an abiding interest in the lives of children, and faith that in the crucible of the classroom, the truth and beauty of those children would emerge. If invited to give their minds and hearts, they would give everything.

In earlier years, when I first began asking the kids to focus on autobiographical narrative, I would ask them to write down their dreams, figuring it would be a way to turn up ideas and excite them. They dutifully brought in crumpled notebook papers with sloppily scrawled dreams from the previous week. But when it came time to read, they were reluctant. No one wanted to share anything. They were practically hostile to the notion of self-disclosure.

"Why should we have to read?" an eighth-grade boy, Jason, complained. "It's our own private world." Lacking confidence to press them, I volunteered to read mine: a long, tedious description of parachuting into Yankee Stadium. I should have known—generally, no one's nighttime dreams are very interesting at all, except to the dreamer. But I blundered on. About half way through the second page, an eighth-grade girl interrupted acidly, "This is really boring."

I should have confronted her rudeness, challenged her unwillingness to venture anything of herself, asked her why she hid herself behind her criticism of me. But my belief in what I was doing had completely drained out. The kids didn't feel safe, and neither did I. And truth be told, she was right. It really was *boring*.

Later, I saw another possibility: that buried under the inappropriateness of her interruption was the possibility that she was bored because it wasn't about *her*. She wanted to speak about herself, know about herself, or at least hear what her peers had written. But she was also afraid of that. They all were. To speak about oneself, one's inner thoughts, was a risk. So her snide contempt masked something more primal: *I have something to say. Can you make space for me to say it?* It took years for me to learn how to make a classroom in which such longing for self-disclosure and reflection could take place.

So I persisted in the belief that adolescents, no less than anyone, perhaps more so, desperately wanted to be heard, seen, known. Some parents, with their eyes on the future or SATs or the specter of college admissions, repeatedly challenged me: *how will this help my child?* What did the private and personal have to do with learning in school and measurable academic achievement? Occasionally, and especially when I first began teaching, parents felt that kids writing freely about themselves was too much, too raw and intimate. They feared for the fragility of their children and also for the tension and reality of their own lives being exposed. However, they discovered over time that their children loved coming to the North Branch School, that their children loved to write and to feel their powers of creation. The reason was simple. Their children got to be themselves at our school more fully than anywhere else. The school was safe—safe for laughter, tears, revelation, embarrassment, pain, inappropriate humor, love. The school was small, intimate, a kind of surrogate family, a place where the kids could invest and be themselves and venture to new understandings of themselves. And over time, parents discovered that when the tender and beautiful truths of their children emerged, they felt relief more than mortification. They got a glimpse into the hearts of their children and had the privilege to witness them growing towards greater affection for and understanding of their peers and the community. They saw their children learning that they could not love each other until they knew each other, and that when they knew each other, they protected each other. Bullying and intolerance, which fed off of fear, could not propagate in such a school. They saw boys being tender, vulnerable, soft. They saw girls exuding strength, courage, assertiveness. When kids shared the comedies and tragedies of their lives, or felt safe enough to admit weakness or to laugh at themselves, or to talk about love and loneliness, they understood that it was the essential foundation to an environment of human closeness. As the students discovered this, so did their parents.

Slowly, I learned. A classroom devoid of emotion was a dreadful place where students mostly marked time. Conversely, a classroom where the inner lives of children was given primacy was fascinating and compelled devoted interest. When the deeper, fragile, or hidden regions of students were brought to the fore, the classroom came alive. Through speeches like Katelyn's, Haley's, or Bennett's, it was clear that extraordinary epiphanies of the heart were not so elusive. And when kids came out of their hidden places, they loved how they were seen and known. I saw it, the kids saw it, the parents felt it, and they were grateful.

When I saw Brody with his face full of freckles sitting terrified at the table, he did not look like he could possibly be twelve. His hair was uncombed, and his Etnies skateboarding T-shirt was stretched at the collar and stained with food. He pressed himself against the back of the chair as though he were trying to separate from the table, shrinking into as small a form as possible, praying that I would not see him.

"Brody, what's your name?" I asked him.

"Brody," he said, staring straight at me with wide blue eyes.

"Brody last name?"

"Brody Linford."

"Middle name?"

"What?" he stammered.

"Brody, what is your middle name?" I asked slowly.

"I don't have one." His face flushed a hot red.

"Really?"

"No."

"Brody, everyone has a middle name. I will tell you mine, if you tell me yours."

"I don't have one."

He hadn't blinked. He was shaking. I knew he was lying because I'd seen the forms his parents filled out.

He stared at me again, his lips locked and white.

"Why are you telling us you don't have a middle name?"

"Because I don't have one."

In *King Lear*, Regan describes Lear's erratic behavior. *Tis the infirmity of his age; yet he hath ever but slenderly known himself.* Brody was not old or infirm. But in his adolescent terror, he but slenderly knew himself; he was unable to bring himself to utter a third of his given identity. Lear asks the Fool, "Who is it who can tell me who I am?" And the Fool answers, "Lear's shadow."

Adolescents—my students, Brody Linford—were shadows, lurkers, mumblers, flimsy cutouts, imposters, champions of platitudes or pieties parroting slogans of products, disciples of a cheap pop culture. Unless called out, they waded in the shallows of themselves. The task was how to help them find their shape, ignite them, help them grow from slender shadows into full being and know the brightness of their names and their deepest selves.

"Okay, Brody no-middle-name Linford. What is your idea about living a good life?"

"I don't know." His voice was flat, as though no emotion whatsoever inhabited his body.

"Jesus, Brody, we've been talking about it for three days!"

"I don't know."

"Okay, what'd you do this summer?"

"I went to a camp in Maine."

"Was it fun?"

"Uh, yeah, I guess."

"Were all the kids nice?"

"Yeah. Um. Well, not all of them."

"Who wasn't nice?"

"Um, this kid."

"Did this kid have a name?"

"Micah."

"What wasn't nice about him?"

"He was a jerk."

"To you?"

"Yeah."

"To others?"

"Yeah, but mostly me."

"What'd he do?"

"He locked me out of the cabin."

"That sucks. What else?"

"He teased me."

"And?"

"He pantsed me."

"Yanked your pants down? In front of people?"

"Yeah. Like the whole camp."

"Anything else?"

"He stole my stuff."

"Like what?"

"My clothes. My shoes. My hat."

"He sounds like a real swell kid. How'd you feel about him?"

"Feel about him?" The word "feel" from his mouth sounded foreign and unsavory.

"Yeah. After he took your stuff. Did you feel anything?"

"What do you mean?"

"I mean, how did you feel when he did all that to you? Pantsed you in front of the whole camp?"

"I don't know."

"You don't know? How you felt?"

He shook his head.

"Brody, that's kind of weird. He treated you meanly, humiliated you, took your stuff. That's a lot of mean shit. Were you pissed at him?"

Brody Sanford stared ahead with terror in his eyes.

"Sadness? Anger? Humiliation? Embarrassment? Even a little itty-bitty smidgen of discomfort?"

In a quiet voice, no longer staring but looking down at the table, he said, "He made me feel like I was a little kid."

The door was opening, and he stepped in tentatively. In those words was all the frustration of having felt small and all the yearning to become big.

"How?"

"When he teased me in front of the other kids."

"How'd he tease you?"

"He called me a little faggot. And everyone laughed."

"Jerk. Now we're starting to understand. Did you want to do anything to him?"

"Um . . . yeah."

"You can tell us. You're free here. Everyone here is on your side."

"Anything?"

"Anything."

"I guess I wanted to push him in a puddle and shock him with a cattle prod and fry him until his eyeballs popped out." The class exploded with laughter, not at Brody, but for him. Brody looked down at the table with a small smile.

"Brody, *that* is expressing your feeling! That's it, that's perfect! So, what would you call him if you could call him anything?"

"You mean, like a mean name?"

"Yeah, I mean like a name. Like any name. You have permission. Is there anything else you would like to say about him?"

"Um, yeah, he was a gelled-up butt-munch douche-bag waste-of-oxygen."

Again the class burst into laughter. The student laughing the loudest was Yebsera, his eyes flashing with brightness as he rocked back in his chair, his head tilting back. To make his classmate laugh so was Brody's power to move his classmates, entertain, make friends, express his uniqueness.

"Brody, you can write a speech about him. You can write anything you want to write about him, okay? You're free to do that. You have to express yourself. But you can't just call him names. You have to tell us what happened, and what you learned about freedom and a good life from being treated like that by some gelled-up butt-munch."

To know Brody's name was not enough. Nor his knowledge, or whether he could absorb content and engage in curriculum, whatever that might be. For him to become himself—to find out who he was and who he could be—we had to also know his experiences, his past, his humor, fears, anger. His way of expressing himself. He was not merely a student, but a person first. Who he was was the foundation. From there, we pressed as quickly and intensely as possible to come to know him by rooting around and trying to get into the marrow of his life. His classmates now had a way to know him as well.

We came to know Brody as he came to know himself. He wanted to be strong and heroic. He'd already done something great simply by demonstrating his fragility, toughness, and wit. He'd already helped make school inhospitable to bullying. He'd shown the class what side to be on. Everyone was with him. He was ours, and we were his.

Ariela was an eighth grader. Her father was a high school Spanish teacher; her mother was from Spain and taught Spanish at Middlebury College. Her mother had been diagnosed with cancer when Ariela was seven, and her parents divorced when she was eight. Ariela was grave, rarely laughed, and was an exceptionally hardworking and brilliant student. She sent me a note one Sunday night.

Tal, she wrote, *I was wondering if I could read part of a speech by Martin Luther King in class sometime.*

Of course, I wrote back. *What's your inspiration for wanting to read it?*

I just read it and it relates to what we have been saying about how we should live and it seems important.

Sure. We can do it in the morning before class. Or after lunch. Or whenever we have time. But remind me.

I had attended middle school in the late 1970s, when strains of a more open or "progressive" school movement were still in vogue. In an unconventional, multi-aged seventh/eighth-grade class, learning for me had been alive. Each week we were issued a long list of work and projects to accomplish, and we were given responsibility to finish it as best we could. We signed up for as much as we thought we could, and the culture of the class encouraged us to do more. We took field trips to Civil War battlefields, ethnic restaurants, and historic homes. We studied mushrooms, spiders, constellations, ferns, and Oriental rugs, topics that usually were chosen by our teacher, who had a famously eclectic set of interests. For independent study, I made apple sauce, conducted a fencing workshop for my classmates, and rode the Atlanta city buses to map urban neighborhoods. We read *The Great Santini,* and later, Pat Conroy and his father, Santini himself, came to visit. We wrote autobiographical narratives about our lives and our stories were read to the class to acclaim and joy, and then published in a literary magazine. Often we chose our own topics of study. I had a great interest in Martin Luther King and American Civil rights, the fighter planes of World War II, Thomas Edison, and the history of ice hockey—so I was granted the opportunity to study these in as much depth as I could and then present to any interested classmates. There was high status and celebration associated with completing our work independently and sharing what we learned. What I did mattered to my peers, and I felt they were interested in me. In essence, I could be a teacher to my peers, and that made me feel powerfully able. So, though I was not a conventionally exceptional student, I excelled in those two years. I was liberated, trusted, and my affinities and inclinations were at the center of the curriculum. I was supported by teachers who knew me, and evinced as much interest in learning new things as any student in the room. And because of all that, I loved school.

Ariela's desire to read a Martin Luther King quote in class one day did not surprise me. In fact, that was what I hoped and expected to happen.

The next day, the kids piled back into the classroom after lunch. Yebsera stood by the table, asking me about punctuation corrections on his speech. Bennett, wearing flannel pajama pants and flip-flops as he often did, laughed and wrestled with Callum over who got the chair at the head of the table. Callum was grabbing for Bennett's hat, which Bennett could not seem to exist without. Jasper trotted in with a bone in his mouth. Many in the class were sweaty from playing soccer on the field, cloaked in the joyful vigor of physical contact, their cheeks red and knees muddy.

Ariela sat quietly at the table, watching me, her face and serious, sharp blue eyes framed by her long mane of unruly, curly hair, waiting for class to begin. A sheet of paper rested facedown on top of her binder. She looked at me skeptically. *Will he get to me? Will he remember?* For Ariela, class was a place to be serious. In the tumult of chairs shoved back and books placed on the table, she looked straight at me.

"Is now a good time?" Her voice was barely audible over the noise of her classmates settling into their seats.

"Let us get through a few things. Then you can."

I was thinking, of course, that we must keep on with our plans: the speeches that needed to be read, the place descriptions we needed to start, the important business of explaining, yet again, the difference between *there, their*, and *they're*.

As important as these were, I was sure as well that whatever impelled Ariela was the most important thing that could possibly happen. Her desire—any student's initiative or yearning—would almost always be more important than my or any teacher's imperatives, and I was going to make sure we had time for her to read and to find out why it was important. This was the unplanned deviation we longed for.

At fifteen minutes before three, there was a pause.

"Are we going to do something else, or are we done?" asked Nolan. "You said Ariela had something." Nolan was thin and smooth-cheeked, with long blond hair and his shirt buttoned up. He sat forward, back straight, both feet on the floor. He carried a copy of the Constitution in his pocket, and was our resident presidential scholar. Intuitively, he had his finger on the pulse of the class, on the time used or remaining, on what we should be remembering. Ariela looked at me with huge eyes, her mouth closed.

"Thanks, Nolan. Yes, Ariela. Do you want to read the thing you told me about?" I asked.

She nodded, and when the class was focused, she began to read without any introduction. Since it was unplanned, it was authentic—something sacred blossoming from the everyday clutter of the end of a school day. None of the students in the room knew why she was reading it, but they were all listening.

The problem is with man himself and man's soul. We haven't learned how to be just and honest and kind and true and loving. And that is the basis of our problem. The real problem is that through our scientific genius we've made of the world a neighborhood, but through our moral and spiritual genius we've failed to make of it a brotherhood. . . . the real danger confronting civilization today is that atomic bomb which lies in the hearts and souls of men, capable of exploding into the vilest of hate and into the most damaging selfishness. That's the atomic bomb that we've got to fear today. Problem is with the men. Within the heart and the souls of men.

When she was done, the class applauded respectfully, then looked to me, tentative and unsure of what to do or say. "So why did you want to read this?" I asked.

"Because it seemed important. Because when I think about what we said for our speeches, about what we need to live good lives, what we said sounded like we were trying to create a moral law for ourselves. And I know we don't always live up to what we say we believe. So it seems like it's important to ask again what our moral law is."

"What do you mean by 'moral law?'" I asked

"I don't know. The laws of our souls? How we approach life?"

"Okay," I began. "So, what is *your* soul law? All of us—what law do we govern our lives by? I don't think we're talking about which side of the road to drive on, or what font size we use, or not stealing. What is the one law that exists for you, that you live by, something sacred, that cannot be broken?"

Tentatively, then all at once, nearly a dozen hands lifted. Activated and awakened by Ariela's reading, they already had ideas. Who could test that? Who could measure that?

The next day, my aim was clear. To magnify and amplify, to keep Ariela's initiative alive in the room—to make it a fire that kept burning.

We found the original source recording of King's sermon. It was from 1954, in a church in Detroit, the first known recording of any of his sermons. The historical backdrop was racial segregation throughout the nation and the expanding nuclear arms race with the Soviet Union. I wanted them to know about that history, yes. I wanted equally for them to feel the sound of the words and understand what Ariela had given us. So we listened to the entire speech.

King's voice spoke from long ago, his cadence slowly building in power: urgent, hopeful, alive. In our room, his words were alive.

The class was quietly spellbound. In the pauses in the sermon, we could hear his audience murmuring encouragement: *Amen! Help him, Lord!*

"What might it mean that Ariela wanted us to hear that?" I asked. "What did it do to you when you heard it?"

"It was wicked cool to hear his voice like that," said Bennett.

"I never heard Martin Luther King speak," said Yebsera, with his still-strong Amharic accent. "I mean I heard him say 'I have a dream,' but I never heard him saying like, his ideas."

"It's strange to think about all those people in the room listening to him," said Nils. "They were there!"

"I wonder if it felt like they were in the middle of history happening," asked Callum.

"I was thinking that I want to be like Ariela," said Katelyn. "I want to do something important in the class. And I think Ariela was right. We need to think more about how we're acting. We're always complaining or blaming others. But the only thing we can fix is ourselves."

"Katelyn, you're doing something important in the class right now," I said. "Just by saying what you're feeling is important. The hard part is living it."

"If the problem is our hearts and souls," said Nils, "then that is something we have power to change."

"Isn't that what he was telling us, that we are not yet great, but we can become great?" I asked. "You all can be great souls. Like him. Or Gandhi. Or Ariela."

"I think Ariela is a great soul," said Katelyn. "She's giving us the greatness of who she is."

There was no Unit Plan or Rubric, because imposed structures would kill the thing before it could begin to grow. I would help them, make space, and encourage them. I would not stop asking them to bring forth what was inside them. When the classroom was theirs, it became a living thing.

When I first began teaching, moments of improvisation—or of giving over the direction of the class to the students—were rare. It was not because my students were any less able or inspired, but because they did not yet perceive themselves as free, and I did not know how to conjure such a feeling in them. Coming from conventional elementary schools, they were accustomed to having a curriculum set for them, with every moment structured and dictated by teachers. I had not learned that if I gave them power, freedom, and responsibility, they might actually use those gifts to noble ends. Instead, like most teachers, I controlled the class, set the agenda, and made sure there was not an empty moment. Most questions I asked had reasonably accessible answers. I was afraid, like most teachers, that nothing would happen unless I planned it or scripted it. Moreover, cloaked in the insecurity and self-consciousness of adolescence, my students did not feel like they walked on solid ground—and my insecurity fed theirs. I took this as the natural developmental state of things: that they were reluctant and unwilling to take risks. The consequence was that I did most of the work, and it was not terribly noteworthy.

Over time I learned to trust the students. I allowed for empty space, and I put the burden on them—to express their inner compulsions and desires, to make something happen. I discovered that they desired to be heroic, and that they possessed a sort of emergent Odyssean impulse. They wanted to be great and travel far. Simultaneously, they were questing for their own solid ground, a place on which they could stand and move the world. They wanted to make an impact, to create and transmit their culture and experience, and leave behind some kind of great work. And when I gave them time, encouragement, and trust, they seized their chances.

Every day we held a morning meeting that preceded classes. It was informal, sometimes a Quaker-esque gathering of relative silence, sometimes a ritual of closeness and community, sometimes a cornucopia of comical adolescent digression, current events, and personal accounts of happenings from the day or night before. We did not squander fifteen minutes taking role or making announcements or playing card games until the first bell—anyone could speak about anything. They responded by putting forth perceptions, ideas, feelings, wonderings, commentary. They talked about the news, dinner the night before, their siblings, and their struggles and accomplishments in school or out. They reflected on grandparents, pets, their classmates, the weather, and themselves. Sometimes there were tears, other times we laughed uproariously. They brought their lives into school each day, and whatever they brought could be woven into our learning.

Each day, I simply asked: "Who has something?"

One morning their conversation concerned how all of us, especially children, were constantly filled with the useless knowledge of our material culture. They remarked on how they felt assaulted by directives on what to buy, and how to act or appear, and how they were bombarded by consumer messaging. My students knew the release dates of the next Hollywood blockbusters, that Dodge equaled *Grabbing Life By the Horns*, that Subway meant *Eat Fresh*, that McDonald's was *I'm Lovin' It*, that owning a Cadillac was all about *Break on Through*, that

Bill Gates had been temporarily surpassed by Jeff Bezos as the world's richest man.

"I heard that kids see like three hundred advertisements a day," said Nils. The accurate number of advertising and brand exposures was actually somewhere closer to two thousand to three thousand per day, along with up to forty thousand TV advertisements per year. So I tested them.

"What's the latest product John Keats is putting out?"

"What are you talking about?" asked Winn.

"What's the new hit song by Duke Ellington?"

"Oh, oh, didn't Rihanna do a song with him?" offered Katelyn.

"Katelyn," I said, "that would have been cool, but Duke Ellington was a jazz composer. He's dead."

"Oh, oops. But I totally love Rihanna!" she said. Duke Ellington and his contributions to American culture were, as yet, of no importance to Katelyn Sawyer-Brown.

"Okay!" I said. "What country is the Dalai Lama from?"

"Burma!"

"China!"

Nils's hand was raised. His long hair, parted neatly in the middle, was tied back in a ponytail. He rarely wore shoes and sometimes had a cloth kilt wrapped around his torn jeans, which were covered in black pen doodles and lyrics by Ani DiFranco.

"Nepal?" he offered.

"Close!" I shouted back.

"He's like the pope of Buddhism," Nils said.

"Yes!" I shouted. "There's hope yet. Who can name five famous scientists?"

A few hands went up.

"Oh, wait," said Bennett. "Newton. And Einstein. And um . . . oh shit. I can't think of it."

"Archimedes! Archimedes!" shouted Winn. "That's the quote in Rose's room!" Any time Winn made a connection, she was ecstatic.

"Aeropostale?" shouted Bennett. "He was like a Greek philosopher?"

"You idiot!" shouted Callum. "It's not Aeropostale, it's Aristotle!"

"How many of you know what the number of the latest iPhone is?" I asked.

Virtually every hand in the room went up.

"How many of you know what the sound and the fury signifies?" No hands reached for the sky. They looked at me with blank eyes, and then clamored for me to test them on slogans of products about which they were, it appeared, veritable geniuses. They were excited by how much they knew. IBM? *Think Big.* Geico? *Fifteen minutes could save you fifteen percent or more.* They knew Taylor Swift's birthday, but not names of America's great jazz musicians or any female scientists. They spoke with intimate familiarity about iPhone's Siri, but they did not know the rudiments of spiritual seeking.

"You guys are freaking hopeless!" I called out amid laughter and shouting. No one seemed to hear. Morning meeting ended and we headed off to class.

Later in the morning, after science class let out, Callum burst into the big room.

"Tal, I have an idea! We should have someone recite a poem every morning at meeting after we say the good things. Like what Ariela did. That way we can start filling up with a different kind of knowledge, like poetry knowledge."

"That's a great idea, Callum."

The next morning meeting, we began—our small revolt against the rapacious encroachment of popular consumer culture, a humble attempt to take a stand and move the world. Callum held a piece of paper in front of him.

"This is a poem by Rumi," he said. "I'm studying him for my project." He looked at me as if to ask, *What should I do?* I didn't know how it should go either. We were beginning something and we had to see what would happen.

"So should I just read it?"

"Yeah, man. Just go for it."

Callum read the poem. *In your light I learn how to love. / In your beauty, how to make poems. / You dance inside my chest, / where no one sees you, / but sometimes I do, / and that sight becomes this art.*

The class applauded respectfully, not quite knowing why Callum was reading them a poem by a Sufi mystic, or even what a Sufi mystic was.

"So what we'll do is have someone sign up to read the poem every morning," I said. "Who wants to read a poem tomorrow?"

The next day, Bennett read Frost's "The Road Not Taken." *Yet knowing how way leads on to way . . .* the words echoed into the school. Callum's idea led us on, and that was how we began to find our way, poem to poem, every morning.

We asked students to build their learning around what mattered to them. We asked them to become seers and seekers of beauty and truth. Truth, and the beauty of the truth, was not to be found in a textbook, on a test, or in a chapter summary. Lesson plans, rigid schedules, final exams, standardized testing, PowerPoint presentations, the Internet, even instructions from me—none of these were truly necessary. Truth and beauty would be found in the full amplitude of lived experience and in talking about and recording what we found.

Once my students left our school, there would likely not be time in high school to spend hours each week in the search for beauty, or to invent rituals, particularly one that required the reading of a poem every day. Conventional schools held assemblies, pep rallies, and awards ceremonies, occasions driven not by the immediate imperatives of students, but by administrative or institutional needs. No matter where my students headed after the North Branch School, education for them was going to be less personally engaging. The self and the soul would no longer be central. I knew this because they wrote and told me.

"How's high school?" I asked.

"It's *okay*," they said. "It's *soul-grinding*," they said.

But it was clear: a connection was severed, channels to the heart closed up. The system—grades, credits, tests, schedules—imposed its demands.

A former student, Courtney, once wrote me after she graduated from North Branch; high school, she said, was barely tolerable. But now, finally, in April, after a routine and stultifying year of tenth grade, she finally had a real reason to write to me.

Something interesting happened! she exclaimed, and she described how her substitute teacher had discarded the lesson plans he'd been issued and instead spent the entire two-hour block describing his experiences as a soldier in Vietnam. He told them of his feelings—guilt, terror, sadness, patriotism, pride, shame, doubt. He answered their questions, he allowed their curiosity to open him up, and he spoke with direct honesty and the truth of himself.

Courtney told me she then wrote him a page-long letter thanking him for that class. Courtney was not a great student of war, nor fascinated by history; no, she wrote ecstatically, *It was real. He was telling us about him. For a whole hour we had a real conversation.*

My students, like all adolescents and teenagers, clamored for that kind of contact with life. As they approached adulthood, they hungered to feel and inhabit what was to come. They wanted to slip the skin of real life on and see how it fit. They wanted to achieve authentic, dimensional being, to know about love and suffering, to feel like they could be part of history or to have a hand in making it.

❦

Ruby was a ninth grader, in her third year. She'd grown up in upstate New York and was close to becoming a "forty-sixer"— one who'd climbed all forty-six 4000-plus-foot mountains in the Adirondacks, a great feat of endurance and commitment. She'd started climbing when she was five years old.

One morning she told us, with a flush of bright red in her cheeks and prideful excitement in her voice, that on the coming weekend she was going to climb her forty-sixth and final peak.

At lunch I was tossing a baseball with Bennett and Cole in the field.

"Why would anyone want to climb forty-six mountains?'" asked Bennett with derision. "That's so dumb. What's the point?"

"What do you mean, what's the point?" I asked. "It's incredible."

"It sounds dumb to me."

"You sound jealous to me. You sound like someone who hasn't yet found his mountain to climb."

Later in class, Ruby raised her hand. "Can I bring up something?"

"Sure, be my guest." I sensed she was mad, and if her anger led to conflict, then that had to be allowed to happen. Dissension and anger were a necessary part of the whole. It was doubly important that a girl take a stand. It was so easy, and so often the case, that adolescent girls held back from taking a public stand and acquiesced to the voices and directives of boys. I wanted Ruby to be bold, to take ground and hold it.

Ruby looked around the room, hesitating. "Um, Bennett, did I hear you ask Tal why would I climb the forty-six 4000-foot mountains? Did you really say it's dumb? *Really?*" Her face was blazing red.

All movement in the room was arrested. Bennett looked down at the floor, his face flushed.

"Um, yeah. But . . ."

"Well, it pissed me off that you said that!" Ruby continued. "It's the most important thing I've ever done. Jesus!"

There was a long silence in the room. I waited for them. They had to define the limits of what was acceptable. They had to stake a claim for what they believed was right and good.

"I think climbing those mountains is awesome," said Nolan.

"It *is* awesome," said Ruby. She was on fire. "It's what I do. It's part of who I am. I'm proud of that."

As gently as I could, I asked, "What else could you have said, Bennett?"

There was another long pause.

"He could ask, 'How did you do that, Ruby?'" offered Nils.

"Or, 'What's the tallest one you've climbed?'" said Katelyn.

"He could have said, 'That's awesome,'" said Yebsera.

"My question is: 'Why would you *not* climb the forty-six mountains if you could?'" I asked. "Why would any of us ground ourselves when we could be on a mountain top seeing for 150 miles in every direction?"

We waited again.

"I'm so proud of what I've done," Ruby said. "A lot of those mountains I climbed with my dad and my mom. I'll have it for the rest of my life." She was staring at Bennett.

"That was dumb of me to say," Bennett said finally. "I guess—um—" and he broke off again, staring at the table.

"The only big mountain I've ever climbed is Mount Abe," said Katelyn. "And I only did that once."

"I'm jealous," said Haley. "Hiking isn't something my family really does because my dad's heart is so weak. So when I think of her doing that, it makes me think of my dad. And it makes me think about how strong Ruby is."

"Tell us more," I said. The class knew about her father's heart condition, but I wanted them to know why it mattered now. Why was she thinking about her father when Ruby was talking about Mount Marcy?

"I'll never get to climb a mountain with my father," she said. "He'll never climb a mountain. Never be able to, I mean."

"Can you understand that?" I said. But I wasn't talking to Bennett. I was talking to all of them. "Ruby is mad to live, to go to high places. She's been blessed to share that with her mom and dad. Shouldn't we all be living with that kind of fierceness? Haley knows what it's like to not have that. She's telling us that it's a treasure."

"I look up to my uncle," said Nolan. "Because he's always going out in the early morning to climb mountains before sunrise. I want to live like that, not be someone who just slept my life away."

There was a pause. "So . . . Bennett?" I didn't know if he had anything more to say, but the door was open. He stared at the table, glanced up and scanned the bookshelves.

"Well, now that I'm thinking about it," he began, but he paused, looking down at the table. "I think I am a little jealous of Ruby, actually. It'd be awesome to do that. I wish I could do that. I shouldn't have said what I did. That was just really dumb."

"You can set your path in the other direction," I said, softly. "Ask her about it. Inquire about what it means to have a great goal. To live it out. Let her tell you what she learned when she comes back."

I told them about Mozart's antagonist, Salieri. "He was the patron saint of mediocrity. He was bitter and broken because he was never great and always played it safe. Mozart was filled with passion and fire. He took great risks and was fully alive. Do we really want to be nothings, slugs who just leave a silver stream of slime behind us? Or do we want to evolve into giants of the best that is in us?"

"I guess the second one," said Bennett. He was smiling.

Over and over, I saw that conflict and tension were not only inevitable, but necessary. Martin Luther King, Jr. wrote in "A Letter from Birmingham Jail" that tension was a prerequisite for social evolution. *I must confess that I am not afraid of the word "tension." . . . there is a type of constructive nonviolent tension that is necessary for growth.*

Adolescence is a series of small crises of great psychological, developmental, and social tension. It was imperative, then, to not be afraid. To avoid those developmental shifts and frictions would be to sidestep the crucial life energies surging in the kids in the classroom. Tension and conflict, once named, expressed and clarified, gave way to greater, deeper, more loving awareness and more nuanced understanding. Behind anger was always something beautiful or fragile that needed to be expressed. And behind guilt or sadness lay immense affection or devotion, which, expressed improperly or not at all, dried up and shrank into dark corners of consciousness. I often explained to parents: if we want them to grow up and be true to themselves, they need to begin to learn about the courage and directness that entails.

Hannah was a seventh grader, petite and pale with freckles and orange hair angled up in a mohawk. She lived alone with her mother. Her father lived in Florida and she'd never met him. Hannah wore square-framed glasses, which continually embarrassed her. But she wanted to talk about what she was feeling. Her face would turn red when she spoke, and she was desperately dependent on the word "like" when struggling to find words to say how she felt or what she understood. But no matter how difficult it was to articulate her feelings, she remained undeterred and relentless, reentering moments when she felt herself tested and held in tension. Her willingness to go back into herself made her stronger as she went forward. She learned about herself, and the class learned along with her.

Hannah's speech recalled how, when she was very little, she spent days with her aged grandmother. To Hannah, to remember those mornings was to feel as though the two of them were the only people in the world. She remembered how she lay in the bed with her grandmother listening to the morning songs of birds, and how her grandmother told her the name of each one. Then they would rise from the bed, and Hannah would help her grandmother slip her bony feet into her slippers and hold her as she stood on her thin legs. They would walk into the kitchen together, where they made breakfast with real lemon in the tea and honey on the toast. Her grandmother would feed her old dog the toast under the table, against the rules, yes, but Hannah understood: her grandmother felt something deeper for the old hound, and Hannah felt something deeper for her grandmother.

Then Hannah scampered off to play and watch her TV shows. She had forgotten her grandmother, left her, momentarily, to do a childish thing. She was, after all, still a child.

Her grandmother followed and found her and said, "I didn't know where you went. I was looking for you." Hannah recalled that her grandmother seemed afraid and confused.

Hannah was sure she had committed some treacherous betrayal. And when, months later, her grandmother died, Hannah could only think about how she had left her grandmother to go watch the Disney Channel.

Now, looking back, Hannah wrote, *I hate what I did. I left her alone. I abandoned my Nana to watch a stupid TV show.*

"Why did I do that? Why did I do that?" she asked, standing before us and clutching her speech, her lips quivering. Her speech resolved to love everything and everyone, always, with as much fierce devotion as she could, because she knew that the world she so loved was fragile and would someday be gone.

"So did Hannah do a bad thing when she left her grandmother?" I asked the class afterwards. "I mean, is the feeling that she did a bad thing for not having stayed by her grandmother's side the right feeling?"

"She was doing the things little kids do. How could it be a bad thing?" answered Nolan, pushing back his bangs under his black San Francisco Giants ball cap. "There was no way for her to know what it all meant. I guess it's normal to feel guilty, but she isn't guilty of anything."

"Then what's behind the guilty feeling?" I asked. Hannah watched this conversation, her cheeks flushed, her gaze moving from Nolan to me, and then to the others. To hear what others thought was an experience in itself, a making of waves. She asked, *What did I create? What have I given?*

"It's love for her grandmother," said Bennett. "What she's feeling now means she loved her grandmother. She feels guilt because she feels responsibility. She feels responsibility because she loved her."

"Or, she loved her, but feels bad about the one time when she thinks she didn't love her," I said.

"But that still means she loved her, no matter what she did one time."

"It seems like she loved her grandmother as deeply as a child can love," I said, pausing. "So is that an answer for how we should live? To love deeply? To be responsible to the ones we love?"

"She has to remember what she felt when she was listening to the birds," said Winn.

"That was the most important thing," said Nolan.

"So she has to think about the power of her love for her grandmother, and doing that means feeling pain as well?"

"Yes."

"Could she hold multiple feelings now? Acceptance that she had a childish impulse, and also the knowledge that death comes, and also her deeper impulse to be good and loving? And remembering those times that she wrote about? Can all feelings live in her simultaneously?"

"Well, if they do, then she'll be really aware," said Winn. "Her love is still alive. Like, she's feeling it now. She never stopped loving her grandmother. It's right there in her speech."

But there was more.

"It makes me think of my grandparents," Brody said, his voice nearly a whisper.

"I don't have much of a relationship with my grandmother," said Nils.

"What Hannah had, I wish I had," said Haley.

"Say more," I said.

"I mean, to have that much love, to love someone that much. To have had that."

In the space that followed, in the brief silence between the end of that sentence and the next, a door was opening, and the boundaries of the common expanded. Hannah's feeling, expressed in a speech, was a rare song—a true, resonant story about companionship, and old age, loneliness, and love. We might not have ever spent time with an aging grandparent, but we learned from Hannah about listening to the names of birds, about the power of actions and inactions, and the greater depths of feeling with which we might live.

Those were living lessons we would remember.

On a cool morning in late September, I faced my students as they gathered around the table.

"What are we going to do this morning?" Winn asked.

"We're going to read a poem. No one move. Don't even blink. It's going to make your hair catch on fire. You will never be the same again. You will be changed."

I wasn't smiling; I wanted them on edge. Hair catching on fire didn't always happen, but it was always the intention. An epiphany every day, if not every hour.

"This poem is by Robert Hayden. It's a sonnet. A sonnet is a fourteen-line poem. This one's about Frederick Douglass, who was a former slave who became a great orator and activist against slavery, an abolitionist. He spent his life trying to abolish slavery and fighting for the rights of African Americans. But that's not the only important thing. What's also important is what the poem makes you feel *right now*. Think about yourself in this world. Think about what this poem is telling you. *That* is why we are reading it. What you feel and think when you hear a poem or story is why we read poems and stories."

There was silence in the room. I held the poem just over the top of the table.

"This poem is a doorway, a portal, a threshold, a transporter to another realm—"

"Tal," said Nadia. She pulled her hair behind her ear.

"What?"

She placed her hands in her lap, her back straight. "Can we hear the poem?" She was shutting me up and smiling at the same time.

"Okay, I'll read it now. So listen . . ."

When it is finally ours, this freedom, this liberty, this
  beautiful
and terrible thing, needful to man as air,
usable as earth; when it belongs at last to all,
when it is truly instinct, brain matter, diastole, systole,
reflex action; when it is finally won; when it is more

than the gaudy mumbo jumbo of politicians:
this man, this Douglass, this former slave, this Negro
beaten to his knees, exiled, visioning a world
where none is lonely, none hunted, alien,
this man, superb in love and logic, this man
shall be remembered. Oh, not with statues' rhetoric,
not with legends and poems and wreaths of bronze alone,
but with the lives grown out of his life, the lives
fleshing his dream of the beautiful, needful thing.

Hayden had taken from Douglass, and I gave them what Hayden made. Yes, I was trying to awaken their hearts with those fourteen lines. Because the poem was, as all good poems are, about the passion and vision with which we must live, or that we must discover. In short space, with immense force and energy, "Frederick Douglass" celebrated a heart of greatness. *Diastole, systole.* The poem, in its motion and rhythm, was itself a beating heart, the heart of a man in all of his nobility, sounding in our ears, the pulsing music of a great man whose dream we might flesh.

For an hour we dwelled in it and deciphered it. What *was* the beautiful, needful thing? Where would we find it? How could we make it? I didn't ask them to raise their hands, but they did.

"When he talks about the beautiful needful thing," Nils said, "we could say that whatever we wrote in our speeches is our own beautiful needful thing."

"You mean, your speeches are where you talked about that which is needful to us as air?"

"Yeah."

"So what is it we have to do?" I asked.

"We have to find the beautiful, needful thing," Nadia answered.

"Yes, that's what we have to do."

Not every class and not every poem elicited epiphanies. There were days when I did not know how to precede. Days when all our energies seemed run-down. There were days when they stared blankly, mornings when they had not read the literature assignment, entire classes in which I labored desperately to keep the conversation alive. Their minds could be infuriatingly dormant, their tongues tragically lazy. They could be more excited by someone's new haircut than, say, the 274 words of the Gettysburg Address. A fidget spinner was infinitely more riveting than Hemingway's Old Man, and his dream of the lions on the beach. A new rumor had its own incandescent magic that I was often powerless to outshine. How many times had I found, at the day's end, a clementine peel cut into a hundred perfect half-centimeter squares and scattered across the table? If they ever brought that kind of deep focus to a sonnet by Shakespeare, they could have been Elizabethan scholars.

The mornings of our days were spent in science and math classes or literature classes, in groups divided for geometry or algebra and literature, or in free work periods. The work periods gave them time to work together, alone, or with me one-to-one. During the days, students moved freely about the school, into the office to make copies, to one of two computers to print photos of volcanoes, to the basement to paint a poster board, to the piano to play music at lunch. The sounds of Coldplay or Mozart and Adele and Scott Joplin and the ubiquitous "Heart and Soul" filled the rooms of the school. Soccer balls in the corners, backpacks piled in the entry on an old church pew, an aquarium with two skittish piranhas named Luna and Jesus, a single bathroom with an excellent selection of reading material: the 2009 *World Almanac*, a 1978 *National Geographic*, and a copy of Gary Larson's *Cows of the Planet*. No permissions, no hall passes, no intercoms.

Most afternoons of each day were scheduled simply as "All Tal": the whole school together in one room, a two or three hour potpourri of literature, history, art, philosophy, project presentations, religion, and creative writing.

Discussions in class were most often improvisations and only loosely planned. We *planned* emptiness. We allowed for large swaths of time and tried not to overly control what happened. And because it was being created in the moment, there was always a sense of nervous anticipation, both in myself and in the students. If we were lucky, vistas opened and the classroom came alive.

I linked our conversations to other ideas from other classes and helped them see how their ideas and theories were connected to philosophical explorations of the historical past. They were inquiring about morality, community, friendship, matter, spirit, the nature of love and meaning in no less serious a manner than Plato or Schopenhauer because their lives *were* connected to the world. I wanted them to see the relations between things, and particularly their relations to each other. I could sprinkle in theories, historical context, facts, or wisdom based on my experience, but it was the combustion between universal ideas and their particular lives that provided our richest material. When they understood that they were budding philosophers, they became impassioned and invested.

These conversations happened continually—in the middle of lit class, at lunch, after school. One led to another and the next morning we would pick up where we left off. By this method we built up a natural accumulation and accretion of ideas, ongoing discussions that were personal, emotional, and intellectual in nature. From constant questioning, we built scaffoldings on which understanding grew.

I did not have a degree in education, and I had not studied the Socratic method, but over time I discovered that such a mode of constant, direct inquiry allowed the students to feel as though they were creating knowledge, that they were feeling their way forward as part of an ancient and noble tradition. My role, in the ideal, was to help them constantly arrive at a state of *aporia*: puzzlement, doubt, an impasse, or a new awareness of their previously held beliefs.

Socrates believed that aporia was good because it fostered and sharpened questioning and renewed hunger for knowledge. It broke down shallowly considered ideas, theories, or misinterpretations so students might move beyond their common or unquestioned knowledge. To arrive at such a point, Socrates believed, was purgative. One might see what one did not know, and so the desire to investigate and question further would grow. Jacques Derrida defined aporia to be the location of "undecidability," where things or ideas came apart. Others characterized it as a kind of trauma, a wound. The literary theorist Valiur Rahaman believed aporia was a creative force in art and that it put the artist at the point of "edgeless-ness." I loved this idea of edgeless-ness, which led us in the direction of infinitude. Thoughts, ideas, and possibilities could expand in ever-widening circles. As Emerson wrote, "under every deep a lower deep opens." My job was to keep us at that edge, where we could dive for the treasure for as long as we liked.

Rose taught math. She came to our school with no formal teaching experience; her gift was an ability to care about children as much as math, and to do both with reverence, unrelenting hard work, and child-like openness. She had grown into her teaching, which partook not only of the Pythagorean theorem, proportional reasoning, and data analysis, but also of Pascal and Aristotle, stained glass and toothpick bridges, Fantasy Math football, Chinese kites, and medieval labyrinths.

Lately, she and her geometry class had been looking at a reproduction of Raphael's "School of Athens" to understand three-point perspective.

"We should have a North Branch pantheon," Callum said one morning.

"Who would we put in it?" I asked.

They called out names, mostly people we had learned about the previous year. "Bucky Fuller!" "Abigail Adams!" "John Coltrane!" "Mother Teresa!" "Joe Strummer!" "Lucretia Mott!"

"Derek Jeter!" shouted Cole.

"Justin Bieber!" shouted Katelyn.

"We will *not* have Justin Bieber in a pantheon!" Henry called out. He was the school troubadour, his pants rolled up, his socks mismatched, carrying his guitar from class to class, playing bits of blues and the latest chords he'd learned. He took it as his duty to enforce good taste in music.

"Justin Bieber could be a North Branch hero," Katelyn asserted.

Amid this discussion, Ariela's hand was raised. I called on her and the hero discussion died down.

"I've been really liking how in math Rose has been teaching about Plato's cave and Socrates," she said.

"That's a cool thing to learn about in math," I said. "Did you guys know that this is a kind of Socratic classroom?"

"Is that your teaching style?" asked Nils. His emphasis on "style" suggested that he was not convinced that I had any kind of organized pedagogy.

"Partially," I said. "Except you guys are not yet quite Greek scholars. You are average, run-of-the-mill middle schoolers, so my art takes more art."

"How does it work, Socratic-ism, I mean?" he asked.

"I ask you a lot questions, even when I have an idea of the answer. It's a form of conversation. I try to keep some tension and pressure on you, and your task is to listen and stay open to what you discover, and try to see what you hadn't seen before as it becomes clear. Along the way I try to learn things from you, too."

"Can you, like, do it on us?" he asked.

The day before, I had observed the ninth graders in a science lab at tables set up outside. They had been wearing goggles and aprons and were all armed with hammers. With varying degrees of attention to the task and lots of broken rocks, they'd been immersed in a joyful sense of doing something.

"Okay. Let's see. Callum, yesterday in science, describe what happened."

"Well, yesterday Henry and I were doing the lab about the hardness of rocks. But it was really cool, because we were doing the lab the way we were supposed to, and we were figuring out everything, but we were also playing around, and laughing."

"So what?" I asked.

"I don't know. It was like we had a special bond. Like we both knew we wanted to do well, but we could have fun doing it."

"What is this feeling?" I asked.

"Safety is what I felt," said Henry.

"What do you mean?"

"Like I knew he wouldn't drag me down, because he cares about me and what's important to me."

"It's sort of like I can float out on my own," explained Callum. "But Henry would pull me back if I started to screw around."

"Should that be our goal here?" I asked.

"You mean, to be able to be free but also float out, but not disconnect ourselves?" asked Nils.

"Yeah."

"Why?"

"Because that only gets you so far. And people can only go so far with superficial jokes. There's a limit. And I want to get somewhere."

"And?"

"And I know that if something important happens, that the important thing won't stay hidden."

Katelyn picked up the thread. "I hide the deeper parts of myself when I only focus on what is fun or what I am happy about."

"What's wrong with expressing happiness?" I asked.

"Well, I'm not giving my whole self."

"What's wrong with that?"

"Because then I don't show the other things inside me."

"What's wrong with only showing a certain side of yourself?"

"I don't ever resolve or figure out the deeper things. And I drive everyone crazy."

"Then you're only a shadow of yourself?"

"And stuck there," Bennett interjected, "because you don't go to the hard things or the things with meaning."

I held up a tattered sheet of homework, a hastily scribbled math assignment.

"What happens if someone only shows this?"

"It's just a piece of garbage," said Nils.

"What if this is the best that person can do? Do we accept it or not?" I asked.

"That's not good enough," said Ruby. "Anyone can take care of a homework assignment. They should, anyway. Because that's part of showing that we care about what we're doing here. If we don't care about a math assignment, then what *do* we care about? What's the point of being here?"

"But why should you care what someone else does?" I asked. "What difference does it make whether someone else does good work or not so long as *you* do?"

"We all have to care about what others are doing," Nils asserted. "That's what this school is. Caring about each other."

"It's like what Callum was saying. If someone doesn't do their best work, they are apart, and we're not together," said Bennett, twirling his baseball cap on his finger. "We have to bring them into us. We can't let one single boat be separated from the big ship."

"But how do we make that happen?"

"The root of the root," said Nolan.

"What?" I asked.

"We have to get to the root of thing. To the bottom of what's the matter."

"Even if someone does a bad thing?"

"Especially if someone does a bad thing."

"Why?"

"We have to believe that what someone does has a reason," he said, staring straight at me. "A root. And that the root has a root. And we have to get to it."

Dust-motes floated in the sunlight and flies buzzed over us in the early, still-warm October afternoon. The table was crowded with backpacks, notebooks piled on top of sketchbooks, and the residue of lunch.

When they were settled in, I began. "When we grapple with our fears, we find things we didn't know existed."

Nobody said anything.

"That makes sense," said Nils, after a moment of silence, though he didn't seem inspired or convinced.

"Words which are flowers become fruits which are deeds," I said. "That's a line by the poet Octavio Paz. If you make a move, if you put something into action, even if it is scary, but especially if it is good, you can make something beautiful and real."

They looked at me.

"So . . . beautiful and real is . . ." Winn began. She sat pressed against the table, eagerly recording every quotable remark said in class. She wore lace skirts and scuffed cowboy boots. A scattering of freckles drifted down her nose onto her cheeks. Her brown hair was in two braids, and she wore her John Deere trucker hat. Her pencil was poised over her notebook.

"You make something great by telling a true story," I continued. "Inside the stories in your speeches is the golden honey. If you can find and taste it, you can become heroic. A famous scholar named Joseph Campbell once said, 'We are all Galahads, you know.'"

Winn carefully transcribed those words into her composition book.

"Do we mean a good life as in 'do whatever the hell you want, when you want to do it?'" I asked. "Or do we mean a good life is to live in a mansion with a heated pool and a new iPhone 14 and 800 Insta Snapchat followers and have no worries? Or do we mean good also includes responsibility, duty, happiness, expression, truth, openness, or generosity? Are we talking about something for ourselves, or for all of us? Are we talking about a shining and inanimate thing—or are we talking about what we do?"

There was a long gap of silence. No answers, no arms raised. It was possible the discussion would go nowhere.

"Here's an example. What is most important, a rare Stradivarius violin enclosed in its protective case, shining and perfect, a monument to human craftsmanship? Or the fiddle of man who lived a hard life as a coal miner, a fiddle handed down to him by his father that he takes off the hook on a winter night and begins to play an old song his father taught him?"

"The rare violin has value and beauty in how it looks or in what it's worth if you sold it," said Bennett. "But the coal miner's violin has value and beauty because of its history or what it did."

"I'd take the beat up fiddle any day," said Callum. "It's got human love in it."

"What is human love?" I asked.

"Human love is . . ." began Henry, but he stopped.

"Human love is what one human creates with another," said Hannah.

"Be more specific," I said.

"The coal miner's fiddle has the love between the father and the son in it," said Callum.

"Is that more human love than the person who made the beautiful Stradivarius?" I asked.

"The most important thing is the music the instrument makes," said Nils. "But the expensive violin could have human love given to it by whoever made it so beautiful, because there is love in how a thing is made."

"Neither one of them is a 'good violin' until a human makes it good," said Bennett. "It all has to do with what is put into it for the violin to be living a good life."

"So both the fiddle and the Stradivarius have potential?" I asked "They only have real value by what is played on them?"

"Yeah, I guess."

"Whether we are rich or poor, short or tall. Whether we are beautifully crafted and polished or beat up and weathered, the question is: can we play our lives? Can we make music that is really ourselves, something that flows from us, played over the strings with soul and love?"

"Yes," said Yebsera. Adopted from Ethiopia when he was nine, Yeb presented joyful happiness on some days, a fearful dread on others. His mother and his brother had died of AIDS. I knew these facts, but I did not yet know Yebsera. I wanted him, and his life, entirely in the room.

"How do you know, Yeb? How do you know how to play your life to make it a good life?"

"I don't know."

Socratic inquisition meant nothing until it opened my students up. Unless they let the experiences of their lives rise up in them, they were treading in still water, believing a thing, but not knowing why. The answer, the source of whatever knowing he had, was in him. The trick was to find a way to help him bring it out.

"Yeb, is there anyone who you know whose life played over the strings and made pure music? Who lived an authentic life?"

"What does 'authentic' mean?"

"Someone with a golden heart. Something real and true and nothing fake."

"Yeah."

"Who?

"My mother."

"Your birth mother in Ethiopia, or your adoptive mother here in Vermont?"

"My birth mother."

"Do you have a picture of her?"

"Yes. On my dresser."

"Where is she now?"

"She's dead. She died when I was like, seven."

"Why do you keep a picture of her on your dresser?"

"Because I want to remember her?" he asked, unsure of this most essential truth. The hesitance in his answer suggested that to remember her was to awaken something at once terrifying and essential.

"Because why?

"Because she was strong. Because she tried to help us live."

"Us?"

"My brothers and me."

"How'd she try to help you live?"

"She walked fifteen kilometers every day to sell baskets she made so she could get us food. She took them to a market to sell them."

"So how was she living?"

"She was living for us. Not for herself." There is a long pause after this, a silence in the room. One tear slid down Yebsera's cheek.

"Behind that was what? Why would she do that?"

"Because she loved us."

"Was your mother someone who was trying to live a good life?"

"Yeah, yes, I think so," he said finally. "Not like a famous hero or something. Not like a rich person. She did live a good life."

"Did she have a golden heart? Does she have a golden heart?"

"Yes."

"Do you know where that golden heart is now?"

"No. Wait, what do you mean?"

"Where is that golden heart now?"

"I don't know. It's gone. She's dead."

"Or maybe. . ."

"Maybe her golden heart is—I have her golden heart?"

"Do you think so? Do you feel it?"

He shrugged.

I looked around. "What's Yebsera telling us? What's he giving us?"

"It's a message that we need to find our own golden hearts," said Winn.

My students occasionally found their way to moments of supremely beautiful epiphany. Yet they were still so fragile, so vulnerable to the smallest slights, tone of voice, or subtle glances. They were on the cusp of adulthood, yes, beginning to wear the mantle of responsibility, purpose, and achievement. But if given permission, raw, inchoate feelings roiled in them and it only took the simple question to tip them.

In the Grail legend, Percival's essential question—*What ails you?*—was the simple question that needed to be asked. It was the key to unlocking his power and healing the wasteland. With middle school kids, the question often was, "How do you feel? What's up? What's the matter?" Just a few steps past the monosyllabic or glib response—hovering just behind the ubiquitous and dismissive "Whatever" or "Fine" or "I'm just tired"—were large knots of feelings, inner landscapes laden with doubt or insight, confusion or clarity, a new idea, or a line that sang. To ask adolescents "How do you feel?" moved them in the direction of their powers.

Henry read his speech about how he fought and battled with his younger brother, how he did all in his power to negate his brother, to go back to the prelapsarian time when it was only Henry and his mother and father—the *holy trinity,* he wrote. But he could not get rid of his brother, and their relationship eroded over time into a never-ending series of vicious battles in a lifelong war: who sat in front, who cheated in the game, who teased whom in a soccer game with friends, who ignored whom, who weaseled out of getting in trouble.

Games of backyard soccer became violent. The force of fists, the force of cutting words at twilight in the grass—Henry was relentless in his honesty. He beat his brother up whenever he had the chance; he felt he was monstrous to his brother; sometimes he felt he did not deserve to live. He also held onto a clawing belief that he and his little brother would never again get along, and so he relentlessly punished him. The story was filled with a sense of powerlessness that it would never change. They would never go skiing together again, never give the other a compliment, never return to the childhood Lego table where they had once played peacefully in the fantastic cities of their imaginations. But from those truths, he envisioned the opposite of hopelessness. At night, he'd look up at a skylight above his bed.

When I gazed into the gateway of that window, when I had the courage to do that finally, I didn't want to see the dragons and devils camping out on my roof, I didn't want to see myself miserable, having failed myself. I didn't want to see my teachers disappointed, my mother hurt, my friends ditched, my brother in pain. I wanted to look into that window, and see nothing but myself, smiling back at me. A wink would be nice, like a kind old wizard expressing how he approved, but was too wise to try and use words. Maybe one day I could look at the big picture, all the parts of me, the good and the bad, then understand it, understand why, and smile. I just hoped that day would come soon.

I asked, afterwards, as always: "How did hearing that make you feel?" One by one we went around the table.

"My brother is older, so now I know how he feels sometimes," said Bennett.

Winn looked up from her class notebook where she was writing a letter to Henry. "It seems like brothers can be really brutal. Like physical cruelty, I mean." For some of them this may have been familiar. To Winn it was a window into darkness.

"I'm the older brother, and I never really thought about how it might seem to my younger sister," said Nolan. "I feel like I can see the other side."

They were asking, *How is this me, how am I that? Am I different, or the same?*

The phrase "I know how he feels" came up again and again because Henry's story had made it safe for them to see themselves with clarity and honesty. They could recognize their own feelings through it. Along with memorizing academic concepts, impersonal histories, or mathematical formulas, they were learning to see themselves. As Henry waded into the taxonomy of conflict and growth, he gave them a way to order the hierarchy of their own experiences.

I asked them to each take a turn afterwards to say one feeling they felt as they listened. *Mesmerized. Strange. Like my own brother. Sad.* Then I came to Hannah. She was in the back of the room with her chair turned slightly away from the table. Her mouth moved but we couldn't hear her words.

"Did you say 'The same'?" I asked. Sometimes they cried, sometimes they resisted. Sometimes their voices shook, sometimes they spoke in whispers.

"Ashamed," she said, louder this time. Then her face reddened, and she began to cry. The tears, as always, brought the class to a rare, intensified focus. Some portion of Hannah's soul was vibrating and trying to speak, and they were going to listen.

"Did you feel ashamed because the story made you think about how you treat your brother sometimes?" I asked.

Yes, she nodded.

"Like, sometimes you're mean to him or you're too busy to play with him?" Her admission required vulnerability. I wanted her to go further, to see what it had to teach.

Again she nodded.

"Why is that?"

Through tears, as quickly as she could say the words, she said, "Sometimes I'm so mean to him and I don't know why. I want to be nice to him, I want to play with him. He always wants to play with me. I don't want to hurt him. I want to show him I love him."

"But maybe there are reasons?" Winn interjected. "Maybe you're growing up and you have new things to do."

"Maybe. I guess. But I still hurt him and yell at him."

There was no answer. The story had pierced her deeply, but also revealed her humanness—to her and the class. As she saw the shape of her "bad" feelings, she also saw ideals towards which she might move. In a brief moment, she had a glimpse of who she was, and who she might be. This was learning by way of the heart.

Hurt, shame, suffering, guilt, and doubt, I had learned, were great teachers, forces that pushed, shaped, and tested. As my students explored those darker regions, they found what darkness was, as well as their own incipient power to find lights that marked a way home. The deepest learning happened when they learned to see themselves truly.

Two days later, we were still working on a draft of Bennett's speech. His was the last one, and he wasn't happy with what he had. A good life for Bennett boiled down to a single final sentence: *A good life for me is to stand up for what I believe.*

"But it seems kind of boring so far," he whined after handing it in. "It's like the most boring-est speech anyone has ever written."

"There's nothing wrong with the idea," I said. "But it is pretty damn boring. You sound bored when you talk about it right now. You're not standing up for anything right now. You're just saying the words. It's not *alive*. There has to be some more compelling way to get it across."

"Yeah, probably."

"Do you have a model for this superhuman that you wish to be?"

"Well, the stories in the Bible, I guess."

"Is the Bible important to you?"

"Yeah, well, I mean, I know a lot of the stories."

"Why don't you use them in your speech?"

"Can I?"

"Yes, Bennett, this is a school; we're interested in ideas, history, myths, heroes, and even religion. Why not? You're free!"

"So, can I use the story of Samson?"

"Do you know it well enough to use it?"

"Yeah."

"You'll have to sketch it for us. Most of us are religious ignoramuses. Can you get it across to us and make us feel it? Can you relate it to yourself? Can you make us believe that you would like to be Samson?"

"I think so."

"Then go for it."

"Um, Tal, also, can I use the story of Jonah and the whale?"

"You want to go into the belly of the whale?"

"Yeah."

"It's dark in there."

"I know."

"Why do you want to go in there?"

"To be strong like Jonah. To show it can be done."

"And?"

"To not be afraid. To show everyone about courage."

"Bennett, you can be our Biblical scholar. You can retell the entire Old Testament if it helps you say what you need to say."

"Okay."

"But why do you want to be this great biblical hero? You gotta tell us more."

"I don't know." He looked down, then up.

"Was there ever a time when you weren't a hero?"

"Well, in elementary school I was picked on by Yebsera."

Yeb looked across the table at us, his head cocked slightly.

"We would always be playing soccer," Bennett began, "and then he would start to punt the ball into my face. He would come up really close and laugh and then punt it at me."

"Did you fight back?"

"No. I was afraid. I didn't want to get in a fight or get in trouble. And I thought if we fought we would never be able to be friends."

"Did you quit?"

"No, I was afraid to. Cause they'd call me a pussy."

"Is he telling a true story, Yeb?"

"Yeah. I kept doing it because it made Jason and the other kids laugh, and Bennett would kind of laugh, too. So I thought, like, he didn't really care." Yeb's voice was quiet.

"And now what're you finding out?"

"He didn't like it. I guess nobody would. I wouldn't like it."

"Nope, nobody would like it, even if they were laughing," I said, and Yeb nodded.

"So, Bennett, you want to do something now? This is why you want to be Samson? To keep Yeb from picking on you? To be a hero tough guy?"

"No, to keep anyone from picking on Yeb."

At this, many heads lifted up, a new frequency vibrating in the room. This was a revelation. He wasn't talking about his *own* fears and needs; he was talking for everyone. Yeb's eyes widened. I was flabbergasted.

"What? If he was the one who picked on you, why are you standing up for him?" I asked.

"Because he's my friend. I want him to be my friend."

"But he kicked the ball at you," I said. "I don't understand."

"He was my best friend in elementary school. I mean, he kicked the ball at me, but we were also best friends."

Yeb was looking down at the table.

"So, if he feels safe, then he won't do what he did again. And then you'll be safe? And for everyone in here?"

"Yeah, so they don't have to feel what I felt."

"Then we'll all be safe," said Hannah, quietly. She understood.

"You guys," I said, "do you all see this? Bennett wants to be Samson, Moses, Jonah, and David all in one. If he describes his feelings and where they came from, and we feel them, he becomes heroic. It's power and it's risk and it's love." He was living out Hayden's dream of Frederick Douglass: "*visioning a world / where none is lonely, none hunted, alien.*"

For Bennett to become himself, to soulfully demonstrate his faith in the highest good, he had to become unsafe, feel tension and the weight of things crashing down. Bennett risked all this by calling Yeb out, and calling himself out, and by pushing past his outer edge.

Days later, Bennett read a final draft. His voice rose with strength and clarity. His words stilled the room, made his classmates gaze at him and look at each other to see such power emanating from him.

He said: "To you, the class, I want to be a great, loving cathedral, the arms of a welcoming sanctuary."

FALL

I Dwell in possibility —

—Emily Dickinson

OUR SCHOOL WORKED BECAUSE ALL TWENTY-SEVEN of us could squeeze around the big wooden table and have a conversation. Everybody had a chance to speak. In literature class, all of the eighth and ninth graders leaned in with their copies of *Animal Farm* and a one-page response about the reading selection, usually twenty to twenty-five pages for each class, which they had been assigned to read twice. Year after year the copies of our books—battered, torn, and taped—were passed down. In the front covers, they saw names going back eight or ten years. To read the names was to look at growth rings of the school, all those who had sat at the table before doing this same thing, this intimate intensity of trying to understand what an old book could teach us. I told them to fill their books with notes and underlining and commentary. Many of them clamored for books that were worked over. Often they found messages written by previous students: *Dear whoever gets this book. I loved this book. There is something amazing on every page. I hope you will love it too.*

Callum raised his hand. He wanted to talk about Boxer, the great, loyal workhorse of *Animal Farm*. He started to speak, but was unable to form a sentence, his lips tightening, his face reddening, tears dropping out of his eyes. No matter how much he wanted words to flow, he could not find words, torrents of feeling dammed up inside. No one moved, no fidgeting, no doodling. All eyes were on Callum as he tried to form his words.

"Say it Callum, whatever it is. It doesn't have to make sense. Just let it go out." I didn't know if he could find words. Again, was I pushing him into a corner. But I believed *something* was in him.

Callum looked up at the triangular window above us, where clouds passed across the blue, the tendons in his neck showing taut. Then, slowly, he looked down, bowed his head, and spoke.

"Boxer works so hard. Harder than any one. And he doesn't even have a reason. He does it because he's so strong. He never gives up. He's being used. But what does he have? What if no one loves him? What's he going to get out of it in the end?"

Callum's head hung over his knees, his shoulders sagging, as though he were the exhausted beast. Ruby put her hand on his shoulder.

"Callum," I said. He looked up slowly. "You understand this book. You're understanding something far more important than knowledge about Soviet totalitarianism. You're feeling it. You're being opened by the book. Your mind and heart are alive to it."

I wanted him to know that his feelings, whatever form they took, were important. I tried to think of what to say next.

"See, Callum, I don't have a lesson plan. The lessons come from *you*."

"Why do you have such strong feelings for Boxer?" asked Nadia. She spoke tenderly, like a sister. "It's like you love him, and he's a real animal. Like he's your brother."

"I feel like he's my brother. He works so hard. And no one sees it."

"You see it," I said. "And we're seeing it because you're seeing it."

The book for him was a living thing. There was nobility in his communion with Boxer, with the loving affinity he felt for the great beast. His was not the response of an academic, but of a feeling child.

The next class, Katelyn began. "I was thinking about what Callum said last time. And I was thinking that maybe why he loves Boxer is because Boxer is so pure. And that is how I think of Callum. He's like the purest one here."

"What do you mean by pure?" I asked. "Pure like undiluted or clean, or pure of heart?

"Like pure of heart," she said.

"How do we purify our hearts?"

"By forgetting all the dumb stuff and focusing on the important stuff," said Katelyn.

"It would be feeling like Callum did about Boxer," said Winn.

"I think it would mean to be like God," said Nils. "Like, the Buddha or Martin Luther King or something."

"You mean a person who gives or lives for others?"

"A pure heart would be someone who gave everything to the cause without questioning or worrying about what they got," said Henry.

"That's what I want to do," said Hannah. "I'm tired of being someone who stands around. I want to be a domino that falls and makes something important happen."

"But something is wrong," Callum said. "They should love Boxer, because he was good. But nothing good happens from him being good. They worked him to death. How could they do that? That's what he got for being the best one of all."

"Do you guys think Boxer's actions have meaning in the universe?" I asked. "He gives everything with noble strength, and then he dies." My question was for them, but also for me. What did my actions mean to the universe? I taught for thirty or forty years, and then I died.

"If Boxer makes us feel what being pure-hearted is," said Nadia, "then his actions had the greatest meaning of all."

Nils suddenly leapt up. "We're talking about how we enlargens the heart!"

"Do you mean enlargening the heart?" I asked. Nils loved twisting words around into meanings that suited him.

"No, I mean we have to *enlargens* the heart! That's what we have to do! That's the meaning of Boxer!" Nils was vaulting with his vision.

"So, how do you do it? This *enlargens*, as you say?" I asked. I got up from my chair and pulled a book of James Dickey's poems off the shelf. "Listen to this poem and see if we can find anything. It's called 'Them, Crying.'"

I read them the poem, which began, *In the well-fed cage-sound of diesels, / Here, in the cab's boxed wind, / He is called to by something beyond / His life.*

In the poem, a man enters into the heart of a hospital—*the still, foreign city of pain*—because he is drawn to the sound of children alone, crying. He is drawn into what others feel, and when he lets himself be drawn there, the small cages of his world become bigger.

"Let's write the meaning on the board!" Winn cried out. She scampered from the big room table and scrawled in huge letters the class's summation:

You will enlargens the heart when you know the superhuman tenderness of strangers.

I told them to write for ten minutes about whatever they understood or felt about enlargens. They hunched over their papers, their copies of Animal Farm at their elbows. When they were done, I asked Callum to read first, and he gave us a poem as clean and hard and lucid as a poem could be.

Wake up to quiet.
Feel the immense difference
of the warm green blanket
and an autumn breeze.
Which is better?

As you close the window,
hear the misjudged crows
cawing in delight.

Don't you wish
you could be one of them?
I do.
The day's beautiful,
no sun, overcast, windy.

If I were one of them
I would be closer to what I love.

Maybe Callum was getting closer to what he loved, or finding words for it. I knew in time that they would remember this book—and not only because of what I taught, but through seeing Callum grapple with it. A story was happening before them, to them. *Animal Farm* was not just an artifact to be analyzed; it was a doorway that lit and enlarged the hearts of the students around the table.

"So, listen," I began. "The other day we were talking about the roots of our feelings, and how those feelings come to be, and how what is behind them shapes how we act."

There was a pause.

"Do you guys want to hear a story about a kid who went here?" I asked. There was vigorous assent. A story, particularly about one of their predecessors, was always a fruitful way for them to see themselves. Not only did it activate large areas of their brains, it also let them be kids again. Just to sit and listen and feel that they were part of an ongoing story.

"There was a boy here. He was very strong, gritty, tough. We had a large set of old metal lockers that needed to be moved. He brought them down the basement stairs all by himself. He accidentally smashed his fingers on the door frame, bloodying his knuckles, and then dragged the lockers across the basement, cussing the whole way. When the lockers were in place, twelve of his classmates came racing and shrieking and squabbling to claim a locker. He was standing there with his fingers in his mouth trying to soothe the throbbing pain. 'I call this one! This one's mine!' a girl, Akilah, was shrieking. 'I got the best one! I got the best one!' Not one person said thank you to him for dragging the lockers in. This sent him into a rage, because all these selfish so-called friends were not appreciating his work and they were only fighting over the best locker. He was disgusted at their selfishness and his invisibility. So, in anger, he went outside to where Akilah's bike was. He took an Allen wrench and slightly loosened every nut and bolt on her bike. That day she rode home, the bike fell completely apart, and she nearly crashed into a logging truck. She could have been really hurt. She could have died."

They looked at me in bewilderment.

"So what is the meaning of this?" I asked.

"He was *pissed*."

"The other kids were jerks."

"Is that all?" I asked.

"It wasn't good, what he did," said Henry.

"But he was mad for a reason," said Haley. "Like there was a real root to his anger,"

"What was the root?"

"No one thanked him."

"He felt his efforts were unappreciated and rejected."

"So what's important?" I asked.

"Noticing and appreciating the efforts of others and not just thinking about ourselves constantly."

"How did he respond when he *didn't* get noticed?" I asked.

"With something hurtful, mean, destructive."

"Did it solve the problem?"

"No, it made it worse!"

"What if we said that by sabotaging the bike he was actually trying to bring the issue up?"

"What do you mean?"

"By screwing up her bike, he was trying to say that something was bothering him."

"That was a destructive way to do it, then," said Katelyn. "He could have just brought it up without screwing her bike up."

"Why do you think he did it that way?"

Nadia raised her hand. As always, she had been listening carefully, only entering the conversation when she had found her bearings.

"Because, it was like what Katelyn said. That was the harder thing to do. If he said that he was hurt and rejected when he did a nice thing and that he needed someone to say thanks, that would be him admitting he needed other people. That would make him feel vulnerable, or weak."

"Meaning he would be showing his feelings," said Nils.

"Yes!" Bennett blurted. "Just like Carl Tiflin in *The Red Pony*. He gets hurt, and he feels he might show his tender feelings, so he hurts things because he is afraid to show his feelings." Since we had begun *The Red Pony* Bennett had come alive. It connected to something in him and he brought it up every chance he could.

"Exactly!" I said.

"That's what the kid did," said Nils. "He hurt someone instead of showing his true feelings. Well, he showed his feelings, but in a kind of screwed up way. Or unscrewed way."

"He felt disconnected. And he disconnected her bike," Bennett said. "He took things apart."

"So we should be putting things together?" said Nolan.

Hannah looked perplexed. "But how do we do that?"

"We have to just keep trying," said Bennett.

"So now what?" I asked. It was ten o'clock. Time for break. We'd been in morning meeting for an hour.

"Ruby," I asked, "do you have the poem?" Ruby had signed up to read the poem that morning and had been holding a book—*The National Poetry Project*—throughout the entire discussion.

"I do," she said.

"Let it rip."

"Nolan," she asked, "can you read his name? I can't pronounce it." She held the book out to Nolan.

"Rabindranath Tagore," Nolan read slowly. "'Gintanjali 35' is the title."

This is what she read:

> *Where the mind is without fear and the head is held high;*
> *Where knowledge is free;*
> *Where the world has not been broken up into fragments by*
> *   narrow domestic walls;*
> *Where words come out from the depth of truth;*
> *Where tireless striving stretches its arms towards perfection;*
> *Where the clear stream of reason has not lost its way into the*
> *Dreary desert sand of dead habit;*
> *Where the mind is led forward by thee into ever-widening*
> *   thought*
> *and action*
> *Into that heaven of freedom, my Father, let my country*
> *   awake.*

All around the room eyes were up, awake, watching, looking at each other.

"Wow. Holy crap," I said. "Read it again."

She read it again.

"Ruby, did you have that poem picked out already, or did you pick it after you listened to everything this morning?"

"I had one but I decided to read this during our talking."

"That's incredible. That poem related to everything we just talked about."

"I guess so," she said. She was beaming.

I was once told that I was demonically possessed, that my teaching was full of wild swings of passion and force, loving and tender, sometimes transformative, though sometimes imperfectly expressed, or expressed in unorthodox ways. My experiences in the extreme, which I incorporated into my teaching, included my occasional depression and anxiety, the birth and parenting of my own children, the pain of two divorces, the life I had lived apart from my children, the distance from my daughter, who lived on the other side of the country, my father's Alzheimer's disease, my mother's struggle to care for him, the discovery of a lasting love at a relatively late stage, my journey to become a teacher and start a school, the stories of my former students, my many mistakes and missteps as a student, my childhood, my travels, my relationships to my parents as a child and as an adult, and my relationship to my brother and friends.

The animus of my teaching was the aggregate of my experiences: love, loss, death, growing, striving, failing, grieving, winning, losing, giving my heart and soul—music, art, poetry, history, comedy, nature, and everything else. It included shoveling snow, making paintings, changing diapers, coaching soccer, driving in the rain, mowing grass, making love, cooking hotdogs, reading in the middle of the night, opinions about gluesticks, John Coltrane, watching a mother robin make a nest on a window sill. It included all of me. I was going through Erikson's stages of development just as much as my students were.

"You guys are going through the fourth and fifth stage," I told them. "I'm coming out of six and headed into the seventh."

"What does that mean?" Nils asked.

"You guys are working on 'Identity vs. Role Confusion'. You don't know who you are yet or where you fit in."

"What do you mean?" asked Winn. She had on her John Deere hat but it was pulled around backwards. Strands of brown hair straggled from the sides. Her eyes were squinted, not in distrust, but with curiosity upon confronting something strange.

"I mean, you once were a little kid in the nest of your family. A baby bird in the nest with no feathers. You were weak and vulnerable, but protected and warm and fed. In a place of safety. In adolescence you begin to fly a little. But it's scary to fly for the first time. You don't know what's out there, or how strong your wings are. You know you're a bird, but you don't know how you're going to feather out."

"Huh? I don't get this," said Yebsera.

"I get it, I get it!" cried Winn.

"You're waiting for your plumage. Wondering if you'll get a mate. Worried about predators. Or if other birds who aren't in your family will accept you."

"So, middle school is where we are joining our first flock?" she exclaimed, smiling broadly.

"Yes. Exactly. That's what you guys are working on."

"And what are you working on?" asked Nils.

"I'm working on intimacy, isolation, and trying to be productive and not stagnate."

"What's next after that for you?" he asked.

"Ego-integration or despair. Or good old death."

"What do you think you'll get?"

"I don't know, but I'll let you know when I find out."

❧

In middle school, I had been lucky to have teachers who allowed long, winding discussions and digressions. I had teachers who exclaimed with joy when I wrote a beautiful line. In seventh grade, I wrote a story about my grandmother, who was in a nursing home. It was a series of remembrances of witnessing her decline. My writing teacher sat with me one day. The last paragraph needed work.

"Is there any way you want to change this part here at the end?" he asked, holding my story in his hand. I read the line and rewrote it in my head. Then I said it aloud.

"The lights were going out slowly in her eyes."

My teacher exploded. "*Yes!* Hot damn! That is perfect! Now *that* is writing!"

I felt my body warming at the praise, this thrill of being seen. There was nothing amazing about the new line. It wasn't luminous or syntactically revolutionary. My teacher was celebrating something else: the process and my developing powers of creation.

Later, he told another teacher, his mentor, about that moment when he'd helped me. He brought me to his mentor's office, who looked up from his work and exclaimed, "Bubba, I hear you're a hell of a writer!"

I was shy and only nodded. But I felt that warm feeling coursing through my body again.

Maybe moments like that made me want to teach. Maybe the good I could do had to do with leading adolescents to finding their creative powers, and believing that every moment in school possessed such possibility, and that I could bring my own life into the classroom.

As I was willing to bring everything from my own life, I asked them to do the same. I was not only their teacher, I was a human being, someone relatable and accessible—and to the extent that my humanity showed, they could learn from that. In me they saw one whose eyes were trained on something at once invisible and possible, unique to me, but also part of the vast human story, and connected to them as well. I showed them what it meant to be possessed by a vision—and one having little to do with test scores or achievement gaps or preparing them for tenth-grade English. My vision had everything to do with believing that they could discover something in themselves that might save the world.

Some days I arrived with a thought in my mind. Maybe a line from a poem, or something I had read in the news, something that had happened the night before, an encounter with a stranger, an old story I remembered that made me wonder or question, or a famous quote.

"Listen," I said to them, "John Keats, a poet in the 1800s, once wrote this in a letter. He said, 'several things dovetailed in my mind, and at once it struck me, what quality went to form a Man of Achievement especially in literature and which Shakespeare possessed so enormously—I mean *Negative Capability*, that is when man is capable of being in uncertainties, mysteries, doubts, without any irritable reaching after fact and reason.'"

By their expressions, none of them grasped the meaning.

"I don't care as much if you remember who John Keats is, or when he lived, or if you know what Romanticism is. I do care about what he's saying. I care about you caring about what he's saying. I care about your lives and how they can become great. I care about you understanding these words because they can change your life. Being in uncertainties, mysteries, doubts: this is the state of being an adolescent. Do you think we can be in that place? Of negative capability?"

"To be in a negative place?" asked Haley.

"No, to have the strength to live in what you don't know, to accept it, move in it, to laugh with it, to rise and fall with it. To be able to accept not knowing things."

"Can you read it again?" asked Nils. I read it again.

"So," Nils said, "he is saying it's a kind of power to be in uncertainty."

"Yes. Or in doubt. Or mystery."

"How is it powerful to admit you don't know?" asked Bennett. "School is all about having to know things."

"How do you know?"

"Because at my old school I was bad at reading and bad at math and those things were hard and everything that happened to me revolved around me not knowing how to do those things."

"Why didn't everything in school revolve around what you *could* do?" I asked.

"I don't know."

"Why do schools spend all their time troubling with things kids can't do? Why don't they trouble with the things kids *can* do?"

"I don't know."

"Shakespeare didn't take standardized tests. He was busy writing plays for a theater troupe. He wrote his plays to get across to people the hugeness and complexity of being alive. His plays asked questions. His characters were mad, raging, dying to understand themselves. The characters must have been parts of him. That's how he became a man of achievement. I want you to be men and women of achievement. I want all of you to be men, women, and children of achievement. I want you to rage and be mad to live. But who can be great enough to be in not-knowing and still know that is the place to be?"

I *was* mad for them to understand. Acquiring facts and skills was not the sole aim. To have a free imagination and a mind that quested—that was the aim. Could they accept that some things began as and remained an awesome mystery—that not every-thing would be readily or rationally comprehended? I wanted them to stay open, not resisting. Accepting, for instance, that the answer would not always come in the first sentence, the first paragraph, or the first page, or the first day. Sometimes we would be lost. We would write the wrong words, cry tears of rage or frustration, grope in the darkness. That was part of our becoming.

Schools can be masterful at leading students to see or dwell in their failures, shortcomings, or deficiencies. Usually these revelations revolve around academic skills—the ability to remember information, take tests, summarize texts, follow the course.

At our school, we were after something entirely different, something more soulful, which was no less than the essence of each one of them. They had not formed solid foundations of self and identity, and so their thoughts were dominated by incessant questioning—which was good—and self-castigation—which could overwhelm them. *I'm too short. I'm no good at math; I'm afraid to speak in class; I'm boring; I'm afraid to tell people when I feel put down; I'm too fat, too pale, too thin. My nose is funny; I'm mean, I snap, I lose track; I don't listen well; I have too many thoughts; I'm not organized; I don't understand abstract concepts; physics makes no sense to me; I'm not cool; my clothes make me look like a dork; people don't understand what I like; I feel apart from others; I disappoint my parents; I'm too easily distracted; I'm weird, unlovable, unsure; I'm obsessed with things that drive others crazy; I don't understand what others like; I only show a part of myself; I'm judgmental; I'm weak, frail, afraid; I'm terrible at sports; I can't keep up; I'm slow; I cry easily; I'm always last; I can't cry; I anger easily; I don't have a good vocabulary; I get overwhelmed. I'm a slow reader; I'll get left behind; I worry about everyone else; I don't get it. I'm a bad friend. A bad student. A bad classmate. A bad daughter or son.*

Even at age twelve or thirteen, they had stories to tell, and they possessed wisdom, even if no teacher had ever called it that. They had lived in myriad places and states of mind, hundreds of mental conflicts and inner monologues, thousands of memories, a million perceptions. This was the motherlode. By engaging what they believed to be true, or opening up the classroom to what perplexed, mystified, or disturbed them, the ground was opened for authentic, intellectual exploration. If we could find the vein of right feeling in these magnitudes, the larger abstract concepts arose before us, born from the concrete realities of their actual lives. When we talked about their lived experiences, we could talk more truly about "Love," or "Freedom and Responsibility," or a "Good Life." They were willing to enter such conversations, to devote themselves to them even, but they did not always know how to begin. I found myself imploring: *Your answers to these questions have everything to do with life and death. Life depends on how you answer these questions, in how you apply yourself, in how much you are willing to chase it.* The only expectation was a belief: each of them had something to offer that could add to our understanding.

For adolescents, understanding the good life also included contact with the world outside of the classroom. Hilda Billings was a "town elder," born and raised in Ripton. For many years she'd been the postmaster in the village. She gave a talk, which the school attended, about growing up in Ripton during the Depression. She told stories of Robert Frost, who she knew. She then read selections from her gardening diary, in which she'd recorded interactions with him from the 1950s. She told how Frost, when he used to come into the post office in the village, would be highly disturbed by the posters of the FBI's "Most Wanted." Apparently, she explained, he did not feel comfortable with the idea that there were so many bad people in the world, or, perhaps, so nearby. So Hilda rearranged the posters, hanging them on the back of a door so that Frost, and any other postal customers, would not have to see them.

A few Fridays later, we walked through town to Hilda's house on Maiden Lane. We walked up Robbins Crossroad, past the town cemetery, onto the Natural Turnpike, down Peddler's Bridge Road, and climbed up into Hilda's yard, which sat on a small hill above Sparks Brook. In the distance, the slope of Robert Frost Mountain was gray under a blue sky, the sun so bright we had to shield our eyes as we looked up.

A massive two-hundred-year-old maple in Hilda's front yard had been taken down and we'd come to clear the limbs and move and stack the wood. Two tons of maple lay in the grass, piles of browning, crisp brush, heaps of wet sawdust, and broken limbs and un-split chunks of soon-to-be stove wood.

Hilda appeared from the kitchen door and met us. "I'm so thankful for you coming here. I don't think I could get all this cleaned up by myself. We're sad about this old tree coming down, but it will keep us warm."

"We'll get the job done," I told her. In order to move the wood, we formed an assembly line. The material—chunks of still wet and green wood weighing upwards of seventy pounds apiece— did not move in what one might term an efficient, methodical, or swift manner. Our line was more like a disjointed, confused caterpillar. We bumped up against each other, moving too fast or too slow, standing idly as one chunk of wood moved among thirteen kids, as Callum stood for a full minute straining to not drop a chunk of maple on Nils's foot while Nils was engaged in boisterous conversation with Bennett about whether he could dream in slow motion. If we had been a bucket brigade, the house would have burned to the ground.

"Wait! I am *not* ready!" someone shouted.

"Ow, this one is too heavy! Take it! Take it!"

"Move it faster!"

"Bring the wheelbarrow!"

"Look how strong I am!"

"Where's the cart? Who's driving the cart?"

"Who's the weak link here?"

"You're the weak link!"

Soon we were covered in fragments of bark, arms scraped and bleeding. In one hour, the yard was clear. We towed a dozen cartloads of sawdust and leaf-litter and dumped them into Hilda's overgrown garden, gray with stalks and weeds and a few rotting green tomatoes. Then we climbed on top of the stump, which was nearly five feet in diameter, and Hilda took a picture of us.

That tree had lived when Thomas Jefferson was alive. That tree was old when Robert Frost traveled into the village to pick up his mail from Hilda, who was then a young woman. Hilda, who outlived the tree, laughed as she watched us chucking sticks of firewood into her cellar to season, to be burned a winter hence.

In the first years of the school, a girl named Alycia attended North Branch. Adopted from Tampa Bay, a tough punk kid in black, graffitied combat pants, she said "fuck you" liberally and half-humorously to anyone who pestered her and she told us how she liked to scare kids in elementary school. All of these behaviors indicated a child who did not feel entirely safe in the world.

"I would kick them behind the baseball backstop if they didn't do what I told them," she claimed. Some of her words were braggadocio; sometimes it was to make us smile; sometimes it was to keep us at a distance. Yet she was closed and shy. She mumbled; she hid her black-lined eyes behind thick dreadlocks.

In seventh grade she was listless, sleepy, cranky, and unable to complete her work. She was sick at least two days a week, it seemed. At school she never sat up at the table. She hunched over in the corner drawing at a battered wooden desk. She showed her drawings to no one.

I checked in with her every day in her corner.

"What're you drawing? I asked.

She narrowed her eyes.

"Come on, lemme see."

She looked down at her hands, which had formed a protective wall over her paper. Then she opened her hand, like a little gate opening.

On the paper were Japanese manga drawings. Faces with large eyes and great, oval pupils, with spiked hair hanging over dark, shadowed cheeks.

"Those are cool, Alycia. But why do they have such big eyes?"

She sneered at me, but there was a little smile at the edge of her lips.

"Because, that's how they are."

Each day, Alycia drew new characters, each with a name and attributes—imaginary children who, according to her, were all fighting for their lives.

"Well, I still don't get why they have such big eyes and little noses. And why are they always so angry-looking and carrying guns?"

"Tal, shut up. You are so dumb. I am going to hurt you. These are my friends."

"Really? But they seem kind of rough and tough."

"They're my *friends*."

"The friends you wish you had?"

"Maybe."

"Do you ever draw regular people, ones that look more real or something?"

"These people are real, and yes, I think I will have to hurt you."

I assumed she would rather be seen than ignored. Gentle provocations with little smiles were the best I could muster to connect with her. Often she complained. About the weather. Or perky, eager students. Or her assignments. She talked about music she hated, food she hated, styles she hated, people she hated.

We were on a day hike through the Breadloaf Wilderness

in the fall. I was behind her, pestering her, trying to lure her out.

"Hey, Alycia, how come you're always talking about things you hate. Why don't you ever talk about things you love?"

"Like what?"

"Like all these beautiful leaves and trees and these ferns right here where we're walking."

"Tal, I don't like hiking and I don't like leaves." Her voice was edged with irritation.

"Why don't you talk about what is cool or neat-o or beautiful?"

"Yeah, right."

One day in November, after the kids had all gone home and after I had packed up my books, I walked out of my classroom to find Alycia waiting for a ride, standing at the window, looking across the field outside the school. A stone wall ran between our field and the neighbor's pasture, where his four cows were grazing under a single apple tree. The late sunlight fell across the field of dead grass and brown ferns, illuminating the tops of the hemlocks on the hill. The sky was filled with gold-limned clouds. Alycia was watching trees light up.

"Alycia."

She didn't look at me, but kept staring out.

"You're looking at that. That's beautiful, Alycia. Look at that. See *that*."

"Yes, Tal, I see it. I see it. Okay. I get it."

I smiled at her and she smiled back. Later that night I got an email from her.

tal, after you left i stayed in the school and waited for my mom. my shoes were wet and i didn't want to wait outside so i sat on the bench and looked out the window. by then it was getting darker, the sky was a deep blue/purple. i sat in silence for a while there and just watched. but then there was a break in clouds and the sun shone down onto the field one last time. it was orange and yellow which contrasted well

*with the sky. it was truly one of the most beautiful things
i have ever seen. and I'm sorry i didnt say it before. It was
pretty yes but i didn't say it was beautiful because it's hard.
but when I saw the field when i was alone i found myself
saying "i really can't hate this, it is beautiful" out loud to
myself over and over again. i suppose I'm telling you this
because you showed me (finally) that i really should get used
to saying things like that without fear.*

love Alycia

Weeks later during her study period, I approached her at her chair in the corner.

"What'cha drawing, Alycia?"

She slid her spiral notebook a few inches across the wooden desktop. Filling up an entire page was a ballpoint pen drawing of the face of a boy with true-to-scale nose and soft lips. There was no shadow, no spiked hair draped over and hiding the light—two human eyes stared straight off the page.

"That's a person!" I said. I picked up the notebook and looked into the drawing. "That's great, Alycia, that's really good."

That night I got another email.

*im so happy!! i can draw real people! i never thought i could
do that. thanks for bugging me about it. if i practice i may be
able to draw something i am proud of*

Alycia

I thought about Alycia often, about how she learned, how she carried tenderness inside the hard shell. About how she grew and how she could see herself growing; about how she wanted to make a life of which she was proud. She reminded me of what teaching could be. Its supreme expression was in those rare instances when the hidden impulses and yearnings of a student were awakened and stirred. Alycia reminded me of what a living school could be—a sanctuary of unpredictable collisions where children could feel their own lives opening before them.

Fall moved forward. After a hard frost, the field would be silver-white in the morning before the sun warmed it. The kids arrived cold and breathless, excited and noisy, shouting as they came through the door, anticipating the winter and snows to come. But Yebsera had been in a morose funk for weeks. He hated the cold, for one thing. *I'm so dumb,* he said, for another. *Everyone is smarter than me, he said. I don't get this poetry junk,* he said. He'd spent a lot of time in math and science classes disconnecting himself from what was going on, acting like he didn't care, goofing off, trying to make Callum and Bennett laugh. In short, letting his fear become a reality, goofing off so he didn't truly fail, and ignoring actually doing the risky, difficult work of mastering the art of the manual compass.

Growing up in Ethiopia, he'd never attended school. He'd learned a handful of English words. He'd spent a lot of time playing soccer in a grassless field with a ball made of rags. He'd stolen bananas from the market so he and his brother could eat. His image of himself was reductively negative: he was a child, he was uneducated, and he was a thief. He believed he might have been responsible for his mother's death. He did not believe he was ever born to be smart. And he was sure he'd never catch up to his peers.

We were in lit class, reading *The Red Pony*. He sat moping, away from the table. I paused our discussion about Billy Buck and Jody Tiflin, knowing he was telling us something without using words. Our class could not proceed until all of us were together.

"Yeb, why aren't you saying anything? What's the matter? Why are you sitting far away?"

"Nothing. I'm just tired."

"That's a load of manure. What's going on?" He stared at the floor, then looked at me.

"I don't get this book. Everything is all like, metaphorical and stuff," he mumbled.

Sometimes they cried, were bewildered, or they resisted. Sometimes their voices shook, sometimes they were maddeningly difficult to reach.

"Well, Yeb, you feel like you're dumb, then just feel it all the way. Be dumb, and see where that takes you. You're driving us all crazy telling us how dumb you are and then acting pissed off. See if you can try even harder to believe you are stupid."

"What?" His head picked up. He was listening closely enough to hear the strangeness of my suggestion.

"You've already decided. So be dumb. Continue to believe you're dumb, all the way. See how that works. See if you want to keep feeling dumb, or if you want to find out if there's anything else."

"Okay. I feel really dumb. I suck at math and I suck at English. I'm like the stupidest kid in Vermont . . ." his voice trailed off, void of energy.

"Congratulations. So you're dumb and not so hot at solving a math equation. In science you say, 'Forget about longitude and latitude, let's be dumb together.' You've been acting like a dumbass, screwing around with everyone, making jokes like you don't give a damn. *Why?*"

"Because I *am* dumb," he insisted irritably. "Why should I even try?"

"You sit there and space out and goof off and make jokes, Yeb. Because then, if you fail, it isn't because you're dumb, it's because you space out, goof off, and don't care. Yes?"

"I guess."

"But you end up feeling dumb anyway?"

"Yeah."

"So how's your plan working so far?"

"Not so good," he said, speaking towards his lap.

"If someone was afraid they sucked at soccer, would your

advice to them to improve be to tell them to zone out, tell them they suck, to screw around, and quit. Would that make the feeling of being crappy at soccer go away?"

"No, they would still feel like they sucked at soccer, and they would still suck at soccer."

"Would them believing they were stupid and saying it over and over to everyone in the universe make them smarter?"

"No."

"So is your technique of dealing with feeling dumb a good one?"

"No," he said, now smiling. "I still feel dumb."

"So you can keep doing what you're doing, or you can change course. Fixate on something else. Why don't you tell us, or tell yourself, how you actually *are* smart."

"Huh?"

"Maybe you don't know a lot of fancy literary terms or about magnetic zero, but you know a lot of stuff I don't know or that anyone knows. Tell us something you do know. See how that feels."

"Tal, I don't know about anything. I'm dumb compared to all these kids."

"Come on. Try. *Try!*"

"No, I'm stupid. I can't write like the other kids. I have to get help like every two minutes. I don't know big words."

Big words. As if they defined intelligence. What taught him that? I was frustrated, and irritated, because only he was blocking himself.

"But you might know something they don't know," I said. "Like, maybe being smart isn't *only* about being the first to figure out the math equation."

"Uh, okay." He was stopping in his tracks. Reason would not get him to the place he needed to go. He needed to go into himself.

"So tell me what you know. What you actually know, your soul knowledge."

"Like . . . like, I was adopted and stuff? Like what I know about Ethiopia? My brother? You mean like that?"

"Yeah, like that. What do you know about your brother?"

"You mean about the facts of him, or about feeling things?"

"Jesus, Yeb, *anything!* Feelings or facts. Help me out, man. Help yourself! All of us are here with you."

"Well, my brother, like, I guess I love him. That's a fact."

"You know about love? Yeah, like that. What you know about that. I don't care about you knowing what you *think* I want you to know. I want you to tell us what *you* know, what *you* understand."

He sat, unmoving. Pencils rested on the table. Winn wasn't taking notes.

"There's my mom. I know about her. But she's dead. And I already talked about that."

"Yeah, but we don't really know about that," I said.

"It'd be good to hear about her," said Ruby. She spoke softly. "You can tell us about it if you want. We'll listen."

We waited again.

"So she made us fried bread in the mornings. It was called *injera*. It was really good. I liked the smell of it. And we'd have tea. And that would be all we had to eat all day."

He paused.

"And I told you about the baskets she made."

"We remember."

"And she would walk so far to sell them." His voice was tinged with pride and wonder.

"And we played soccer all the time. That's all we did. And there were horses where we played. But they were sad and starving. I always felt sad when I saw them."

"All that soccer you played was how you got so good, huh?" I said, winking at him.

He nodded, and the faintest trace of a smile played across his face.

We listened to his story. We listened to him. His life and his stories were true and could not ever be wrong. When he held those truths, he came closer to his elemental self, and we came closer to him. Rabindranath Tagore wrote: *This discovery of a truth is pure joy to man—it is a liberation of his mind. For, mere fact is like a blind lane, it leads only to itself—it has no beyond. But a truth opens up a whole horizon, it leads us to the infinite.* No less than any other student, Yeb had inside of him intimations of the infinite.

We asked him more questions, about his younger brother, who had died in the bed they shared. He remembered their ragged blankets on the floor where they slept. He remembered the city of Awassa and his fear of the hyenas at night. He remembered the boys he played soccer with, the wooden posts that stood for goals, and the long days on the dusty clay fields where the horses ranged. He remembered his shoes—no shoe-laces, torn along the soles. He told us the things he possessed, the molten core of his being.

"Your knowledge is your power. Your experience is your power. Now go home and write it."

"What?"

"You have so much to tell us, and we'll be ignorant until you reveal it. You have more knowledge in your left pinky than most people will find in a lifetime. We'll see the world through your eyes. So quit screwing around in science class and get your ass in gear." I smiled at him again.

A week later, he returned with a draft of a scene he'd written. I asked him to read it to us. He sat back away from the table, his eyes moving down the page as he read in a small voice.

> *Tal asked me, "If I keep thinking I'm a dumbass, what will happen?"*
>
> *"I don't know," I said with a groan.*
>
> *He looked me dead in the eyes and said, "You'll be a dumbass."*
>
> *Then he kept going, to add that I was not yet a dumbass.*

He told me I had powers, I had powers and ways I can use them.

"Well," I asked myself, "what do I have for powers?" Well, I know what pain feels like, I know how hate feels, I know how you can lose a brother or a mother, I know how to love, I know how to be mean and harsh; I have knowledge, feelings, ideas, I know about being rich, being poor, leaving your true home, I know the feeling of desire, of a person's desire for guitars and sports. I know how to have friends, I know how it feels to not have friends, I know how it feels to get rejected from a girl, and from a family that doesn't want you. I know how it feels to leave your best friends behind, and I know the feeling of coming back and giving them a warm hug that makes the hot tears flow down your cheeks.

When we were reading Bennett's speech, I was proud of him and how he did it was great. I commented on it and gave him feedback. I compared his speech to Dante, and the circles of hell, which Tal had told us about.

Tal asked me then if I was stupid and a dumbass? I looked at my fellow mates, who also sometimes feel like I do, and I said, "Hell no!"

As he read, I could feel my heart caving, making space for him. When my students gave themselves, affection came easy. We were opened to the love he felt for his far-away home, the love he felt from his mother, and it overflowed in our classroom. Joyful applause filled the room. All around the table his classmates were looking at him with affirming eyes: *Hell yes, you do have powers.*

"Yeb," I said, "you're a boy who heard your friend's speech and compared it to Dante. That's something special."

He looked at me, not blinking, his mouth half open. Yebsera had to feel the contours of his life, use what he already knew, and hold it close. The further he pushed his life away, the more shallowly he lived. *The Upanishads* directed: *Know thine own*

Soul. In order to know their souls they had to look back—which brought them to fear and strangeness but also to rooms, like the captain's quarters at the bottom of the sea where treasures were stored.

"Yeb," I said. "Right now, you are as smart as any boy in the world. Do you think there is another boy in America right now who is writing about his comparison of a classmate's speech to Samson and Dante? Do you think there is anyone in the world who knows what you know, and feels what you feel? Is there anyone who can move a class of people like you just did?"

He shook his head and shrugged simultaneously.

"Nobody else ever did that, Yeb," said Bennett.

"When you think and write like that you are with the gods," I said.

He shrugged his shoulders again, and gave the class a half smile.

"We have powers and we are naming the powers," I told them. "These are the powers we might use to live a good life."

At lunch that day I watched Yebsera playing soccer on the field, baiting his mates with the ball, then dashing to escape, the ball stuck magnetically to his feet, laughing as he ran.

We were reading the poems of Mary Oliver. Our aim was not to become perfect readers of poems, or critical analysts. I did not care if they could memorize poetry terms, identify forms, or count syllables. We read Oliver's poems, or any poem, to slow down and change our ways of perceiving. We read poetry to learn how to look and listen, and keep listening.

"Tal," asked Nolan, "are we going to keep reading Mary Oliver poems?"

"Yeah, probably. Why?"

"Because I look forward to these lit classes more than any other class. Every day when it's Mary Oliver poems I look forward to school."

That was music to my ears. "Really! What do you love about them?"

"Just because the poems are so good," he said, as though it was blatantly obvious.

"Which ones?"

"'White Flowers' is pretty cool."

"Why do you like that one?"

"Because, like . . ."

"Like?"

"I don't know."

"Then next lit class read us the poem, we'll find out. But you have to think about it and write about why it's important to *you*. You got that?"

"Got it!" He saluted and walked out of the room.

I had not chosen "White Flowers" as a poem for the class to read. But since Nolan had chosen it, it became crucial to go into it.

He read the poem to us in Tuesday morning lit class. He stumbled over some of the words, but in his voice was a hunger to give us a feeling he'd found in the words of a poet. The poem came to a close with the final lines:

Never in my life
had I felt myself so near
that porous line
where my own body was done with
and the roots and the stems and the flowers
began.

There followed a soft applause and then quiet.

"Nolan, can you tell us why you read that one?"

He took a sheet of paper from under his binder and read.

As you hear in this poem the woman in the field wakes up and is one with the flowers. Where there is only the faintest line between her and the white flowers. We need to be one with each other. I need to be one with everybody. I want to barely be able to see the line that divides us, we and me. I want to feel like we are all one. We are all around this fire together.

He stared down at the table. Nadia looked up and smiled as he finished.

"Wow!" I said. "Holy crap! What do you guys think?"

"That's really good," said Ruby.

"I feel that way sometimes," said Henry. "But a lot of the times I don't. There are times when I feel like I'm not connected to anybody."

"But there are, like, lines that divide us," said Nadia, and she emphasized *us*. She looked at Haley, her best friend. "When I heard Haley's story about her running and thinking she was ugly, I didn't feel like there were lines dividing us."

"You mean," I said, "that when someone opens up, the walls between us disappear?"

"That's when it feels like we're around a fire together," said Nils.

Nils was a ninth grader, a modern-day thirteen-year-old Vermont hippie. His mom cleaned houses and sang in local folk bands. His dad was a sound engineer and worked part time at the Vermont State Apiary. Nils occasionally wore a skirt over jeans, which were patched and torn and had song lyrics penned on the thighs. He was gangly and thin, his shoulders scooped in around his chest, and he wore his mother's old

T-shirts emblazoned with Frank Zappa quotes. He moved rapidly, bumping into tables, stumbling over chair legs, talking and gesticulating at the same time—philosophy, George Carlin routines, singing lyrics to Ani DiFranco in a falsetto one morning, bellowing "Let's Get It On" by Marvin Gaye the next, tripping over his own feet, which were often bare, his torn Chuck Taylors kicked off into a far corner of the school. He wore wire spectacles and spoke exceedingly fast, as though there were a thousand ideas he wanted to touch and comical debates he wanted to have. He loved to spar with words, puns, and colloquialisms, playfully twisting them and turning them inside out, seeking roots and meaning. He'd come to our school because he wasn't happy at the Union middle school where he'd spent seventh grade. I didn't yet know why, but he was looking for a place to take him in.

One day in class I said: "My old pal Bobby Dylan said, 'He not busy being born is busy dying.' Do you know what he means?"

"That we need to get off our asses or we're going to rot," said Nils.

"Something like that," I said. "If you're on Facebook or Instagram more than two minutes a day, you already are. Rotting, I mean. Or like this: is it possible to be born, or see with newborn eyes, every single day?"

"So, you mean we got to dance," he said.

"What do you mean?"

"I'm talking about, you know, like we got to move if we want to be really alive." He bobbed his head and snapped his fingers like he was trying to dance in his seat.

"Yeah. *Yeah!* That's what I'm *talking* about. I'm talking about being conscious of every moment."

"I think Bob Dylan is being hardcore," said Bennett. "If you slack off you're dead."

"You'll be rotten meat," said Nils.

"That sounds gross," said Yebsera.

"We're talking about how if we spurn growth and experience, *nothing* happens. 'Nothing comes from nothing,' is what King Lear said. Something inside must be growing constantly or you start to rot and decay."

"What does 'spurn' mean?" asked Yeb.

"Rejecting things, not taking what is offered," I said.

"But what is the *something*?" asked Nils.

"You have to figure out what the good something is," I said. "You have to be listening for when the something happens and say, 'It's happening.'"

But what is '*it*'?" asked Nils. "What is the *something*?"

"I could never tell you what it is, but I can know it for myself. When I think of 'it,' I think of an unknown place. Like this." I rummaged around on the bookshelf behind me until I found the poems of Wallace Stevens.

"This is called 'Prologues to What is Possible,'" I said, and I read them the first stanza.

There was an ease of mind that was like being alone in a
    boat at sea,
A boat carried forward by waves resembling the bright
    backs of rowers,
Gripping their oars, as if they were sure of the way to
    their destination,
Bending over and pulling themselves erect on the wooden
    handles,
Wet with water and sparkling in the one-ness of their
    motion.
The boat was built of stones that had lost their weight and
    being no longer heavy
Had left in them only a brilliance, of unaccustomed origin,
So that he that stood up in the boat leaning and looking
    before him
Did not pass like someone voyaging out of and beyond the
    familiar.

He belonged to the far-foreign departure of his vessel and
  was part of it,
Part of the speculum of fire on its prow, its symbol,
  whatever it was,
Part of the glass-like sides on which it glided over the salt-
  stained water,
As he traveled alone, like a man lured on by a syllable
  without any meaning,
A syllable of which he felt, with an appointed sureness,
That it contained the meaning into which he wanted to
  enter,
A meaning which, as he entered it, would shatter the boat
  and leave the oarsmen quiet
As at a point of central arrival, an instant moment, much
  or little,
Removed from any shore, from any man or woman, and
  needing none.

"How is freedom like the 'ease of mind that was like being alone in a boat at sea?'" I asked. "How is freedom like a 'brilliance, of unaccustomed origin . . . like someone voyaging out of and beyond the familiar . . . like a man lured on by a syllable without any meaning?'"

"How can a syllable not have any meaning?" asked Nils.

"It could be like a whisper, or a moan," said Nadia. "Or a song."

"Maybe it's saying we need to venture out to a place that's not known," Bennett stated.

"That's good, Bennett," I said. "It's like you're beginning to use that speculum."

"What's a speculum?" he asked.

"A glass to help you see things you can't. Inside a body. Or the way the planets line up."

"But he's talking about a glass boat that's on fire!" Nils nearly shouted. "He's talking about One-ness!" He smiled, delighted to be overwhelmed by the impossibility of arriving at a fixed definition.

He continued. "Where *is* the place he's going? What is the *it*? What is the *something*? Where is that boat *going*?"

Nils had no fear of following the lure of the "far-foreign departure" or of abandoning the shores, asking questions that had no known answers or location.

Given the chance, they would talk of all the small, soft things they loved: the old, tattered blankets, the one-eyed stuffed bears, the simple words their parents called them—"my little peanut" and "sweet one." They would talk of their precious toy Hot Wheels they'd once clutched in their sweaty hands, the ragged black Puppy made from an old sweater that they'd gotten when they were two and still kept. I knew all this because I asked.

"What is the most treasured thing you have? What do you still have on your bed?"

Before they could arrange their defenses, I made them close their eyes. "How many of you still have some sacred thing, like a blanket, pillow, or stuffed animal on your bed?"

All of them raised their hands, even tough guys in lacrosse shirts.

"Open your eyes."

Then they saw the truth, looking around the room, all of their hands raised. The fact was, they were as close to childhood as they were to growing up. They held on to old threads, the sounds of waking up at home, those first smells of Saturday morning. To remember together was a kind of communion and belonging. They could see that they were part of the "family of things," as Mary Oliver wrote. They wrote of these things over and over, as though they were still rubbing the soft place on the back of their fluffy bunny's ear to remind themselves of something they should never forget.

We allowed ourselves freedom to digress, go deep, meander, get off schedule, ditch the plan. There was playfulness in our days, chaos as well as purpose. One morning meeting we discussed possibilities for a social experiment that might relate to the idea of freedom itself. One idea: we could severely restrict one freedom (say, going outside) while completely allowing another (say, the freedom to blurt anything you wanted, at any moment). Other ideas were proffered—from being forbidden to speak all day to running the school like a jail.

"IT'S ALREADY LIKE A JAIL IN HERE," I hollered. "You have to do what I tell you, and you can't leave until a certain time when we say you can!"

The idea of being roped to someone who wasn't a close friend garnered support as the best idea.

"And we could have one person be blindfolded, and one not," said Nolan.

"I still want us to run the school like a jail!" shouted Bennett, who couldn't let the idea go, probably because he could envision bossing everyone around.

"WE ARE ALL IN PRISON!" I shouted. "FEEL THE WALLS CLOSING IN! WHEN THE DOOR SLAMS BEHIND YOU, YOU KNOW IT'S REAL, BROTHER! CLANG! IN THE HOOSEGOW!"

The discussion dissolved into shouting, and then we went to lunch.

The next day, Nolan raised his hand in morning meeting.

"So I was lying in bed last night thinking about the idea of being tied to someone all day, and I thought that last year I would be all worried about who I would be with, but this year I realized that I would be happy with being with anyone."

"Can we all be someone anyone would want to be with?" I asked. "Can we all be a person others would take pleasure in being with, or feel safe being with?"

"Why do you always look at me when you're asking us the hard questions?" Ruby asked.

"Because I like to look at someone who reacts, like you, Ruby, who smiles and nods and listens." I scanned the faces at the table. "Sometimes others of you freaking clowns look catatonic. You know what I'm saying?"

"You're saying we're clowns," Nils dead-panned.

"Damn straight!" I shouted. "But get back to the point: Can we all be a person all others around us would take pleasure in being with? Is that possible?"

Instead of running the school like a jail or tying ourselves together, we decided to make a museum linked with our year-long study of freedom and revolution. The idea was to have each of the students "find" or "discover" historically valuable objects relating to the topics they had chosen to study. In truth, each of them had to manufacture a historical artifact and invent a story about how the item came into their possession. Their museum artifacts had to realistically mimic the age and condition of an object that might have come from that era. In this way, history came alive, and the students were making it.

We staged the exhibit at a local coffee shop. On the walls were a homemade broken portion of the Berlin Wall and a runaway slave poster "from 1855." Henry had studied the 1961 Freedom Rides and replicated a part of the Greyhound Bus that burned in Alabama. Together, Henry and I poured motor oil on polyester fabric, then singed it black with a blow-torch. Bennett studied revolutions in music and donated Woody Guthrie's "actual" guitar on which he'd painted the words, "This machine kills fascists." Hannah contributed a 1796 Phillis Wheatley poem written in her hand. There were the journal entries of American Revolutionary soldier Joseph Plumb Martin, and a fragment of 1200 BCE Iraqi vase that had been looted during Operation Iraqi Freedom in 2003. Amazingly, the museum also featured the actual ears of Vladimir Lenin, created by Ruby, who was studying the Russian Revolution.

"These ears are very important because Lenin was an important historical figure," Ruby wrote in the text that accompanied her artifact. "We have what he heard through. It's like listening to history!"

Nolan donated one of the white carnations that had been placed in the barrel of the guns of National Guardsmen during an anti-Vietnam protest on the Pentagon steps in 1967.

"We not only have objects of war and violence, but also of peace," he wrote. He also donated a Students for a Democratic Society armband worn during the Days of Rage in Chicago in 1968, which, he fibbed, had been worn by his mother's cousin.

Some of the artifacts illustrated the role violence had played in revolutions. Katelyn, who'd studied the French Revolution, "found" a wooden brace that supported the guillotine by which Marie Antoinette was beheaded. And there was an unused Molotov cocktail made by the Polish partisans who opposed the Nazis during the Warsaw Uprising in 1944. We didn't tell anyone that the gasoline was really apple juice.

Our school did not look or feel like other schools. There were no intercoms, no long, windowless halls, no narrow metal lockers. No blank walls, hall passes, planning rooms, demerits, or detentions. There were no written rules. We elected to deal with each problem as a unique circumstance, each with its particular context. No day was like any other. There was noise, and there was movement, there was unpredictability, and there was laughter.

In the small window of time in the morning when classes were switching from math to science to study, Callum and Bennett wrestled in the doorway to the big room.

"Tal, check out how I'm whupping Bennett's ass!" shouted Callum.

"And I'm helping," called out Cole, who was wrapping both of them in a bear-hug. They loved to wrestle and I understood why. Physical closeness was hard to come by if you were a fourteen-year-old boy. They were moving away from their parents, but had not yet found their way to romance. They needed that closeness for comfort and safety.

As they wrestled and laughed, Hannah walked in. She'd taken a Vermont Trailways bus to Concord, Massachusetts to visit Walden Pond over the weekend to research her project on Thoreau and take pictures.

Callum, red-faced under Bennett's grip, looked up at Hannah as she entered the room with a stack of books in her arms. He released Bennett and looked up.

"Hannah! How was the visit to Walden?" he called out. He had remembered.

"It was awesome. We sat in the chairs when no one was looking."

Ruby came in from math and wanted to talk about her project.

"Tal, Tal, Tal, can I focus on Bobby Sands? I found out all about him. Oh, and I have U2's song 'Sunday Bloody Sunday.' Can I play that?"

"Of course, that's great." The noise of break, the release from class, the joy of being at school—it was a dervish of swirling adolescent energies.

"Oh my god!" Katelyn called out from across the room. "I have to start researching my project, like soon!"

"You better, and that project better be GREAT!" I said.

"But Tal, I'm such a bad reader," she moaned. "I'm so slow. I'm like—"

"Tal, do you like my John Lennon drawing?" asked Yebsera. He was holding up a pen drawing of a stick figure with long hair. "I made it so I can fit in with all the cool hippie kids. Like Nils." He looked at Nils, who looked up from his computer.

"You can be a cool hippy kid, Yeb," Nils answered. "You practically already are."

"Yebsera, I'm helping Ruby on her project right now. I can't look at your drawing."

"So you don't like my John Lennon drawing?" he said, smiling broadly.

"I can't say cause I haven't seen it! Lemme see it."

He held it up. "That's an awful drawing," I said, smiling back.

"Tal, are you racist?"

"No, Yebsera! I am busy helping Ruby!"

He was laughing now. "Callum, Callum!" he called. "Help me make this new drawing on the board. We're gonna show Tal who's boss." He quickly scrawled something on the whiteboard.

"Tal, do you know what this is?" he said. "Callum helped me draw it." He had drawn a crude six-fingered hand with the middle finger extended. "It's the bird, Tal. You know what THAT means!"

"Yeb, that hand has six fingers! So it's not a bird, and it does not offend me. I have a strong ego to protect me from you clowns."

"You don't like me, do you? Because, because I'm black!" he shouted. "Isn't that right Callum? Tal is a racist teacher! I'm going to tell the principal, Tal. I'm telling on you."

"But Tal *is* the principal," Ruby said, shaking her head and laughing, her eyes wide open.

"Now you REALLY have problems, Yebsera," Callum said.

Yebsera was the only black student in our school, which, I was sure, added to his sense of isolation. Once he had announced to the class, "Me and my brother are like the only black dudes in this whole state!" He'd said it with a smile, but behind that smile I was certain there existed a depth of anguish and loss as he negotiated adolescence in a mountain town in rural Vermont.

But now he was doubled-over in laughter, happy to be playing and at the center of fun, happy to have Callum and Ruby at his side.

Nolan burst into the room from math class.

"Oh my god, my game I made for math is so cool. It's called Geome-trictionary," he said. "I think I'm going to market it."

"Yeah, we played it and it's really fun," said Yebsera.

The noise of conversations rose—benign chaos, gentle teasing, adolescents being themselves. This was part of why they loved coming to school.

"Hey everybody!" called Henry as he walked into the room. "My guitar is in tune."

"You should play 'All Blues' by Miles Davis," said Callum. "That song is sweet."

"Miles Davis is the boss, and *he's* black!" said Yebsera, looking at me with narrowed eyes.

""I love Miles Davis. And I love YOU!"

"Tal, you are a white poetry teacher who is racist!"

"Yebsera, I am not racist. I *am* Miles Davis. Ask Henry."

"You're not Miles Davis," Henry said, feigning pity and shaking his head. "You're just another old white man who's our poetry teacher."

"Play 'Chameleon' by Herbie Hancock!" said Callum. "That song is sweet too!"

Henry played the first chords.

"Herbie Hancock is black!" shouted Yebsera. "See? All the cool people are black!"

"That's some nice playing, Henry," I said. "And Yeb, you are absolutely right. Miles Davis is cool and so are you."

Around and around it went, amid laughter and loving put-downs, while Ruby stood by my chair, smiling, waiting patiently to talk to me about her project on the Troubles in Ireland.

In class, I noticed that Brody was unusually withdrawn. He was normally quiet, but now he was on edge, irritated, cornered.

"What's going on, Brody?" It was time for literature class, but I had to address him. The curriculum came second. My presumption was that the truth, whatever it was, would be interesting, if not enlightening.

"I don't know, like, people are criticizing me," he said. He looked across the table at the shelves behind me. He was hesitant. To draw him out would take some work.

"People? That's kind of a big group. Which people? You gotta be specific or we don't know what you're talking about."

"Like, the class, I guess."

"Criticizing you for what?"

"Everyone says I'm lazy or I don't care or something."

"*Everyone?*"

"Some people, sometimes."

"And they say you're lazy? That you don't care?"

"Yeah."

"Is it true?"

"Well, sometimes it is, but not always."

"But you feel they're not seeing the times when you aren't?"

"Yeah."

"So you feel like you're not getting something inside and important across to them?" I asked. "That they have a picture of you, but you feel that you're working hard and that you're not lazy."

"Yeah, I guess."

"They have one idea of you and it's not complete."

He shrugged.

"But you're feeling bad, and you know you're more than what they see."

"Yeah."

"And who here has the power to change that picture?"

"I do." There was a pause. "Yeah," he nodded. He finally looked up. His face was red and his eyes were watery.

"Brody, what matters is the truth you know of yourself."

He nodded.

"So when *do* you work? When are you all out?"

"At hockey. Because I really care about it."

"Tell about that. About hockey." Here was a way in. He hesitated, unsure of how much to say or show.

"I want to make it to the NHL," he said finally.

"That's awesome. Did you write your goal down?"

"Yeah."

"When you go to hockey practice, are you thinking about your goal?"

"Yeah. When the coach says to do laps for conditioning, I always skate the hardest so I'm first."

"If you do that every time, you'll become better than others over time. If you keep doing that you'll be great, whether you make it to the NHL or not."

He nodded.

We knew Brody was quiet. He was sleepy and slow in the morning, distractible during the day. None of the kids at school had ever seen Brody playing hockey, but I had. He was small, and low to the ice, but he glided. He snaked and curled behind and between other players, in perpetual motion, and when he had the puck it was virtually velcroed to his blade.

The story they knew about him was incomplete. They knew he played hockey but they had no image or sense of it. They did not know about how he travelled all over the state, or his games in frigid rinks on weekends in Missisquoi, up near the Canadian border, or what it was like to have practice until ten o'clock on a school night. Since they didn't see it, it was as though that part of him did not exist, and he felt that.

I looked at the class. "You guys understand that it doesn't matter if he does or doesn't make it to the NHL, but that he has a goal? He knows what he wants, and he works for it?"

The class nodded, feeling the seriousness of Brody's dream.

I looked around, trying to figure out how to get to whatever was in him and bring it out.

"Hey. Someone go get that poster in there." It was Brody's poster, a "freedom" collage he'd made for class. I'd looked at it the other day. It was extraordinarily detailed, with ten quotes pasted on, each arranged in a jagged, downward-falling zig-zag. One of the quotes was from Rousseau: "Man is born free yet everywhere he is in chains."

If Brody's soul was embedded in his poster, neither I nor anyone in the class had truly seen it. All of us, in the rush of our days, had unwittingly made him feel invisible, even though his work was hanging on the wall and he was sitting at the table before us.

"The poster there, above the printer." Henry left the table and pulled the poster off the wall.

"Brody, tell us what you were thinking when you made this. What's this here?" I held the poster up so everyone could see it.

"Well, the eye-shaped thing, that's an eye. It's what I see. See how the eye is split and there is that whirlpool going down through it? That's how I sometimes feel. Water going down or draining out."

"What about this?" I pointed to the cut-out face of a man, the size of a passport photo.

"That's James van Riemsdyk of the Flyers. They're my favorite hockey team."

"Van-*what*?" I asked. I was willing to be stupid in order to ease the tension. It let the class feel and fill the role of being the most serious listeners.

"Tal, you're such a freaking idiot!" Ruby called out. "He's telling a story."

"Alright, alright. Okay, so tell us about the guy. Why's he on here?"

"Well, he was really poor when he was growing up. He never had much money and he couldn't afford new sticks, and when he broke one he would use duct tape so he could keep using it.

And he built his own rink behind his house so he could play all the time."

"And you admire him for all that?"

"I feel like him sometimes."

"Even though he's not the most famous player? Because he's kind of under the radar?"

"Yeah. Because of that."

"Tell us more."

The class listened as Brody told us everything.

"Well, the guy in the corner is me."

I put my finger on a nine-year-old's drawing of a USA hockey player holding up a trophy.

"We got it. You're that kid holding up the trophy. What else?"

"Well, the arrow sign pointing says 'one way,' because there is only one way to go."

"And the poems and quotes?"

"Well, I arranged them like water dripping down, going from cup to cup, and they all end up at the bottom there, where the water is made out of words."

"Awesome. What else?"

"Well, that shoe, it's kind of corny, but what it says—'Looks good . . . feels good'—that's sort of how I feel, like people see me on the outside, but what's on the inside is much different."

"What else?"

"That ice climber."

"The dude in the crevasse?"

"Yeah, that's me trying to climb up."

"Do you guys get all this?" I asked the class. "Brody's put everything here with intention and consciousness. His poster is the map of him. There's a whole story here. None of us have read it until now. It tells us that what we see is not really always what's actually there. Or, maybe what's actually there is greater than what we see. And that we have to see better."

Brody's poster was a constellation of feelings, hopes, and dreams. True, in the first half of the conversation, I was doing the work; I was saying for him what he had not yet been able to say. But his words of explanation came easily, already formed, as they must have been, since, in the poster, he'd already said them.

I handed Brody his poster and he held it over the edge of the table. I did not know if he felt better; no expression passed over his face. He fingered the corner of the paper, looking steadily down.

In the process of making the school their own, every action the students took could be read as an attempt to make a place for themselves in the world they would one day inherit.

I entered the building on a Monday morning. The lights were off, but in the gloomy quiet I heard the sound of tape being ripped somewhere near the basement stairs. I turned the corner to find Winn crouched on the floor of the doorless broom closet. She had removed everything from it. Mops, a rolling bucket, paper towels, and cleaning supplies were piled haphazardly next to the stairs.

"Winn, what in the sam hell are you doing?"

"I am taking this space over and making myself a room here," she said, as though there was no other option.

"You're making a *room*?"

"Yes. My room. But anyone can come in. You're welcome, too."

"But Winn, the room is four feet by three feet. It's a closet."

"That's okay, it makes it more cozy! I can pay you rent if you like!" She smiled and turned to the wall, where she'd taped pictures of Leonardo DiCaprio and Kanye West. A feather boa was draped around the small window. She'd hung a bulletin board covered with pictures of her half-brothers, step-brothers, and friends. On one wall, surrounded by dried flowers, was a picture of her, maybe six months old, in the arms of her father. He lived in New Hampshire.

She'd made a room of her own, an adolescent cocoon, a safe home away from home, and filled it with images of her life. If she ever felt alone or lost at school, she had refuge. The door was open. No one was walled in or out. Anyone was welcome.

The sun was out after a hard, cold rain the night before, streaming in through the high window. Cobwebs hung faintly in the light. The door slammed and opened as the morning began. Shuffling down the basement stairs first, the students entered the room with energy and excitement. Bright faces, smiles, computers, and binders. Once they were gathered around the table, I asked them: "What thoughts, any thoughts, have you had since three o'clock yesterday afternoon? Write them down."

I waited for them to scratch out a sentence.

"Can I write more than one thing?" asked Katelyn.

"Of course."

"Now read the sentences you wrote," I said. The room quickly filled with their voices reading a collective journal of the previous twenty-four hours.

> *I am worried about my cousin, who had a motorcycle accident*
> *a couple of days ago.*
> *I wasn't sure how to talk to my brother last night because he*
> *was being so quiet.*
> *I need to look harder at my friends to see them.*
> *I loved playing Frisbee in the rain yesterday, and I found*
> *out Brody is really good.*
> *A military recruiter came to my sister's high school yesterday,*
> *and she thought that it was wrong for the military to be*
> *recruiting in her school.*

I was listening to my brother talk in the car on the way home, and I realized he is growing up fast.

Their thoughts came easily. They were aware—without being tested or taught—of the fleeting fragility of life, of change and the process of growing, of beautiful or troubling things they encountered; they were free to see and to choose—a power both infinite and liberating. Above all things that school might validate or honor, this was most vital.

The structure of our days and the openness of the conversations allowed them time to develop awareness of the moments in which they felt most alive—to become cognizant of emotional currents around and within.

One morning, Katelyn plopped herself down in my office.

"I'm sick of it!" she pouted.

"Sick of what?" I asked.

"Sick of my life."

"Say more. That's pretty damn vague and general."

Her voice became quieter and her pouting vanished. Tears dropped out of her eyes.

"My dad is . . . I don't know. I never see him. He's kind of an ass."

"What's he doing?"

"Driving trucks. I guess. I don't know."

"I could kick his ass," I offered. "I'm pretty tough."

She rolled her eyes and half smiled. "Forget it. My dad would kill you."

"What about your mom?"

She shook her head and looked down and stared at the floor. "I have my grandmother. She's really tough." She looked up at me. "She's strong. At least I have that. Someone to take care of me and my sister."

"You *are* lucky," I said. "She's doing alright, because you're doing alright. You're doing great, actually."

"Thanks," she said. She sighed and stared into the big room

where her classmates were getting ready for morning meeting, then wiped the tears off her cheeks.

They continually lifted veils to reveal deeper feelings. They spoke of comfort and pleasure, the joy of being alive to the presence of others, and they described pain and suffering as well as the beauty of the morning sun or the blessings of their families—or the emptiness they felt. They told of gifts of kindness they received and cruelties they witnessed. They grappled with ghost figures of past experiences and touched the fullness and possibility of what was before them.

All morning, they worked and moved. In math, they built houses of clay from geometric plans they'd sketched on paper. In science, they looked through microscopes at the cells of onions, dirt from the woods, and strands of their hair. Eric, the science teacher, watched bemusedly as they struggled to master the controls of the microscope. He stood by patiently while they explored and shouted at what they suddenly saw. We drew portraits in which we mimicked Picasso's "Girl Before a Mirror." Soon enough, in the silence of the basement, with Cray-Pas smeared on their fingertips, they gazed at richly-hued portraits of themselves.

At lunch they played in the wet field, the green faded to brown, now littered with windblown twigs. Only a few golden beech leaves still hung among the black and silver limbs in the woods. When the bell sounded, they came running, some barefoot or in socks, chattering, their cheeks red.

It was a Friday afternoon, the clock moving towards three. The weekend beckoned.

"We've been talking about important moments and thoughts. You've been talking about things you see and feel. Now, tell me one important moment from this week. Where you were, what was happening, what you felt or realized, how it changed you. You have thirty seconds to think about it."

I waited, watching their faces. Hands went up.

"Yes, Katelyn."

"I was sitting in front of my stool, painting it. I was thinking about how I knew it wasn't what I wanted it to be. It was that painting of a world, right behind you."

We'd been painting mandalas on the round seats of the stools we used in the art room. Hers was in the corner, and we looked over at it. "I was in the big room," she continued, "and I had a paintbrush with black paint on it, and I was painting mountains across the continents, and little rivers, and I was thinking it was kind of gross, the mountains didn't look good, and I didn't like how it was coming out, and it was cheesy and dumb, and I looked at Hannah's and Ruby's and they were more of like an abstract design. And I realized I didn't like what I had done. I wanted to change it because this year, I want to do everything in a way that I am proud of."

"It's admirable that you tried to make your mandala something specific and from the real world," I said. "I wish I had done that with mine. Maybe if I'd painted a chicken or a hummingbird it would've been better. A chicken would have been better. I'm questioning what I did too."

"Mine is totally gross," she said again. "I want to do something great."

"You're conscious of what you're trying to accomplish. You're striving. You're self-critical. You're not afraid to say, 'I can do better.'"

She looked down at her paper where she had doodled a flower with spirals of petals growing out from the center. She didn't react or look up. Sometimes the movement and growth came slowly, with cumbersome, frustrated motions, starts, stops. And I thought, *this is also what school is for.*

"Okay. Anyone else have another thought?" I asked. Five or six more hands up.

"Yes, Yeb."

"So, on the gravel pathway coming back inside from playing Frisbee at lunch with Callum. He was behind me. And as we were walking in, he said, 'Good job, Yeb.' That felt good."

"Sketch out the whole scene," I said.

"What do you mean?"

"A picture of words. You were at the center of the universe. You were the sun and the world was orbiting around you. What was the first ring around you?"

"The school?"

"No, I mean, yes, the school is there! But, I mean, what is the absolute first ring around you, as objects in the world radiate outward. Your moment occurred at the central place, but describe everything around it."

"Oh, I guess the pile of firewood we collected the other day for the bread oven. That's where we were."

"Yes. And then what?" I implored.

"The grass."

"Yes. And?"

"Then more grass, and then the stone wall?"

"Keep going!"

"And the trees and things growing on the stone wall . . . and the windows reflecting the trees . . . and the compost bin in the woods, and the cow pasture, and the woods—"

Everyone began shouting, adding to the list the rings of tiny horizons circling out.

"And the tall trees!" "And the blue sky with purple and gray clouds!" "And the sounds of the cars crunching over the gravel driveway!" "And the shouts of the seventh-grade boys!" "And the sound of the bell ringing us back to class!"

"And there you were at the center of that world," I said, "in a moment of significance. Why did that moment stand out above all the others?"

Here he did not hesitate.

"I guess because Callum and I have never really talked before. He usually just stares at me and I think he doesn't like me. So I was surprised. But it was good." Yeb, frail and unsure, learning meanings of words, was seeing the figure of himself in the swirl of adolescence and a half a world away from his home.

"At the center of your cosmos, the most important thing was being seen by your classmate Callum."

"Yes."

"So you're all understanding the power of each moment. You have to. You have to see that if you're alive, that every moment can be filled with great power and infinite dimension"

"I see it," said Haley, with a little smile of happiness and knowing.

"When you write this weekend, write moments like these, all these moments in the vast and empty universe. Moments that are true and beautiful. When a feeling was living in you, briefly, in the core of your being. Then you'll be doing something great."

The next week we learned about the social structure of meerkats. We were asked by Hannah, as she presented her project, whether honey bees, with their brief few days in the sun, represented a utopian ideal. *Do bees live good lives?* Did we humans, in our long, complicated lives, make anything as sweet as honey? We asked whether we could live peaceably, as Sociable Weaver birds do, in a mud-and-straw nest with four hundred other birds. We learned that the Statue of Liberty stood on broken chains, and that the seven rays forming her crown represented the seven continents. In science, they studied the properties of rocks and dirt, and then put another coating of mud and straw on their bread oven.

Nolan loved history—he was becoming an expert on the US military, current events, war aircraft, and the great battles of American history. He was emerging as the school's un-ironic "Celebrator of American Greatness."

Nolan presented a project on his area of expertise: American freedom fighters. George Washington, Theodore Roosevelt, and World War II heroes John Basilone and Chesty Puller. From these biographical stories, we teased out a handful of virtues that might be included in a "good life." In Washington, for example, they found an incarnation of honesty, honor, integrity, courage, faith, fighting for ideals, leadership—someone whom others would follow, who lifted others who were demoralized, who would not quit.

At the end of the project, Nolan had a surprise for the class. He and I had ordered a new American flag for the school. Standing in front of the big table, he carefully withdrew the flag from a brown paper wrapping.

"We're going to dedicate this flag to John Basilone," he said. He read a paragraph about Basilone's actions in the Battle of the Bulge and explained why Basilone was his hero. Then he climbed up the ladder he and I had brought into the room. Once at the top of the bookshelves, he carefully reached over the loft ceiling and unfurled the flag, hanging it on two nails facing directly across from the gaze of Martin Luther King, Jr. He stood above us with our still-stiff and creased flag hanging behind him, and the whole class applauded.

We heard another story. A story for all of them, born from the story of one of them.

One day at lunch, Ruby approached me at the big room table. "Is it okay if I leave early today?" she asked quietly.

"Why? What's up?"

"Because today is Luke's birthday, and we do a thing every year. We're going for a hike and then we're making dinner."

"Yeah, of course. There's nothing we're doing as important as that." Her brother Luke had died when he was three, before she was born.

At the end of the day, we were discussing how to write about siblings, choosing what to include and omit. Katelyn had written about her sister. Callum had written about Emma, who was in high school. Ruby looked at me and mouthed the words, "Can I go?" I nodded, and she stood up and gathered her neatly stacked books into her arms.

"Why's she leaving early?" Hannah asked.

"We can talk about it tomorrow," I said as Ruby walked out the door.

The next morning in meeting, Hannah asked again. "I mean you don't have to say, but I was wondering why you left early yesterday," she said.

"Do you want to say, Ruby?" I asked.

"Sure." She opened her mouth, but no words came out.

Then she said: "We were going to hike Snake Mountain. It's Luke's birthday. We do something special every year."

"Who's Luke?" asked Henry.

"My brother. He died before I was born."

"How old was he?" asked Katelyn.

"Three and a half."

"What do you know about him?" I asked.

"Not a lot, I guess," she said, pausing, then starting again. "I know that he loved chickens, and that we plant a tree every year for him. And that the oak tree in our yard was planted by him and my parents, and they dug it up and brought it to our new house when we moved. My mom and my dad and my sister all knew him. But I don't really know much." Then she began to cry.

"Do you talk to your parents about it?" I asked, already sensing the answer.

"No, not really, not very often."

"Why not?"

"Because I'm afraid it will make my mom and dad sad."

"And you don't want them to be sad. But you want to know about him?"

She nodded.

"But in order to get to know more about him, you'd have to ask, and then they might feel sad feelings."

"Yeah."

"But you still want to know more? He's important to you too? He's a part of the family? Yes?"

She nodded and wiped the tears from her cheeks. "He's my brother."

In the stillness of the room, we were listening.

A few days later, Ruby stood behind my chair after class. I turned around to face her.

"Hey, Ruby. What's the story, morning glory?"

"I was wondering who I should write about for my character sketch."

"Do you have any ideas?" I had been encouraging them to write about people they knew intimately or who were complex figures in their lives.

"I was thinking about writing about my friend Zoe." Her voice was flat, unconvincing, and unexcited. "Or . . . if I should . . ." and her voice trailed off.

"Well," I began, and I was thinking, S*he's asking to know, she wants to wade in.*

"Ruby, here's what I think. You should write about Luke. Maybe it will be hard, because he's not here. But he *is* here." I pointed to my chest. "He's in there in you. And you know more than you know. He's a presence, and you feel it."

She nodded.

"Then start. If you get stuck, write about what you don't know. List all the things there *and* not there. It'll lead you where you need to go every time. Okay?"

"Okay."

"Go rip it up, Ruby."

As she turned there was a little smile behind the hand that wiped away the tears.

A few days later, she had a three-page sketch of Luke.

"So," I said, "we read these sketches you guys write about the people you know or love, and how you came to know them and love them. But this one, Ruby's, is a little different. It's about someone who is hard to know, who she hardly knew. But listen. Listen to this with everything you've got."

It began: *I never knew my brother Luke. He died before I was born.*

Her sketch was filled with memories and images, valences and echoes—of the words he'd spoken, of the oak tree they had planted for him, of the apple tree they'd planted last spring, of asking her parents to tell stories about him; and about the blue heron, which was Luke's favorite animal, and how whenever she and her family saw a blue heron, they called out to the bird, "Hey, Luke." All of it—every bit she revealed to us—was part of her root system, and by revealing it she made a bloom for us to witness. She was rooted among us, and we were rooted in her.

"You were so brave to write that," Nadia said after the clapping had stopped.

"I feel like I know him, but even more than that, I feel like I know you," said Katelyn.

"I could see you pulling the apple tree out of the truck," said Winn. "And wrestling with this huge thing, and you're trying to make it stay alive. And that's like trying to think about and write about this huge person, and make a relationship stay alive."

"You were scared to write this?" I asked.

"Yes. Because I was afraid to be sad."

"But you did it."

"Yep."

"Are you sad?"

"Yes. But also a little happy. A lot happy. And I feel accomplished."

"And you asked your mom and dad to tell you stories about him?"

"Yeah, in the truck on the way to Boston. I told her I was writing about Luke and I wanted to know more."

"Were you scared to ask?"

"Yeah. My mom cried. But we laughed too. They said it was good to tell the old stories. I liked hearing them."

"Do you know why?"

She nodded. Before she could say anything, Haley said, "You were letting him live."

"Exactly," I said. We sat for a moment, no one moving.

"Maybe it's okay for your mom and dad to be sad when they tell you about Luke. They speak of him and they feel his presence. You give them that chance. There is life all around it. He's still alive in the way he makes them feel. And so he is not kept away. You gave them the gift of not having to be alone with their sadness, or Luke to be alone."

"And we got to know him too," said Ariela.

"He was making us laugh," said Nils. "He's a funny kid."

"It's like we can see him in the oak trees, like you do," I said.

"And we can see him in the blue herons when we see blue herons," added Nils. "Now when I see a blue heron, I will think, *Hey, Luke.*"

"That's a beautiful thing, Ruby," I said. "That is making life."

When I left school on that chilly afternoon, I thought about how warm it had felt in that class talking about Luke. I was thinking about blue herons wheeling over black waters, and about Ruby, who was brave enough to hold the hand of the brother she was still beginning to know.

Rachel Carson urged the inculcation of a sense of wonder in children by simple measures. She wrote: *And then there is the world of the little things, seen all too seldom. Many children, perhaps because they themselves are small and closer to the ground than we, notice and delight in the small and inconspicuous.*

So she offered this counsel: *give your child a magnifying glass.*

I ordered twenty-eight magnifying glasses, of glass and plastic, ergonomic grips, complete with vinyl lens-protective cases. I hoped that what we might see in those lenses would fascinate and ignite wonder.

We were reading Dylan Thomas's "Fern Hill" in literature class. Before we started, though, I sent the seventh graders out to the stone wall to collect bunches of wilting ferns. When they came back, I asked them to look at their ferns and list all the ways they could find out something about ferns. They proffered many ideas: look it up on the Internet or in a book, or ask an expert; observe the ferns in their habitat; observe differences and similarities between ones that thrived and ones that did not; look at them, turn them over, and look from another angle. Then they went a little further: take them apart, disassemble them, rub them on different parts of the body. Smear them, shake them, smell them, taste them. Drop them, bend them, freeze or burn them, blow air through them, count the parts, look for patterns in their construction.

Then I walked through the classroom holding one up and walked out the opposite door. When I returned to the room, I asked: "How much would we be able to say, conclusively, about this plant with just this passing glance, this brief opportunity to know the fern?"

"Not much," was their answer.

Then I gave them each a new magnifying glass and asked them to find out three new things they had not seen before. "Look closely, and carefully. If you discover any new thing or observe anything notable, say it out loud."

The stem fades from light green to reddish to black at the bottom.
The individual leaves and fronds are all the same size and scale as the whole stalk.
The leaf stalks alternate.
There are hairs on the stem.
There are seeds on the back—are they seeds/eggs of an animal or the plant?
There's a hollow tube in the stalk.

They looked as hard as they could, noticing more carefully than we normally allowed ourselves, or time allowed.

Then I gave them copies of "Fern Hill." "We're going to practice the same kind of looking on this poem. All you have to do is see how many things you can see."

I could not say if the purchase of our magnifying glasses produced 280 dollars worth of learning. I could not say if the magnifying glasses helped us understand "Fern Hill" better. But still I asked: what was learning worth, at the bottom line? And how could we measure it? There was no test in the world that could measure the value of spending a morning looking closely at the stalks of woodland ferns and then reading "Fern Hill."

We came to the last line of the poem. *Time held me green and dying / Though I sang in my chains like the sea.* Such a beautiful line, mysteriously loaded, as Hannah said, "with substance." And we could have sat in the room to talk about that substance, to define it with more words that had less music or meaning. Normally that's what teachers did.

Instead, I ended the conversation.

I looked out the window at the beautiful latefall light. The sun shone and the field was beckoning—the field of praise and animals, our field for children and for playing. It was so obvious: if I wanted them to understand the music of Thomas's windfall light and the sun born over and over, I had to send them out to feel it on their faces, the coolness of grass and the warmth of long rays of sun stretching across the field. And if they could not hear the nightjars flying with the ricks, at least they might see the nuthatches in the low limbs and the crows high over the trees and the geese criss-crossing the cloudless sky.

"Go outside into where it is green and golden, lay down in the grass, and meditate about the last line: Ask what it means to sing like that."

Pushing their chairs back, they headed into the day to understand the poem.

Such flowers of perfection, sitting together at our table. From time to time it occurred to me that my students, just beginning to wrap their hands and hearts around the few poems we would have time to read, were growing up before my eyes. They moved quickly through the liminal dimension between the relative freedom of childhood and the weight and responsibilities of adulthood. They could only be held so long in the safe and happy rooms of our school. *So few and such morning songs*, the poet wrote.

"You guys, you have to understand, Adam and Eve appear on page two of Genesis and are sent away, to East of Eden on, you guessed it—"

"Page three!"

"The happy times don't last long," said Bennett.

"So even while we're green and young and alive, we're also dying?" asked Nils.

"Yep," I answered.

"Man, that sucks," said Nolan.

"From the time we started talking about this poem in class to this moment, which has been about fifteen minutes, you are that much closer to your own end."

Some of their faces fell.

"Time is passing. I know for a fact I can only read one book every month. Roughly that means I can read only about four hundred more books in my lifetime. So I better choose my books wisely. And I've only got one life. Six hundred and fifty thousand hours, give or take. So find and make some sweetness. That's the highest thing you can aim for. Sing in those chains while you can."

I had them read "Fern Hill" in conjunction with *The Red Pony*. Time was precious, and my students were young once only. In Jody, they met a boy straddling the gap between childhood and the adult world. His father's gift of a pony is a stepping-stone to the world of responsibility and adulthood.

"Does the horse, in itself, give him spiritual power?" I asked.

"No," answered Henry. "Because it was given to him. It wasn't earned."

"So any power he gains from the pony is not truly *his* power?"

"No, and he can't be great until he does something great," said Henry. "He's still a boy and the pony isn't a horse. Neither one of them has grown up into what they're going to be."

"The greatest thing isn't the pony," said Nils. "It'll be what Jody becomes."

The terrible suffering of Jody and his pony brought them directly back to themselves. There was truth and beauty in these kinds of epiphanies. *That is all / Ye know on earth, and all ye need to know*, wrote Keats. Of all the things I could teach them or that we could pursue, Truth and Beauty was most elemental, the point around which all else pivoted. In debates about pedagogy, such an aim might be considered an anachronism—outdated, irrelevant, neither measurable nor quantifiable. Yet that was what they were coming to discover.

In class we made lists of things both beautiful and true. *Peonies in spring. The way my father's lip curls up when he plays mandolin. My mother looking out the window at the street. My parents holding hands at night on the couch. How anger can evaporate with a kiss. My brother, asleep. Beauty is when my mother took me on dates, just the two of us, during the year of my parents' divorce, and we ate lemon bars in the coffee shop. Beauty is two old men, who are still best friends, laughing as they walk across a cornfield.*

Beauty, according to Haley, was when we laughed on the long hike through the orange and golden trails of Moosalamoo Mountain, even when it was pouring rain. The sound of those happy voices behind and ahead of her were true and beautiful, she said. Resting in the first snow at the top of the ridge, they saw, as Alycia once had, that it was beautiful: a valley below us to the east, the edge of Sugar Hill reservoir showing silver and shimmering through a gap, the trees gray on the rounded slopes in the distance.

"It was beautiful," Ruby said one day in class, "when Hannah sat with Winn at lunch because she was alone."

"I saw you that day when you were sitting with her," said Nolan. "That was pretty cool."

Once at school we were talking about the autumn leaves. Was it true, we wondered, that the colors of autumn leaves were an eternal, absolute beauty—that any human who ever saw those leaves could only arrive at that single, unalterable conclusion? How could it be, we asked, that a single thing could be beautiful to anyone who beheld it? A few weeks later, we were driving back to school from a field trip to the Northeast Kingdom, passing through the Granville Gulch. On either side of the road the hills climbed steeply. Late afternoon sunlight angled through the notches until the trees were afire and incandescent. Henry sat in the passenger seat of my truck, gazing out the window, oblivious to the joking of his classmates in the back.

"What's happening in the way light hits these leaves and

gives us images of colors in our eyes that makes all these people want to come up here and look at the leaves?" he asked, referring to the "leaf peepers," Vermont's annual influx of autumn tourists.

I couldn't answer the question. A week later, on the return from a soccer game on the same stretch of road, he said, "I think I'm beginning to understand."

A student could be terrible at math facts or unable to retain historical concepts. Another child could struggle to distinguish a subject complement from a direct object. A student might have trouble understanding abstract ideas, or they might have poor executive functioning skills. But every child could name the beautiful. When my students named lovely things, cynicism began to die and optimism grew. When they spoke openly of what was closest to their hearts, they opened to each other. Their peers—no longer magazine cutouts or stereotypes—were incarnations of entire worlds, wondrous in complexity, pathos, humor and history, depths opening onto depths.

But they had to practice seeing and saying it. We practiced every day. The hidden parts of themselves were allowed to breathe, an admixture of each of them enjoined to everything else—the particular day, the weather and the wind, polygons and plate tectonics, angles and fractals, "Fern Hill" and the leaves falling to the earth.

We gathered under the trees on a rainy morning by the North Branch River. It ran for two miles along the dirt road that led past the school towards Lincoln. The river was overhung with wet, heavy branches and filled with smoothed quartz boulders. Black pools formed and then poured over the rocks. The browning ferns shivered in the breeze and white trunks of birches glistened in the rain. They wore mud boots and waders and nylon pants duct-taped to their ankles in a futile attempt to keep the waters out. We'd come to explore the way the river moved and flowed for science class. Jasper wandered among our legs in the wet grass, dragging a large stick that bumped into our legs as we conducted an impromptu morning meeting.

"Tal, why are you so grumpy?" asked Nils as we crowded together.

"Not grumpy. Sleepy. Tired. Friday, Nils. Long days behind. Long day ahead."

Nils suddenly leaned into Callum, causing them both to stumble. I gave them a stern, head-masterly glance.

"What?" Callum exclaimed. "I'm awake, eager, and ready to learn!"

Eric lined them up in a phalanx of five rows: five-abreast, each row holding hands. First they followed Eric as he walked, then ran, then changed directions, turning and re-turning. As they imitated the width, rush, and flow of the river, they became human current. In the turns, the outside "water" had to speed up. The inside water had to slow.

They stumbled and laughed. They were multi-hued, their jackets soaked in the rain, the sound of squelching boots. Eric stopped, and they all slammed into each other. They loved having to be connected.

"Oh my god!" shouted Katelyn as she slipped in the wet grass. Ruby tried to pull her up as Eric arranged them again for another demonstration of the river's sinuosity.

"Okay, here's your woodland vocab test," Eric called out to them. "Then we'll head out for your river meditation. What's the word for the deepest part of a river channel?

"THALWEG!" they shouted in unison.

Then they scattered into the woods to find the river, which was filled with overnight rain. They waded in and walked along the bank in the shallow places and into the deeper pools, making observations about erosion and flow rate, ostensibly quietly and meditatively. I watched them move upstream and down, in the river, now a part of it. In the most physical and literal sense, they were immersed in experience.

Then I could no longer see them. But through the misty woods downstream I heard their shouts and laughter and splashing as the water poured in, filling their boots where the river ran deep.

They had meditated in the fields and heard Dylan Thomas speak liquidly of childhood and the physical world: *And the sabbath rang slowly / In the pebbles of the holy streams.* They had walked in the woods under apple boughs and knew something of the tall fields of tall grass, the wet earth, and the dying leaves.

In meeting the next morning, Nils read Whitman's "Give Me the Silent Splendid Sun." He'd chosen the perfect words as text for our learning.

"Read it again," I said, and we listened again.

> *Give me the splendid silent sun with all his beams full-dazzling;*
> *Give me juicy autumnal fruit ripe and red from the orchard;*
> *Give me a field where the unmow'd grass grows;*

The following day, I read a sketch Hannah had written, which itself was a catalogue of Whitmanian beauty. She recounted all the little fractions of a day, the splendid splinters that made life a thing to hold. For her it was the smell of opening a box of tissue, the scented puff arising from the floral-patterned box. Her writing opened in this way—a soft, compact folded order.

> *Someone's twittering laughter in the corner, a girl twirling*
> *her skirt in the field, someone singing "all around the world*

is la la la," a friend sinking her toes into the black sand of Cape Cod . . . the ripe grass, the leaves fluttering down from the trees, little girls prancing under them trying to catch the crispy colors, the spiraling trees, tall and recumbent, every root wrapped around another, everything connected under the dark rich soil, the rocks, strong and solid, the flowers, some dark and pungent, bursting with seeds and scent, others delicate and blushing with pigment, reaching out for the sun, only to close up when it gets dark.

Her catalogue of the small, good things was as bright as the sun. *O such for me! O an intense life! O full to repletion, and varied!* wrote Whitman, and Hannah called back in echo.

"How'd it feel to hear that?" I asked the class.

"It makes me wonder how is it that we go around complaining about how bad the world is," said Callum. "Is it truly something that needs to be complained about, or are we just not seeing it?"

"But there're things in the world that are pretty screwed up," said Nils.

"But what she described is so much more powerful than the wrong things," said Nadia. "I *want* to listen to this."

"Yeah, nobody wants to hear someone complain," said Ruby. "It's like people go around shouting, 'I'm miserable. Help me!'" Laughter filled the room.

"Brody, how about you?"

"I liked it," he said, without blinking.

"Cole?"

"I wish I could write like that."

When their discoveries were born from the crucible of lived experience, their answers could uplift us. They made us laugh, or look at each other across the table and all feel, together, in a single moment, the same bit of understanding. They listened and they raised their eyebrows at each other, smiling, because they were hearing something of themselves in the words of another. The room, and everyone in it, was thrumming with life.

We read Robert Frost throughout the fall. We were so close to the Homer Noble Farm and Frost's cabin that it was not hard to feel that he was "our" poet. When we read Frost, we could imagine him walking in our woods and fields where goldenrod and coneflowers withered and dried.

One Friday, we hiked to his cabin, a log structure with a cedar-shingled roof. We ate lunch on the screened porch looking south down into the mowed pasture. Then we gathered on the floor before the hearth of the fieldstone fireplace in the cabin and listened to a recording of him reading "Directive." We spread out in the fields among the trees and wrote in our journals. And kept him with us into the wet gloom and darkening days of November, reading a poem a week, coming to know his voice that spoke so deeply from the hills around us.

We read "The Road Not Taken." I'd told them that they might possibly want to reject the poem because maybe they'd all heard it before, or had to memorize it in fifth grade. Perhaps, if they had thought about it at all, it was nothing more than a cliché concerned with "not going with what is popular." Some of the kids murmured assent: they had memorized it in fifth grade and believed it to be nothing more than a Hallmark poem.

But we dwelled in the poem long enough to see down the road that "curved in the undergrowth," long enough to ask questions, to let our minds go forward and backward from the present time to "ages and ages hence." We decided the poem was Frost's own voice calling to us from those woods in a faraway time, and telling us, in truth, that there was never any way to know which was the right path. After all, the two paths were really worn about the same. Perhaps Frost was telling us that we had to make a choice, and whatever happened after was beyond all control. At the end of class, Bennett approached me.

"At first I thought this was a corny poem," he said, smiling. "Tal, I changed my mind. It's a kick-ass poem."

That was "negative capability" in action. A mind engaged and taking in new ideas, thoughts, interpretations; discarding previous judgments so that a higher, more refined, capacious, and enthusiastic space opened; a mind, in short, that could be changed, and took joy in being changed.

When we read "The Wood-Pile," we found a poem about going in deep and not holding back.

> *Out walking in the frozen swamp one gray day,*
> *I paused and said, 'I will turn back from here.*
> *No, I will go on farther—and we shall see.'*
> *The hard snow held me, save where now and then*
> *One foot went through. The view was all in lines*
> *Straight up and down of tall slim trees*
> *Too much alike to mark or name a place by*
> *So as to say for certain I was here*
> *Or somewhere else:*

I wanted them to see everything. The shape of a poem. The courage of a human encounter with being lost and alone. The discovery of one's fiery essence. We had a far way to go, and we'd not grow or learn if we turned back. We might get lost, but we still had to keep going and trust we would be held until we found the certainty of ourselves.

"So what are these lines in the woods, this pile of wood all wrapped up?" I asked.

The class decided that these were the lines of his thought and poetry. The woodpile? Man's work, the labor of his hands. The poem was the darker lines on a white page.

"It's like the woodpile is what the woodsman made—" Nils began.

"And words are what the poets make!" exclaimed Winn.

The kids then noticed that the woodpile in the poem was held up by a smaller tree and two falling stakes placed there by the woodsman.

"So why are the stakes there?" I asked.

"On one is the tree," said Nils. "Maybe that's nature, or God."

"And on the other side is the stake the woodsman placed there," said Hannah.

"That's what the woodsman can make from what God gives," said Henry.

"But both God and the woodsman are absent," I said. "So what's the meaning of this abandoned pile of wood?"

Bennett lurched forward, his upper body the head of a horse. "The woodpile isn't going to ever be used, but the poet is using it for his poem!" he said.

"New things will grow from where it's rotting into the earth!" said Nadia. She was rising in her seat with excitement. "Even though it's decaying, it's still living!"

Nils suddenly noticed: "Tal, if you change one letter in the title it becomes 'the *word*-pile'—the pile of wood is the poem that man makes!"

"Oh yeah!" came a jumble of voices.

"The words are the cut trees, or the harvest!" said Ruby.

"The space between the logs that helps them dry are the spaces on the page between the words!" said Bennett, which was a bit of knowledge only someone who'd spent time around wood piles would know.

In a burst of excitement, the kids realized that the poem was unrhymed.

"So what?" I said.

"Look!" they shouted. "It's all unrhymed! Except the first and last words: 'gray' and 'decay.' That's like the tree and the stake that hold the whole pile of words up!" And they were right, there it was: the rhymed bookends of the poem, holding the stack of words in place on the page.

Not every class comes so electrically alive. But that day they were on fire, so to speak, and we had something more than warmth going around the table. The meaning to me was clear. We must not ever turn back; we must always go further. As a school, as a classroom of nascent poetry scholars, we had to press on. Then we might come to a kind of seeing not only about the visible, but about discovering and creating what wasn't visible: the feelings and ideas between the lines, to read what might be living just down the curving path in the yellow wood.

On another day, we gathered at the Robert Frost Wayside, a looping trail crossing the Middlebury River as it ran down the mountain from the Broadloaf Wilderness. There, leisurely hikers could amble along a gravel path and read the occasional Frost poem engraved into US Forest Service plaques.

It was a high blue day, and the mountains were dusted yellow by the last hanging beech leaves on the hills beyond the dry fields. The hemlock overstory rose, darkly pointed in the cloudless, azure sky. We walked along gravel paths to the river where we would measure the water volume and the river's sinuosity. In scientific terms, we were studying *fluvial geomorphology*.

"*Hell-o!* Fluvial geomorphologists in the house, yo!" Bennett shouted, sounding like he was MC-ing a rave. He was excited to be continuing the river studies from the week before.

They splashed in the river with tape measures and stopwatches, recording data on crumpled sheets of paper, calculating the flow rate in gallons per second and liters per fortnight.

Callum walked next to me at the end of the day. "Tal," he said. "Why do you think Buddhism still affects people?"

"You mean, why are there still so many followers?"

"No, I mean, why are so many people still able to feel what it's about? The beginning of it was so long ago."

down, in the river, now a part of it. In the most physical and literal sense, they were immersed in experience.

Then I could no longer see them. But through the misty woods downstream I heard their shouts and laughter and splashing as the water poured in, filling their boots where the river ran deep.

They had meditated in the fields and heard Dylan Thomas speak liquidly of childhood and the physical world: *And the sabbath rang slowly / In the pebbles of the holy streams.* They had walked in the woods under apple boughs and knew something of the tall fields of tall grass, the wet earth, and the dying leaves.

In meeting the next morning, Nils read Whitman's "Give Me the Silent Splendid Sun." He'd chosen the perfect words as text for our learning.

"Read it again," I said, and we listened again.

> *Give me the splendid silent sun with all his beams full-dazzling;*
> *Give me juicy autumnal fruit ripe and red from the orchard;*
> *Give me a field where the unmow'd grass grows;*

The following day, I read a sketch Hannah had written, which itself was a catalogue of Whitmanian beauty. She recounted all the little fractions of a day, the splendid splinters that made life a thing to hold. For her it was the smell of opening a box of tissue, the scented puff arising from the floral-patterned box. Her writing opened in this way—a soft, compact folded order.

> *Someone's twittering laughter in the corner, a girl twirling*
> *her skirt in the field, someone singing "all around the world*

*is la la la," a friend sinking her toes into the black sand of
Cape Cod . . . the ripe grass, the leaves fluttering down from
the trees, little girls prancing under them trying to catch the
crispy colors, the spiraling trees, tall and recumbent, every
root wrapped around another, everything connected under
the dark rich soil, the rocks, strong and solid, the flowers,
some dark and pungent, bursting with seeds and scent,
others delicate and blushing with pigment, reaching out for
the sun, only to close up when it gets dark.*

Her catalogue of the small, good things was as bright as the
sun. *O such for me! O an intense life! O full to repletion, and varied!*
wrote Whitman, and Hannah called back in echo.

"How'd it feel to hear that?" I asked the class.

"It makes me wonder how is it that we go around complaining about how bad the world is," said Callum. "Is it truly something that needs to be complained about, or are we just not seeing it?"

"But there're things in the world that are pretty screwed up," said Nils.

"But what she described is so much more powerful than the wrong things," said Nadia. "I *want* to listen to this."

"Yeah, nobody wants to hear someone complain," said Ruby. "It's like people go around shouting, 'I'm miserable. Help me!'" Laughter filled the room.

"Brody, how about you?"

"I liked it," he said, without blinking.

"Cole?"

"I wish I could write like that."

When their discoveries were born from the crucible of lived experience, their answers could uplift us. They made us laugh, or look at each other across the table and all feel, together, in a single moment, the same bit of understanding. They listened and they raised their eyebrows at each other, smiling, because they were hearing something of themselves in the words of another. The room, and everyone in it, was thrumming with life.

We read Robert Frost throughout the fall. We were so close to the Homer Noble Farm and Frost's cabin that it was not hard to feel that he was "our" poet. When we read Frost, we could imagine him walking in our woods and fields where goldenrod and coneflowers withered and dried.

One Friday, we hiked to his cabin, a log structure with a cedar-shingled roof. We ate lunch on the screened porch looking south down into the mowed pasture. Then we gathered on the floor before the hearth of the fieldstone fireplace in the cabin and listened to a recording of him reading "Directive." We spread out in the fields among the trees and wrote in our journals. And kept him with us into the wet gloom and darkening days of November, reading a poem a week, coming to know his voice that spoke so deeply from the hills around us.

We read "The Road Not Taken." I'd told them that they might possibly want to reject the poem because maybe they'd all heard it before, or had to memorize it in fifth grade. Perhaps, if they had thought about it at all, it was nothing more than a cliché concerned with "not going with what is popular." Some of the kids murmured assent: they had memorized it in fifth grade and believed it to be nothing more than a Hallmark poem.

But we dwelled in the poem long enough to see down the road that "curved in the undergrowth," long enough to ask questions, to let our minds go forward and backward from the present time to "ages and ages hence." We decided the poem was Frost's own voice calling to us from those woods in a faraway time, and telling us, in truth, that there was never any way to know which was the right path. After all, the two paths were really worn about the same. Perhaps Frost was telling us that we had to make a choice, and whatever happened after was beyond all control. At the end of class, Bennett approached me.

"At first I thought this was a corny poem," he said, smiling. "Tal, I changed my mind. It's a kick-ass poem."

That was "negative capability" in action. A mind engaged and taking in new ideas, thoughts, interpretations; discarding previous judgments so that a higher, more refined, capacious, and enthusiastic space opened; a mind, in short, that could be changed, and took joy in being changed.

When we read "The Wood-Pile," we found a poem about going in deep and not holding back.

> *Out walking in the frozen swamp one gray day,*
> *I paused and said, 'I will turn back from here.*
> *No, I will go on farther—and we shall see.'*
> *The hard snow held me, save where now and then*
> *One foot went through. The view was all in lines*
> *Straight up and down of tall slim trees*
> *Too much alike to mark or name a place by*
> *So as to say for certain I was here*
> *Or somewhere else:*

I wanted them to see everything. The shape of a poem. The courage of a human encounter with being lost and alone. The discovery of one's fiery essence. We had a far way to go, and we'd not grow or learn if we turned back. We might get lost, but we still had to keep going and trust we would be held until we found the certainty of ourselves.

"So what are these lines in the woods, this pile of wood all wrapped up?" I asked.

The class decided that these were the lines of his thought and poetry. The woodpile? Man's work, the labor of his hands. The poem was the darker lines on a white page.

"It's like the woodpile is what the woodsman made—" Nils began.

"And words are what the poets make!" exclaimed Winn.

The kids then noticed that the woodpile in the poem was held up by a smaller tree and two falling stakes placed there by the woodsman.

"So why are the stakes there?" I asked.

"On one is the tree," said Nils. "Maybe that's nature, or God."

"And on the other side is the stake the woodsman placed there," said Hannah.

"That's what the woodsman can make from what God gives," said Henry.

"But both God and the woodsman are absent," I said. "So what's the meaning of this abandoned pile of wood?"

Bennett lurched forward, his upper body the head of a horse. "The woodpile isn't going to ever be used, but the poet is using it for his poem!" he said.

"New things will grow from where it's rotting into the earth!" said Nadia. She was rising in her seat with excitement. "Even though it's decaying, it's still living!"

Nils suddenly noticed: "Tal, if you change one letter in the title it becomes 'the *word*-pile'—the pile of wood is the poem that man makes!"

"Oh yeah!" came a jumble of voices.

"The words are the cut trees, or the harvest!" said Ruby.

"The space between the logs that helps them dry are the spaces on the page between the words!" said Bennett, which was a bit of knowledge only someone who'd spent time around wood piles would know.

In a burst of excitement, the kids realized that the poem was unrhymed.

"So what?" I said.

"Look!" they shouted. "It's all unrhymed! Except the first and last words: 'gray' and 'decay.' That's like the tree and the stake that hold the whole pile of words up!" And they were right, there it was: the rhymed bookends of the poem, holding the stack of words in place on the page.

Not every class comes so electrically alive. But that day they were on fire, so to speak, and we had something more than warmth going around the table. The meaning to me was clear. We must not ever turn back; we must always go further. As a school, as a classroom of nascent poetry scholars, we had to press on. Then we might come to a kind of seeing not only about the visible, but about discovering and creating what wasn't visible: the feelings and ideas between the lines, to read what might be living just down the curving path in the yellow wood.

On another day, we gathered at the Robert Frost Wayside, a looping trail crossing the Middlebury River as it ran down the mountain from the Broadloaf Wilderness. There, leisurely hikers could amble along a gravel path and read the occasional Frost poem engraved into US Forest Service plaques.

It was a high blue day, and the mountains were dusted yellow by the last hanging beech leaves on the hills beyond the dry fields. The hemlock overstory rose, darkly pointed in the cloudless, azure sky. We walked along gravel paths to the river where we would measure the water volume and the river's sinuosity. In scientific terms, we were studying *fluvial geomorphology*.

"*Hell-o!* Fluvial geomorphologists in the house, yo!" Bennett shouted, sounding like he was MC-ing a rave. He was excited to be continuing the river studies from the week before.

They splashed in the river with tape measures and stopwatches, recording data on crumpled sheets of paper, calculating the flow rate in gallons per second and liters per fortnight.

Callum walked next to me at the end of the day. "Tal," he said. "Why do you think Buddhism still affects people?"

"You mean, why are there still so many followers?"

"No, I mean, why are so many people still able to feel what it's about? The beginning of it was so long ago."

"So, you mean, why are people touched or changed by it if they are only 'hearing about it' now, and weren't a part of its origins?"

"Yeah. How does it keep going? Doesn't that mean the beginning of the religion was really powerful?"

"I guess so. Same with Christianity. No one here was there when Jesus fed five thousand people with one fish. But people still feel and believe in the power of it. So it must have been really powerful then."

He nodded and kept pace with me. "Tal?" he asked, after we had walked a ways. "Do you know any mystics?"

"Do *I* know any mystics?" I had never thought of such a question.

"Yeah."

"I wish I could say I did. I don't know where you'd find a mystic."

"Could anyone be one?"

"I suppose so. But I don't know how you become one. I think you have to suffer a lot, and have some kind of rare grace while enduring your suffering." I thought of Rumi's saying: *There are a thousand ways to kneel and kiss the ground.*

Callum nodded and kept walking ahead of me as we passed under the gray and golden trees.

Along with geomorphology, they studied orienteering. On Thursday, three groups set out, each at a different pace, each with compasses and GPS units, backpacks, mud boots, food, and water. We only had to go a quarter of a mile on old logging roads before we were deep in the Ripton woods. The clouds were gray and steel, bruised blue and low. We passed through small fields "no bigger than a harness gall," as Frost wrote. Jasper dashed among us, stopping to sniff animal tracks, ears alert, then sprinted ahead. We walked on paths blanketed in wet leaves, under rotting deer stands, through dense hardwood groves, over beds of sodden moss.

The goal was to find "Stopping By Woods," a geocache hidden near a beaver pond a few miles northeast of the school. We'd been there once three years before at this time of year, then, as now, trampling through bogs, knitted together by our own voices, calling out, "We're over here!" They shrieked as they sank deep into the mud and icy waters, giddy, laughing, roughhousing, trampling about like lambs.

On the way to the swamp, stumbling into an old refuse pile hidden in layers of moldering leaves, they found the wrecked frame of an old Dodge. Syrup and oil cans, a great cauldron, and bald, cracked tires were heaped under the wheel-wells, the refuse of some long-gone hill farmer. The rust-brown fenders tilted out like gravestones.

Further on, they were among the reflections of the leaves in the swamp water. They climbed over a beaver lodge and held out their hands to pull each other up. They strode over mosses as green as gold. They smelled decomposing leaves and made clouds of silt rise from the waters.

Even in the remote reaches of the Green Mountain National Forest, they could also be confused, overwhelmed, and unsure— trying to find a way in, trying to connect, wondering who their friends would be, trying to find their place in the family of the school. The younger ones tried to keep up, sometimes barely hanging on, wide-eyed and wondering how they might ever measure up to some older students' capable, inspiring ways. The older ones wanted to inspire, be great, leading the school as they plunged through the swamp. I remembered what Nadia had written earlier in the week.

When we went on the first hike in my first year, I had
no idea what I was doing or what really mattered to me.
I didn't even know what to wear. I thought, 'What am

I doing out here?' I feel like now I can understand the difference between what is real and what isn't.

For older students like Nadia, the goal was not necessarily the geocache, or understanding coordinates on the GPS, it was about the spirit of gleeful motion and going forth. It mattered not if they got wet and cold—they were in love with the going and being out of the classroom in the fall to walk in the woods. "This is hardcore," they exclaimed. "I love my school," they called out. I thought of Brutus' words in *Julius Caesar.*

There is a tide in the affairs of men.
which, taken at the flood, leads on to fortune;
Omitted, all the voyage of their life
Is bound in the shallows and in miseries...
And we must take the current when it serves,
Or lose our ventures.

In such moments, it was impossible to lose our ventures—we were immersed in them. The currents were all around: the dying season, the full waters flowing out of Alder Swamp, the winter fast approaching. Nadia had come to understand the difference between the shallows and the depths, and the necessity of taking the current when it served. These ventures, this time, this voyage of her life, *mattered.*

Ruby galloped in yellow waders. Callum poured water out of his mud boots. Hannah screamed for help as she sank into a bog. Henry pulled a freshly gnawed beaver stick from a dam of mud and grass, holding it aloft like a trophy. Bennett and Cole smeared their cheeks with mud.

"It's my war paint, dude!" Bennett called out.

When they trooped back into the building, their socks were soaking, their shoes squelching. Afterwards, they described the day. "I felt closer to real life," said Haley. "Even though my knee was aching, that was where I wanted to be."

On a cold rainy morning, the school was divided into seven mixed-age groups of four. Eric gave them compasses and a series of waypoints to navigate through in the woods. The ground was clear, but light snow was spitting and swirling. They spent the morning criss-crossing the steep hill to the east behind the school. When they returned, they looked delighted, shouting and exclaiming about their adventure in the woods.

Later in class, Ruby asked: "Bennett, how did you get back so soon?"

"Because," he said pridefully, "we went faster than everyone else." He smiled, filled with his sense of winning.

"So what?"

"We found all the waypoints and we got the right direction," he continued.

"Well, you didn't have to leave me," Winn blurted. She was not usually eager for confrontation, but she'd been abandoned and she didn't like it. The tension was palpable, overwhelming the good feelings from earlier in the day.

"What's going on?" I asked. "What happened out there?"

"Well," began Winn. "I thought I knew which way to go, so I set my compass. Then I figured out it was wrong. But that's the way I started. Then Bennett turned around and told us we were going the wrong way. He didn't tell us what we were doing wrong. He just shouted at us that we were going in the wrong direction. And then he left us. Eventually we figured it out, but by then they were gone and we didn't see them again."

"She didn't know which way to go," Bennett defended.

"So what was the assignment?"

"To get to the waypoints," he answered.

"Was the assignment to stay in your group to find the way-points, or to split up and get to the waypoints first?"

"To stay together."

"Then you didn't follow the assignment, even though you went the farthest and fastest. The assignment was to find them together, and get back together."

"I know. But we figured it out and I wanted to get to all the waypoints."

"That's fine, you did that, you got there first. But you also said you want to be a leader. And you kind of did that because you were in the lead. But is that the only definition of being a leader? Is the leader the guy who goes fastest? Or does the leader make sure everybody gets there together?"

"I don't know."

"Look," I said, "I'm reading a book about the Civil War called *This Hallowed Ground*. In it there's a famous battle. General Lee was the Confederate leader, and his army attacked in these swampy woods called The Wilderness. When the battle started, no one could see anything. It was all trees and undergrowth and smoke and explosions—total chaos and confusion. No trails or landmarks or anything. No one could see the lines or the regimental flags. No one could see the leader, and so the battle lines became disorganized and in some cases it was so confusing that the lines of the same side were attacking each other. Maybe there was a regimental commander charging around in the woods riding a great horse, charging this way and that, out in front. But if he wasn't aware of where everyone else was, it would be death to him and his men. Are you following me so far?"

"Yes." Bennett was looking me straight in the eye.

"Being the first and not seeing the whole picture can lead to disaster. He might have been leading his men in the wrong direction. "

He nodded.

"Do you guys know where the generals were during a battle?" I asked.

"Up high on their horses?" asked Yeb.

"Yes, but where were they with their horses?"

"On high ground?" Nils answered.

"Yes, above the battle so they could see everything. So they could see what was happening and who needed help. See who was in trouble, and see how to move all the pieces so the whole thing worked together. That's what leaders do. They look out for the whole group. They're not interested in glory for themselves, which may *seem* heroic but doesn't necessarily help win the battle."

"I think I understand," said Bennett.

"You were a regimental commander who went charging into the woods looking for glory and not looking out for your regiment or the big picture. You were at the head of the charge, but behind you others in a state of confusion and chaos. There were casualties because of that. You have to be aware of everybody. You can't leave anyone behind, ever. You gotta make sure you move together."

He nodded.

"I was sort of caught between," said Hannah.

"What do you mean?" I asked.

"Well, Bennett was racing to the top of the hill. I could see Winn in the distance, way back behind me in the woods. I could see her because she was wearing her yellow rain slicker. And I thought, *I can't leave her back there*, even if it meant that we didn't find all the waypoints. I knew I wouldn't want to be left behind. So I stayed back with her."

"So you had to choose between two right actions, either finding the waypoints and completing the assignment, or doing what felt right for the people you were with."

I looked around the class. "Every day in your lives you're going to have a moment like this where you have to decide what to do, between right and wrong, between yourself or others."

If we were going to go anywhere, we had to go together.

❦

We planned another geocache hike into the woods. We loaded into three trucks and drove up the dirt roads towards the swamps and beaver ponds at the head of the North Branch River. As we bounced over the ruts and washboards, Nils conducted nine kids in the truck bed in a chorus.

"Obladi, Oblada, life goes on . . ." The song carried in through my open window as I watched them in the rearview mirror bouncing as they sang.

Thoreau liked to use the word *saunter*, from the French *saunterre*, meaning "saints of the earth."

I shouted at them as we loaded out of the truck: "We are the saints of the earth!"

"What?" they shouted back.

On the trail, we walked under the spires of fir trees, working our way to the surrounding beaver ponds. We stepped on a snake that threatened to strike; we helped each other across watery ravines and mud-holes and slippery rocks, we pulled each other out of the cold-water grasses, we navigated in the soft, ferny woods by following each other's voices and tracks. We were in that place where, as Thoreau wrote, "jurisdiction ceases."

"Do you realize we are in a transcendently beautiful place, and we are perhaps the most blessed people on earth? We are treading where no man has trod!" I exclaimed to them.

"Great, Tal!" they called back. "And you mean where no man or woman has trod!"

We found the cache, a plastic bag stuffed in a hollow stump. Inside was a copy of Frost's poems. I opened the soggy pages and read to them part of "West Running Brook."

We must be something.
We've said we two. Let's change that to we three.
As you and I are married to each other,
We'll both be married to the brook. We'll build
Our bridge across it, and the bridge shall be
Our arm thrown over it asleep beside it.

Look, look, it's waving to us with a wave
To let us know it hears me.'

I knew in time they would feel it truly. In a moment of still-ness or remembrance they would know it, because it was in their marrow, and they were in it together. They were becoming something. They went from being twenty-seven *ones* to shift-ing clusters of many—of pairs, threes, and wholes. They built their bridges and were, for those hours, married to the brook, the woods, the blood-colored goosefoot maple leaves, and each other.

One rainy morning we gathered for meeting. The winds the night before had blown the last leaves off the trees. I asked: "What is a religious feeling?"

"What do you mean?" asked Nils. "Like, if we're Buddhist, or when we're in church?"

"Since most of you aren't usually in church, I'm talking about outside of church. So I guess I am talking about a 'religious' feeling in your own experience. Like when you felt an invisible power, something that might have come from a god, if there is one."

"Why are you asking us this?" he asked.

"Because last night I was feeling it, in the time of the leaves coming down. This is always the time of year when I want to be in the vein of a leaf. I want to know what it is to be in the vein of a leaf falling in the night in the rain. For me that is a religious feeling."

"The vein of a leaf?" asked Callum.

"Like on the hike, last week. When we were in the swamps and woods. Was there a religious feeling being there? If there was, write what you felt. If not, write what was absent. Or write about what you feel is something only you and god might have seen."

They wrote for a few minutes and then read to each other. They wrote of their feelings about the silence they found in the water pooled behind a dam; about how it felt to walk alone ahead of the class on the trail; about seeing geese exchanging the lead as they flew over the trees; of no longer caring about being wet; of forgetting the materials we toted—backpacks full of unimportant manufactured objects—and becoming subsumed in the cold flow of waters and woods.

Another day we held class on the stone wall running behind the schoolhouse, where we read Frost's "Mending Wall." The wall was now a tumbling, leaf-cloaked mass sinking into the ground, and some of the stones were in fact shaped like loaves—there we sat with our photocopied poems.

"This might have been the stone wall Frost was writing about," I told them as they shivered in their coats.

"Really?" asked Yeb. His eyes were wide in disbelief. He wore a green knit winter hat with a giant yellow pom-pom bobbling on top.

"Yeah, man," I said with a smile. "Maybe this was the wall." Truly, men like Frost and his neighbor had walked through these woods, over this frost-heaved earth, among wild apple trees and in the dark shade of pines, building and rebuilding.

We decided to ask our neighbor if we could rebuild a portion of his stone wall that ran along Lincoln Road in front of the school. Ruby pointed out that building a wall *up* might seem unneighborly. I told her that in this case our aim wasn't to engage in poetical and ethical metaphysics with our neighbor, but to make something more aesthetically pleasing than a pile of half-hidden mossy rocks covered by beer cans, broken bottles, leaf litter, rotting sticks, and tendrils of rusting barbed wire.

Before we began mending the wall, I ran them through a goal-setting process. *What are your goals for your life? What are your goals before you graduate high school? What are your goals for this school year? What are your goals, or what is your intention, for this week? What was your intention this morning when you woke up? What are your goals in the next hour and a half when we go outside to rebuild our old stone wall?* Then I gave instructions: "Make the wall taller and visible, dig up the rocks, and move the leaves."

We headed out into the cold, gray day in our mud boots and Brooks Pharmacy smocks, which had been donated to the school, with the garden cart loaded with seven rakes, three shovels, two tattered blue tarps, and one heavy iron landscaping pry bar, which we called "God's Nail." Nolan sat proudly atop his father's New Holland tractor, which he had been allowed to drive to school that morning.

Winn stood atop the tumbling wall and read "Mending Wall" from our signed copy of Frost's poems, and then we set to work. The rakers and weeders pulled rotting matter from the wall. The haulers piled leaves, twigs, and detritus on the tarps and dragged it into the woods. Limb- and tree-cutters cut away saplings and vines and barbed wire. The God's Nailers pried up rocks, and the rest of us lifted the heavy stones up onto the wall. We clawed out lichen-covered boulders, fat worms, matted leaves, and an old shovel blade. In one hour, a sixty-foot section of the wall was mended. We posed proudly on top of it with our tools and dirt under our fingernails.

Fall was past. As the days darkened, I read the class Frost's poem "A Late Walk." I told them to imagine him making up the verses in our woods, our fields, walking along our stone wall in late autumn.

> *A tree beside the wall stands bare,*
> *But a leaf that lingered brown,*
> *Disturbed, I doubt not, by my thought,*
> *Comes softly rattling down.*
>
> *I end not far from my going forth*
> *By picking the faded blue*
> *Of the last remaining aster flower*
> *To carry again to you.*

Many seasons hence my students might remember what inhered in the last purple aster from the gardens of summer. Maybe their ears would be so finely tuned that they could hear the rattling of a single leaf, or understand the *whir of sober birds/ Up from the tangle of withered weeds*. Among those last colors and lingerings sounded the laughter and shouting of our time together. In these exalted moments before the swamps froze over, I had sensed in them a growing belief in the power of words, sauntering, music, images, and each other. They were learning that fortunes of faded asters were not far from their "going forth." The flood currents and fields, the walls and the weeds and the singular leaves—all of this was theirs.

Callum read a poem by Keats on a cold, gray Friday, "The Cricket and the Grasshopper," which began with the line, *The poetry of earth is never dead.* In the woods and swamps, the poetry of earth was alive. It flowed and flowed, and we were deep in it.

WINTER

in winter the mountain is a bird
with lavender feathers
and a still heart.

—HAYDEN CARRUTH

ON A COLD, BRIGHT MORNING, when such a thing was unimaginable, Bennett's mother found a monarch chrysalis outside in the school driveway still attached to a small stem. She brought it into school and we re-tied the broken stem to the twig, placed it in a mason jar, and left it on the big room table. It sat there for the rest of the week, turning blacker each day. Though it was unlikely, we waited for the orange of its wings to show.

I could not help wanting my students to suddenly emerge, bold and unfurling, dripping some mysterious elixir of life. It was almost too easy of a thing to say or feel, particularly before the snow flew. But when they set their books on the table to begin each day, I looked at that blackening chrysalis, and I saw them.

On Monday morning, Winn shouted through the school.

"The chrysalis split! The butterfly fell out!"

It lay in the bottom of the jar, its wings pitifully small and curled and damp, it's abdomen thin and gaunt.

"Everyone, get in here! The butterfly is hatching!" Winn shouted again. In less than thirty seconds, the table was circled by twenty-seven adolescents, all of them quiet, looking, unmoving.

"What's going on?"

"The butterfly!"

They leaned in. Haley ran in with a magnifying glass.

"Is it a boy or a girl?"

"You can't tell yet," said Winn. "It's wings are all curled up. Usually their abdomens are really big and full and they pump out fluid to the wings. This one is really thin."

"Is it too late for it?" Brody asked. "Will it live?"

Winn tilted the jar and gently poured the butterfly onto the bouquet of dried flowers and stems.

"Look," she said, "you can see the drops of fluid still on its wings."

They were teenagers, but they still cared as much about a newborn monarch as they did about the longitudinal lines on their papier mâché globes or the pages of *The Red Pony*. And I could not say they were wrong.

Later in the morning, Winn and some others researched how to feed a butterfly. They found sugar in the math room, dissolved it on the science room stove, and during class, Winn dropped the solution on the petals of the flower at the bottom of the glass.

"He's reaching out his tongue and eating it," she announced

But our butterfly could not fly. Its wings remained stiff and curled. The kids made origami butterflies because, they said, ours needed friends. But the following Monday, we discovered our butterfly had died over the weekend. It had spent its life crawling on four legs, carrying its thin body and occasionally flapping it's curled, shriveled wing.

Winn made an origami box and filled it with dried flowers, two locks of hair, and the butterfly's origami friends, and buried it under the maple tree in the center of the school's labyrinth. Ariela had brought in dried daisies, as though somehow she'd known that we would need flowers. She placed them on top of the dirt mound in the middle of the labyrinth.

I found a poem by Emily Dickinson, "The Butterfly upon

the Sky," which Winn read, ending with the last lines: *So soar away and never sigh / And that's the way to grieve—*

One morning, the ninth graders sat around the big table working.

"Tal," Callum moaned. "I don't get why the geometry textbook includes questions about the dimensions of a baseball field."

I began to explain, but Hannah intervened.

"Shush, I know how to tell him." She proceeded to explain how the lengths between the bases could yield the distance from home plate to second base. Then she looked over at me.

"I was explaining better than you."

"You go for it, girl!"

In a quiet moment, I had my first chance to begin reading the drafts of the sketches the kids had turned in. Before I could start, Nils began singing, "You ain't nothing but a hound dog, crying all the time."

"That's great singing, Nils," I said, "but can you zip and go do something, like drill the holes for your Saturn model? We're all trying to work here."

I got to the title of the first sketch on top of my pile of papers: "The Perils of Science." Four paragraphs in, Nils was back. The cardboard rings of his Saturn model were flopping all over the big room and would not stay fixed in place. We made some adjustments, and I went back to the story. At the bottom of the fifth paragraph, Henry walked in.

"Tal, can we talk about my character sketch? I'm all jumbled on what to write about." He showed me what he had and I gave suggestions about how to structure his scenes.

"I think I know what I need to do," he said.

Brody came in late, tired from a late-night hockey practice.

"Brody, how're you feeling?" I asked.

"Broken."

Nadia stood by me to show her Golden Ratio spiral design. She had used Piet Mondrian as her inspiration, who I had mentioned in class one day.

"Hey, Tal, should I color these corners black or leave them white?" Her Lincoln, Vermont, baseball cap was turned around backwards and her eyes were narrowed.

The class and I agreed: make them black.

In literature class reading *To Kill a Mockingbird*, we were transported to the First Purchase African M.E. Church of Maycomb, Alabama, described so marvelously by Harper Lee.

"When she goes into Calpurnia's church, it's like what Atticus says: You have to walk in somebody else's shoes," said Haley.

"And it's a sacred place," said Winn. "My favorite part is how the only decoration in the church is the pink satin banner which says, 'God is Love.' It didn't matter that their church was simple. It had real love in it. That is so cool!"

Ecclesiastical impedimenta were not important when the highest law was *God is Love*. But it was also true that humans were often guilty of not being willing to enter the sacred places of others, or perhaps keeping people out of theirs as a form of protection. We could blunder forward with blinders on, judging or categorizing or blindly accepting what we saw—and then there were children among us, like Scout, as yet unschooled and untainted, who went ahead asking questions with wonder and acceptance.

"I know this seems like it's not related," said Nadia, "but I'm wearing my great grandmother's red-ruby earrings. They were special to her, and she gave them to my mother, and my mother let me wear them today. It makes me feel like I'm closer to my mother and a whole line of women. And maybe that's what's happening to Scout. She's letting herself get closer to beautiful things, except instead of earrings it's the songs at Cal's church."

"I wrote about the graveyard," said Ariela, referring to the brief description of the burial site at the church.

"Why?" I asked.

"Because it said it was a happy graveyard," she replied quickly.

"What was happy about it?"

"She could see the glass in the graves and how it was handmade with what they had," she explained. "And the only decoration inside the church is the pink banner. And they smiled and accepted Scout and Jem. They didn't reject them because they were different."

"And Scout loved their church," said Cole. He didn't say a lot in lit class, but when he did, it gave the class new momentum. "She wanted to go back to it because it was alive and full of love."

"A child can see and feel things that way," I offered, "and that's why children are powerful and so damn smart."

"Like when Scout makes the mob go away," said Nils. "Atticus couldn't do that. But Scout could."

"Exactly!"

In these discussions, they entered the texts as though they lived in the pages. Over and over, their thoughts chimed with rare beauty, without me having to contrive a thing.

A few days later, Hannah brought a book into class, a very old, dark-blue volume with gold gilt-edge pages. It was her day to read the poem.

"Where's that book from?" I asked.

"It's my mother's. It says it was published in . . . 1929."

"Who's it by?"

"John Milton."

"Go ahead."

She read to us the end of "Il Penseroso." The sound of the words, coming from another time, was liquid light, *And let some strange mysterious dream, / Wave at his Wings in Airy stream.* In a moment like this the school was a rare bell, which, on a quiet winter morning, rang with clarities of the highest order.

Current events had a place in our school, but there was nothing formal about it—we simply talked about what was happening when something happened. I felt blessedly lucky. We had created a loving, trusting, committed community. The children wanted to come to school, they looked forward to it, they were safe, and nearly without exception, joyfully happy and excited. When the shooting happened at Sandy Hook, the idea of a nation of schools filled with joy and discovery and trust was darkly distant. Those teachers were doing the good, noble work, and doing it with courage, but a lot of those kids and teachers still did not feel safe inside the walls of their schools. School was not a sanctuary—it seemed a target, and a frighteningly vulnerable one. The children, rightly, came in to their schools on a Monday morning asking questions. *What is going on? Why does this happen? Will it happen to me?*

Within hours of the shooting, the national conversation shifted to politics and policies: the National Rifle Association, gun control, better background checks, stricter licensing, metal detectors in schools, locked-door classrooms, video surveillance, armed guards, armed teachers and administrators. Some of these suggestions might one day make it less likely that an individual could come into a school and commit a violent act. But I wondered if the kinds of solutions being discussed really got to the root of the problem. Metal detectors might keep guns out of the school, but they did not answer the question of why we had come to the point of needing metal detectors in the first place. Controlling access to guns did not in itself ensure that we had a healthy, happy society or happy, healthy, and secure schools and children. And I wondered, as well, would we take the expedient path and place the blame on a few deranged individuals—or would we take the hard, long path and have the strength and wisdom to say: we do this, we are this, we make this?

We could read the statistics—men perpetrated these acts. And we read about it in *The Lord of the Flies*, where a world void of nurturing tenderness led to madness and destruction. As the kids read, they noted that the book, written in 1954, described our present culture—one awash in expressions of male domination centered on violence, control, sexual privilege, and the rejection of tenderness and open-heartedness. I saw nascent versions of it on the playground, when boys found visceral, primal joy in crushing and pummelling each other, and found satisfaction and indentity only in winning. I saw it in boys who called each other "pussy" and "faggot," and I saw, from time to time, how boys tried to brush tears away in class, laugh off being teased, mask their sufferings or grieving with a glib, "I'm okay. It's no big deal."

But our approach—a small school centered around emotional disclosure and intimate bonds—did not allow boys to hide too long or create such a hardened shell. They were called out, face to face with each other, challenged to be honest and real, invited to find their way to another kind of expression. They discovered in themselves fragility, and a deep and human need to express yearning and joy, to be seen, known, and loved. Yes, the boys in our school cried, and when they did, we saw it for what it was: courage and truth and a fierce and pulsing connection to life.

The morning after Sandy Hook, I did not want to talk about Newtown or Bushmaster Rifles or multiple round ammo clips or the NRA or Congress. I did not want to debate, argue, or blame. I did not want to lock doors. I wanted to make something good, something real and translatable to the human beings around our table, in the actual life we had all awoken to that day. I wanted to talk about beautiful things that were in our grasp, that we could make or hold. I wanted the school to do and be what the world needed most. The only way to know a beloved community was to create one. To do that, we had to momentarily set aside facts and statistics, and go inside the heart. I wanted to talk about love.

"How," I asked, "do we make a beloved community? How should we think about what we're teaching and learning in our schools, and why?"

That morning I'd collected a new batch of place descriptions, which was really a misnomer: they'd only had to describe something they felt some place in a moment in time. I decided to read Bennett's to the class, about being in his hall closet with his dog, Chester, in a thunderstorm. He described the darkness, the closeness of the space, the sounds of the storm, and Chester's movements.

The closet door swung shut. I was enclosed with my hound. I could hear his breathing, fast, anxious, scared. Whenever Chester freaked out, his face stayed neutral. But he would start breathing very fast, and he always tried to stay near us. When Chester got like this he went nuts, and sometimes if no one was at the house he would try to chew through walls. I reached out into the blackness of the small closet and found his collar. He was up against the wall, leaning his head toward me, with the end of his snout against the wall, to be as far away from the door as he could be. I moved my leg off the wall, and he moved forward, pushing his face under my armpit, settling down in the corner of the closet in a cozy position. I could hear thunder and it seemed too close and loud for my comfort. Rain pounded on the roof with no pause. Chester snuggled closer as more thunder rolled and more water fell from the sky. I patted him. And he nudged my hand up so he could be under it. Anything to be covered, to be safe and away from the danger. His panting increased. I could barely make out the top of the closet in the blackness. Chester nuzzled closer. After a few minutes, in the darkness, I could feel the dribble of dog drool on my knee. But I didn't care. He needed people around him, and if sitting in a dark closet while he drooled on my knee was enough to calm him down, then that's what I wanted to do.

After he crawled into my lap. I could feel his paws digging into my leg as he positioned himself, considering my presence to be his personal couch. He settled down on my legs and I patted him some more. My hound, what a beautiful pooch. He rested his snout on my knee and made that bored dog look. I put my hands behind his ears and scratched at the fuzziness, when another long loud and frightening rolling of thunder echoed through the house. He moved like lightning and plunged his head into my stomach. He leaned into me in a frightened manner. I moved my hands over his eyes and he calmed slightly. His breathing slowed a little. I uncovered his eyes and rubbed his belly. His panting subsided and then he closed his eyes.

Bennett showed the architecture of his soul—the kind of person he wanted to be: tender, loving, protective, patient. He was as close to himself as he was to his dog.

"If everyone had what Bennett gave his dog," said Haley, "maybe there would be no Sandy Hook."

"Who wants to write the proposal and send it to the Senate?" I asked.

Two dozen hands went up.

The next morning I asked them, as always, "How did hearing Bennett's sketch about him and Chester make you feel?"

"I thought it was really original," said Yebsera.

"That's a thought, Yeb," I said, impatient to get them to move to a more complex or transformative place. "I'm asking: how did it make you *feel*?" To say a true feeling required risk. Yes, to venture a new feeling meant one had to be momentarily alone, but when it happened, it was always interesting.

I looked around, content to wait in the quiet, which had a way of compelling intensity, of raising the stakes. Then Ariela raised her hand. I nodded towards her.

"Well, it made me happy."

"You felt *happy*? It was about a scared dog in a thunderstorm!"

"Yes, well, I wasn't happy that the dog was scared. I was happy to see Bennett being so loving. It made me love Bennett."

"Like, you have a *crush* on him?"

"No! God no!" At this the class laughed. Ariela blushed, but they quieted quickly; they were on the pulse of Ariela's true feeling.

"I guess what I mean is when I see someone being so loving and protective, it makes me feel trust, like I'm safe, too. And then I want to be around that person. I want to be around Bennett. I just felt happy that there's someone in the world who'll sit in a closet with a dog and just stay there to make the dog feel safe."

"They should have dogs in schools," said Henry. "Not for guarding but for petting."

"A Jasper In Every School, that should be the plan," said Nils. "That would be better than teachers having guns."

"They already have a plan called 'No Child Left Behind,'" I said.

"'A Jasper In Every School is better,'" said Nils. "Because kids who got a chance to love something wouldn't grow up to be sad and violent."

"What Bennett did was so simple. Why can't everything be simple like that? Because then it's easy to love anybody."

"Ariela," I began, "hearing you say that makes *me* happy. And I'm not sure why, but I think it has to do with—"

"It's like she's multiplying the feeling," said Nils. "When

Bennett wrote that, he wrote about his feelings for his dog. But it also made Ariela happy. And her feeling happy—and being able to feel Bennett's feelings—that made you happy. That's my theory of the multiplication effect." As he said this he was smiling.

To hear Bennett's description was to imagine a world void of toxic masculinity. His expression was a kind of super-compassion, a clarion call to his classmates saying, "there are Percivals hidden inside us all." The strength he showed did not rely on conquest, or guns, or power; it relied on listening and soft-heartedness.

Later, Bennett wrote about a ditch where he played with his toy trucks, and about building a model airplane with his father in their barn one winter. Nils wrote about drumming alone in a basement when no one was home; Ruby wrote about playing under a piano, watching her mother's feet on the pedals and the sound of Brahms. Hannah wrote about waking up on a screened porch in the Adirondacks and then falling asleep looking at the stars. Nadia wrote about when she was three, being carried by her father on Church Street in Burlington on a day when the winter wind was blowing off the lake. She was wrapped inside his coat, held against his warm body, and she could smell the leather and feel his heart beating inside. When my students wrote such things, we were transported into the place where politics and tragedy ceased, and the new world began. They put love into the world. That was something they could do.

There were many days, and many weeks, when it was difficult to see what we were doing. They wrote stories, they studied winter ecology, they presented projects on historical events, they read novels and poems, they balanced equations. But the larger picture we were creating eluded me. On the nights when I couldn't sleep—wondering how to make Yeb talk more, or how to help Ruby find a thread in her story—I felt as though I and all of the kids were in a dark room with a great canvas spread from floor to ceiling, and we were blindfolded. We were making something—we were fairly certain of that. We moved, ran into each other, shouted in the darkness, everyone putting up colors and marks, but we could not see what we nor anyone else was making. The kids themselves were identities in metamorphic formation, expanding and shifting and growing in ways both visible and invisible. All of it was ongoing, frantic, busy, messy. Add to that the constant inflow of news stories and changing world events, cultural transformations, and the ubiquity of technology, and we had on our hands a large, unwieldy project that was neither measurable nor definable. If the school were a business, we could look at the bottom line and see how much money we'd made. If we were a school operating under rigidly defined standards, we could give a standardized test to see if the students were learning what we set out for them to learn.

In our case, what we set out to learn was mostly governed by the impulses and developmental needs of the kids. As much as life is unpredictable, so too were our days and directions. As my students grew and changed, so too did we as teachers grow and change with them. All I could do was watch them, guide them, and leaven our days with sprinklings of anything that could be creatively or intellectually profitable. *What can I do tomorrow that will keep us riding high?* I asked. *How hard should I be on Bennett, who has hardly worked on his story at all? Should I read Nadia's lit response about feeling lonely? Should she read it? Does her loneliness relate in any way to* To Kill A Mockingbird? *Do we have time to watch the entire "I Have a Dream" speech, and if we do, how much time will I need to explain terms like "interposition" and "nullification?" And how do I tie that in with everything else? Or is it just another splash of color and intensity which we throw onto our canvas, and hope that it finds a place and deepens the picture we are making?*

These were the questions that kept me up at night. But these temporal and day-to-day questions sometimes were over-ridden by more soul-rending existential contemplation: *What is the point? How much of this will they remember? What do I want them to remember? How should they feel at the end of the year? What impact am I making on the world, which, so often, appears dark and crumbling...*

I did the calculations and figured out that over a 35-40 year career of teaching I would only have 350-400 students. In numerical terms my influence and impact seemed shocking-ly small and feeble. My students gathered-in their learning in ways that for the most part I could never know or measure, and to realize this made the task of teaching, or facing another week, sometimes seem impossibly futile and hopeless. To have taught an isolated band of students for only this brief passage of time? To have spent a lifetime at it? It all could suddenly seem so absurd: What difference to the world was I possibly making? What difference would it make to the history of man-kind, whether or not my students understood the rhythm of Mary Oliver's lines or rhetorical cadences of Dr. King?

I read them a story written by a former student called "The Kiss." The boy, Michael, was one of the tough kids in the middle school. Quiet, rough and tumble, athletic, emotionally closed. But in his story he told about a side of himself that he'd never shown, perhaps never even recognized in himself. He described how he volunteered at a convalescent home. He hated it. The old people, so close to death, mumbling and senile, scared him. He wheeled them around the facility, helped them place chips on their bingo cards, lit their ciga-rettes. Onc old woman kept reaching for his hand as he passed her in her wheelchair. She couldn't speak—only dry moans escaped her lips. Her skin was loose, practically falling off her body, he wrote, and so when he saw her he would hurry by. One day, as he was passing her sitting in the hall, she took hold of his hand, pulled him ever so close to her face, and then placed a gentle whisper of a kiss on his cheek.

Michael wasn't sure what to do. He was terrified, paralyzed, never having been so close to death, not knowing how to navigate this sudden and strange interaction. Then without thinking, he bent down and placed a gentle kiss on the soft skin of her cheek. He didn't know what he was doing, but he did what his heart told him was right.

I didn't know if she would remember that kiss. I didn't know if she would remember it five minutes later. But in that second I was glad I had done it, because what I had done in that moment was something she needed.

He'd shocked himself with the tenderness he did not know he possessed. Our discussion centered on how Michael chose to live in that moment. What kind of kiss was this? What had been given, created? How had death been held at bay, even for a moment? Was this the beloved community? What did he create within himself? Could we make life grow out of actions in life? If we must die, how might we also *not* die?

"I have a theory," said Nils. "If we do something great that people will remember, we *are* immortal."

"That's a cool theory," said Yebsera. "So, like, by doing good things you can live forever?"

"But his kiss didn't keep the old woman alive," I said. "This was years ago. I'm sure she's not still alive. He even wrote that she might not remember the kiss five minutes later. And one day the boy will die."

"But that was what she needed in that moment," said Ariela. Her voice was urgent. She needed everyone to believe what she was saying. "He did exactly the *only* thing he could do,

welling of her own tears for him, and she has no idea why, and she wants to know why, and she wants to express all of those feelings, whatever they are and wherever they lead.

So when it came time to write her character sketch on Thursday night, Nadia followed my pronouncement to write from the feeling. *Don't think*, I said. *Don't plan it and don't filter it and don't think about what others will think.* No handouts, rubrics, or imposed structures. "Do what Red Smith said," I told them. "'Writing is easy. Just sit in front of a typewriter, open up a vein, and bleed it out drop by drop.'"

So she did. Only her most true feelings. Some might say an adolescent crush was not an appropriate topic for a school writing assignment. But if we wanted a classroom that was alive, we had to pursue beauty, mystery, pain, or whatever was most true. If we said that one of the truths of adolescence is the explosion of new and sudden feelings and ideas, that they were going through radical transformations, it followed that we had to teach them to understand the nature and process of those changes. Nadia's feelings were real, and they were in her core. They demanded expression, and they were among the essential life forces of the children in the room.

An adolescent crush was to Nadia what falling in love was to an adult. There was no thing more beautiful or mysterious or real. It was undeniable that she, like all of them, would one day navigate intimate personal relationships. To fear those impulses—to say they had no place—would be to cauterize the life-flow of the classroom.

So when I looked down on my pile of papers on Friday morning and saw a neatly typed sketch entitled, "Him," I saw opportunity, as all teachers should when given the privilege to see into a student's heart and mind.

Her paper, in its silence, was as inviting as new fallen snow, the printed text so clean, the single-word title saying, *I have walked out into myself and I left me here for you to find.*

I run down the slope from the school to the big field. There he is. Right in front of me. His long strides come at the ball, Swoosh. Goal, easy as that . . . for him. Sports come easy for him, just like swimming comes easy for a fish. He is graceful and he never looks scared when he is alone on the field. When he runs his arms stay close to his sides, slightly bent, and his hands are free.

He turns around and towards the other end of the field where Callum is holding the football. His brown curly hair is hidden under his black hat. He tosses his sweatshirt to the edge of the field. While we make teams he watches quietly or jokes around with Callum. His team starts with the ball and he kicks it, sending it over our heads and it lands in the rumpled golden leaves. He runs to cover Callum.

We never really talk when we are out on that field, even though there are so many things I would like to say. So many things, but I hide behind my smile. Things like, "You're being a jackass, Bennett!" or, "That was the sweetest thing I have ever seen you do." But mostly I want to tell him that I love his hair, and his smile, and his hands, and his nose, and his mind, and that last lit response he did, and that I see him through soft eyes. But those kinds of words don't exactly roll off the tongue.

I turn, and he is running away from me, across that field. His hair is not hidden under his hat, and his arms stay close by his side as he runs through the gentle, falling snowflakes.

To be aware of oneself is the first intelligence. To be able to describe the contours of one's own thought—and to be able to expand the dimensions of one's heart—is the necessary gateway to greater awareness of the people and things all around. Lao Tze went further: *Knowing others is wisdom; knowing the self is enlightenment.*

Nadia's writing, and her thought—her knowledge of self—was utterly beautiful, utterly enlightening, her most intense rendezvous with her most vivid awareness. Writing about Bennett was as real as her breath and her heartbeat. To know the feeling coursing through her was to find herself in the same place as Romeo: *But soft, what light through yonder window breaks? / It is the east, and Juliet is the sun.* She revealed what filled her sight. A sun, a vision, radiant and alive.

As I sat in my chair reading, with Yeb chattering behind me, I found myself—amid the tumult we call adolescence in that most imperfect place we called school—poised, as she was, at the edge of her most perfectly drawn picture. And all we had to do now was learn from it.

I wanted the class to hear it, of course, but she might be embarrassed. I told her it was marvelous and beautiful, and I asked her if she wanted it read to the class. She became flustered. So I gave her my few small corrections and told her to turn it back in. The next day there was a new sketch. It had a new title, a new character. She'd retracted "Him" and the feelings in it. I was puzzled and frustrated, and when class started after lunch, I wanted to talk about it.

I walked into the big room. The rowdiness of running around and chasing each other began to simmer down. The table was littered with evidence of the morning's work: papers, scissors, binders, water bottles, a Buddhist singing bowl, an empty potato chip bag. I stood in the doorway.

"Uh, so, uh, listen, y'all. "She—" and I pointed to Nadia— "wrote a beautiful piece of writing. I mean, incredible. It was true and tender. It was real. All feelings, a huge risk to write."

I turned to her, where she sat at the end of the table with her notebook in her lap.

"But you don't want it read to the class. Is that right?"

She nodded.

"You feel like it would be a little embarrassing?"

"I guess."

"But what you wrote about, it was a feeling you felt, something real, something true. So why would any of us not feel safe sharing the truth of what we felt? Why would we pull something true back? What's the worst thing that could happen?"

There was no answer.

"How can we strive and believe we're artistically free and true to ourselves if we're afraid of our own feelings, for whatever reason, or afraid of what our feelings might make someone else feel, or afraid of what might happen if we share our feelings?"

The class was silent.

"I don't know why I took it back," Nadia said. She was genuinely perplexed. Just as she was audacious in her writing, she was also willing to examine her actions. "Embarrassed mainly. But also I was afraid that it would confuse him. I was afraid that the class wouldn't understand it. That they would make it be something that it wasn't."

"You mean that you're worried the class wouldn't see the feeling as an honest feeling without turning it into a big kind of rumor-y, gossipy thing?"

"Yeah. I guess that's right."

"The embarrassment part makes sense. It's a new and tender feeling. But if you're afraid the class will mishear it, that the class isn't a safe place for all ideas and feelings, that's not good. We want to feel safe. In life and in everything."

"I just didn't want people to misunderstand it."

"But what if the feelings that you wrote about, which are so true and clear, clarified things? Made us see things as they are, not as we think they are? Maybe your sketch would help all of us see ourselves more clearly. And show why this boy is admirable and how what he did made you feel a feeling. Wouldn't that be the truest conversation we could have? ... But sometimes it's also right that things remain mysterious and unsaid."

"I don't know. What should I do?"

"I don't want you to do anything except do what feels right. I would never make you read it. I think if you did, it could be a good thing. But you have to feel that it's a thing you want to put into the class. If you did, we would want the class to celebrate it and take it in."

"I guess I'll think about it."

"I'm only saying this as a way for us to consider what we're up to. Rumi said, 'Let the beauty you love be what you do.' He was saying we should go all in, all the way. If you make a beautiful thing, or feel it, it should guide you in your being."

I meant to pose questions, to keep up a certain amount of tension. The path to expression had to be examined and continually kept clean. If Nadia never chose to share it, it would still remain with her and in her. Perhaps the next day someone else would put something beautiful into the void.

The conversations about what, why, and how to write filled our days. Children had important feelings and ideas to express, and I didn't see it as my job to give them pre-designed forms in which to do so, but to help them find the forms that were right and true for them.

Hannah stood before me with the beginning of a sketch.

"I'm not sure if what I have is right."

"Let's see what you have so far." She handed me the single typed sheet, a half a paragraph.

"It's barely started. I wasn't sure. I want to write a story about freedom. But I don't know if freedom is a place or a thing or a story. So I think it's probably not what you want."

"What I want is for you to find your own ideas. Freedom is a place, a sense, a feeling, domain, an experience. That's great, perfect. What could be better?"

"But what if it's a kind of freedom I felt just one time?"

"You're talking about a place in time that lives in your mind? Tell about that one time."

"It was last summer. In Michigan. With my dad in our boat. Going over the deep water in Lake Michigan."

"Then write it."

"But it's not a story."

"Just write it! Go for it!"

"But I don't know what the point is."

"Yeah, you don't know yet. It's the start of something."

Later in class I tried to convey how to feel and select the potent details, the ones that rang with power. That very morning, as I had been leaving for school, our family cat, Hendricks, had gotten out of the house, thinking, perhaps, that the good life and true freedom were outside in the woods. Due to dangerous and blissful ignorance, he did not know about foxes and fisher-cats.

"He ran under our deck," I told the class. "I couldn't get him out. I'm always worried when our cat gets out. He might get eaten. I was afraid." I looked at the expressions of my students as I spoke. They stared at me, waiting for meaning. They didn't seem particularly moved or excited by what I had told them. Purposely I had removed the details that would make them feel the fear I had felt.

"Is that a very interesting story?" I asked.

"I guess," said Winn. But she did not seem convinced.

So I retold the story, the way it happened. "My cat got out, like I said. But here's what I didn't tell you the first time. We had another cat a long time ago who died when he got out, probably gotten by a fox. This morning, Hendricks was hiding under the deck, looking for mice, and we couldn't get him and we had to leave for school. I was calling him through the lattice and trying to get him to come to me, and then I looked in the shadows behind him. There, in those shadows, I saw a cat skeleton with a few patches of matted black hair. There were bones covered in damp dirt and the body was draped and twisted over a wire cable. It was our old cat, Elgin. He had gotten lost in a storm the year before, and we'd never seen him again. This was him, these bones were him. He'd probably come back to the house to die alone, under the deck. His body was splayed and tangled over a loose wire in the dark under the deck. He died right under us, but we never saw or heard him dying. The skeleton of Elgin was resting there behind Hendricks, who was only intent on finding mice to eat."

I looked around the table. Their mouths were slightly open, in fascination or pain.

"Which version of my story was more riveting and exciting?"

"The second one," they said in unison.

"Why?" I asked.

"Because it was filled with the details," said Ruby.

"I thought it was the shadows," said Yeb. "And how it was tangled up in that wire."

"I was thinking it was the skeleton," said Nils. "*That* was the reason you were scared," he continued. "You were scared of Garfield becoming a skeleton. The skeleton made you and us feel what you felt."

"Because it was right behind him," said Nadia. "There were two bodies, one living and one dead."

"But the dead form had what? A bigger kind of power?" I asked.

"Much bigger," said Katelyn.

"So what are we saying?" I asked.

"The skeleton has to be shown," said Nils.

"The shadows and dirt. The past history," said Henry.

"Yeah, the bones, the guts, the origins," I said. "The reasons or story living in the background. The story that preceded the present."

In morning meeting, Winn spoke of her grandmother, whom she had recently visited. She told us they'd looked through photo albums and her grandma had lamented that this generation only communicated in the ether of the Internet and ephemeral social media.

"She said that one day we would not have scrapbooks, photo albums, or old letters to hold in our hands," Winn said. "And I was wondering if she was right."

Nobody answered her, so she continued. "Like one day we'll wish we had written letters to each other so we would have a record of our feelings."

I told the class about a letter I had just written to a friend whose wife had died of cancer.

"It's the only thing I could do, the most intimate and feeling-full thing I could do. What would it have been like if I had sent him a text message or an email with the subject heading, 'Your dead wife'?"

"That'd be disgusting," said Nils.

Rose raised her hand.

"Speaking of letters," she said, "I got a four-page letter from a teenager in this school the other day, and getting that letter was such a thrill. I saved it for later in the day. It was like having a full meal to look forward to after eating cheap processed snacks."

"Who was the letter from?" Callum asked.

"From a girl named . . . Ariela," she replied, smiling at her.

The class looked over at Ariela. She looked down at her lap, pursing her lips, uncomfortable with all the eyes on her.

"So Ariela, you just took up the old," I said.

She nodded, suppressing a smile.

Nolan raised his hand. "I write letters to my godfather in Italy. And I always look forward to getting a letter back."

"Save those letters," I said, "because one day they'll be a record of your growing up."

"Ariela wrote me letters last summer," said Ruby. "I loved getting those letters and I kept them."

"Look you guys," I said. "When it's someone's special day, I write that person a poem. I handwrite it on a card. I always want to give something that someone can hold. If I send a friend an email, that's something, but a hand-written poem is filled with feeling, words you might have crossed out, your script and punctuation. You put the fingerprints of your heart on it. And guess what: one time I gave my special someone a book of the love letters written between Georgia O'Keeffe and Alfred Stieglitz. The book is as big as the bible. The letters are filled with two friends, living in a different time in faraway places, in Canyon, Texas, and New York City. The letters are full of life, of waking up on cold mornings, of desert skies, of the joy of opening letters from each other, of the clouds in a storm or the rainy streets of Manhattan, of the clothes they wore and the late-night conversations they had. A whole past world opens up on every page."

"Where's the book?" asked Bennett.

"At home. I'll bring it in. I'll read some of them. Because when you look at a record like that, at these beautiful letters, you have the greatest treasure in the world."

I wanted to keep talking about letters. But the morning was getting late, and we needed to start class.

"So, who has the morning poem?" I asked.

"I do," said Haley. "It's by Mary Oliver, and it's called 'A Letter from Home.'"

"You cannot be serious!" I said. "You had that picked out?"

"Yep." Then she read the first lines: *She sends me news of blue jays, frost, / Of stars and now the harvest moon.*

This was the real news of the "whirling heart," of the vivid, living world. When we talked in the morning, whether about letters or dead cats, each day became a new page of the book we were writing. Pages piling up before us. Poems and stories, artists in cold rooms, envelopes spilling out dry flowers and pain. Conversations about the morning light and the harvest moon and ruby rings, kisses and chrysalises, lovers and students and grandfathers, all of it falling open before us.

❧

On a Tuesday morning around the table, Callum put his earphones in to listen to Allen Ginsberg's poem "Howl." Nadia proofread Ariela's story. Bennett and Nolan argued about whether it was possible to love someone without knowing them, followed by Bennett's epiphany: "All bad feeling comes from absence of love, or the fear of annihilation and existence." Hannah worked on SAT math problems. Yebsera showed me a National Geographic with pictures of combat hospitals in Iraq. Haley tacked up a poster about Jenny Holzer, about whom she was giving a presentation. Winn assembled pictures drawn by child victims of torture for her project. Bennett turned in a lit response that concluded with this: *If you are to sing to me, I am to realize the faults, triumphs, and struggles in your story and weave them into my cloak. If I am to weave a cloak for my own use, I must be able to look to others and then find myself. If I am to weave this cloak I must make it large. Large, to account for the growth of my soul. Large enough to shelter others from the cold. If I am to use this cloak for all it is worth, then it will be torn and ragged at the end of my journey.*

In the afternoon, we talked about a part of Winn's story: her memory of being at *Marrowbone*, a theater production of song, poetry, and story performed annually in the forests in the nearby mountain town of Lincoln. Once upon a time, she wrote, she was an excited little girl of four, more interested in the leaves she collected on a sharpened stick than the strange poetry and singing among the trees. She remembered her little sister clambering in her mom's lap, oblivious to everything except the bodily warmth of a parent. A little ways off, she'd explored and listened, smelling the woods, peeling bark off small twigs, finding the most beautiful leaf in the world over and over. She'd wanted to scamper on and find more leaves, and to find the next path leading to the clearing where there was cider and sunlight coming down through the trees. It was one her favorite memories of her early childhood.

"And when I went to it this year, just last week, it was so different," she said. "There were little girls just like I used to be, and they were collecting leaves, but I was listening to the poems and songs."

Winn was seeing herself growing up before her own eyes.

"And this year I tried to remember words and ideas from every act. I didn't want to forget anything. It was so different from when I was little, when I was just playing around."

"So what did you do?" I asked.

"I started writing down quotes on my hand from the poems they were reading. I was afraid I would lose it and I didn't want to forget anything."

Thoughts and quotes were the golden leaves, and she was trying to save every one.

At lunch on snowy days, they rushed from class to put on boots and mittens in order to get outside as fast as possible to chase each other in the woods or have snowball fights. When lunch was over, I would step outside to ring the bell and the kids would come crashing out of the woods and across the field. I watched as Katelyn sprinted towards me, kicking snow as she came. "Tal, Tal," she shouted. Iridescent blue covered her eyelids and blush added to the brightness of her cheeks. She was breathing hard from running. "I think there's someone at school who's gay!"

She loved to pass information on—the latest about what had happened to a friend at the middle school; whose mother had a new boyfriend; who in our school was mad at whom. I tried to see this not as idle or destructive gossip but for a purpose it might serve: as a link between us, to help reveal us, and her, to the school. If she ended up stirring trouble by passing information on, we'd deal with the trouble she started.

"Really?" I said as we walked into my room.

"Well, I can't really say. But he told me last night he thought he was gay!" She was overjoyed to be carrying the news.

"He told you, huh?"

"But I can't tell anyone because he wants to tell everyone."

"Katelyn, you just told me, you silly goose."

"But you're a teacher. You don't count, and you won't spread rumors. Plus, I didn't say *who*!"

"I know I won't, but how long can you hold onto this?"

She rolled her eyes. "Why would anyone spread rumors? Besides, who cares if someone is gay?"

"Right on. Thank god we're not all the same. If it comes out, we'll all learn something!"

"I know! It's so cool," she said gleefully.

A few days later, I was in my office just before class. Nils stood in my doorway looking at me through his wire spectacles.

"Whatcha need, chief?"

"Uh, I don't know what to write about. I mean, I could write about my dad, but, I don't know, all we ever do is fight and stuff."

"Fighting and stuff is real stuff. You want to tell him what you're feeling because you think he's annoying, but it's more complicated than that. Write about your dad."

"Uh, I don't really want to write about my dad, 'cause . . ."

"'Cause you're afraid?"

He smiled.

"No, because, well, yeah, I *am* afraid, like I'm a total chicken, but whatever. I think maybe I need to write a character sketch about, uh, myself."

"About yourself? Why?"

"Well," and he drew in a breath and began to speak quickly.

"I think I should because I have something that I think I need to say but I can't really say it but I think I can say it if I write it because then I'm writing it and not saying it so that is how I can say it."

"You want to say something about yourself in a character sketch about yourself?" I narrowed my eyes at him. I felt like a co-conspirator.

"Like, yeah."

"Alright! If you want to do it, you have to have courage. I'll make it safe to say what you feel to be true. We're after the truth, right?"

"I have courage and I'm for truth, man. I don't think I can really go on without saying something."

The next morning when I got to school, I found him already in my office.

He was smiling. He handed me a one-page document. I looked down. It was titled "Revelation." I read it quickly. It was written in the third person—the story of a boy who had discovered a truth about himself.

"What does the kid want to do with the document?" I asked, looking back up at him.

"The kid wants to read it to the class."

"The kid wants to read it to the class?"

"Yep, the kid does."

"The kid feels good about that?"

"Yep."

"Not Tal reading it. The kid wants to read it?"

"Oh, yes. The kid does. "

"Okay, kid."

I pushed open my office door. "Okay, let's go! Let's read some writing!"

The class gathered as Nils set the lectern up on the table. He stood behind it looking at his classmates, most of whom he had only known for half a year, and he read:

Tweet! Tweet! The extremely unwelcome sound of birds appears at exactly 5:30 AM. An arm reaches out from under the pile of maroon blankets and smacks a clock off the table. Two hours later, he is once again disrupted by the sound of his mother shouting to, "Get up now, or you'll miss the bus!" *not taking into account the fact that he has a whole half an hour to get his clothes on and out the door.*

The figure arises, and departs for school. He sits at his school desk and absorbs the information being shot at him or, rather, lets it fly past. Home again. And back out the door, to the car, another drive somewhere. The ride there, normally uneventful, is this time blocked out by thoughts swirling around, sucking everything up into a black hole. Something's not right, he thinks. I don't fit in. *The image of a boy keeps popping into his head, and he finds himself in a dream. But* this isn't how I'm supposed to be, *he thinks, allowing the image to leave his mind. And yet, another part of him keeps saying,* Don't even try; it's true, and you know it.

That's when the revelation came. It was the longest second of his life. First his heartbeat quickened, then he started breathing raggedly. Sweat dripped down his face, and in one instant the realization took over. Holy shit. It's true. *It was like an enormously huge weight had been lifted up, and was now being dropped out to sea. He wanted to shout to the world, laugh out loud, shout for all eternity.*

A month or two passed. And he started to wear pink socks to school and wear his hair up. All was beautiful. But alas, gravity kicked in and a voice is heard from across the hall. Ew, what a fag! *The earth stops turning, and then starts again, this time going backwards. He can't hear any distinguishable laughs, but he is sure they are there. He wants to go home and never be seen again. Black socks resume, and he hides behind his own personal fur coat. Life has been harsh, and he is now entrusting you not to judge. To accept. To live with it, respecting it in full. He is me, and he is gay.*

The class erupted in applause. Nils was looking down, but everyone else was smiling. Every hand was up, a hundred comments: *It was courage. It was accepted. It was beautiful.*

Then Bennett raised his hand. "Nils, so . . . I have known you since we were six. I remember when we climbed Mount Abe and pissed into the wind and it sprayed all over us. All I can say is, I'm proud to be your friend."

After school that day, I watched Nils through a window as he stood at the edge of the snowy driveway. A crowd of his friends surrounded him, each of them taking turns hugging him, and he was holding on.

Nils's sketch reaffirmed what I knew to be true: that my students had infinite riches inside them waiting to be brought forth. Nils had made a way to expand the heart of the school—in his word—to *enlargens* it. That's what they wanted most. Life, and growing into life, was their most important work. School was not about things apart from us; what happened in school was us.

When I first started teaching, I struggled to find moments when I was really *teaching*, when something electric and original was growing from the interaction between me and the student before me. I taught in an open classroom—the entry hall, living room, and sunroom of an old Tudor home. The thirty-one seventh and eighth graders had the freedom to choose what to work on, and where they sat, how speedily or deeply to engage with their work.

Once, while trying to lead a class discussion, the question arose: *should we have a class president in our class government or not?*

The eighth graders—veterans from the year before—had clear ideas. In unison, with irritation and vituperation, they exclaimed *Abolish the class president*. I wrote their suggestions down on my clipboard. *The president had too much power.* I thought I was listening. But I should have asked them *why*. An injustice or imbalance of power? Anger? Frustration? I should have pushed them to re-live it, re-say it. They weren't telling me what they wanted—they were saying what they *didn't* want. Instead of presenting their truth in a positive formulation or as a conception of justice and fairness, they were trying to get rid of something without confronting it.

I had not yet learned how to listen for what they were *not* saying.

I remember first moments in class where it began to happen, flashes of tension in my interactions with students, a push and a pull, little conversations that mattered. It was during what we called a work period, and the kids who were not at math were sitting at tables or under the loft, eating snacks, working on question sheets for a study about mushrooms. Some were cutting out paper for posters, others were getting their books from their cubbies.

Daniel Arnott stood before me at my desk. He was tall and lanky, with a mouthful of braces, a crew-cut, shy, and socially awkward. An eighth grader, it was his first year at the school.

"Um, Tal, I don't know what to write my story about. You said we had to write about a big 'problem' or something?"

"Well, not a problem, Daniel. Just something that matters to you. A feeling that was meaningful or intense. You build your story around that."

"Any kind of feeling?"

"Of course. I mean, it could be the feeling of joy or inclusion, or sadness. Or worry. There's always a little journey that lives around a feeling. That's what your story is."

He stood there, his feet together. He looked out the window, then back into the room where his classmates were busy working together, as though he were deciding to make a step.

"I was riding on a bus last year at my old school. We were on a field trip. I was sitting in the back with all the popular kids. We saw a blind man walking on the sidewalk while we were stopped at a light. I wanted to say something. I told everyone to look at him. I said, 'Look at that blind guy. What a loser!'"

I listened.

"We all started laughing at him. I felt so good because everybody was laughing at something I said. Then I shouted out the bus window at him. Just to see if he would turn around." He stared at the floor. "I feel so ashamed."

"Why?"

"Because what I was doing was wrong."

"That's the feeling of your story, Daniel."

"Doing something wrong?"

"Not exactly. The feeling of knowing it was wrong. That's a kind of shame. Knowing that what you did betrayed something in you."

"Shame?"

"Shame, and what's on the other side of shame. Your story is about *why* you feel bad. About a boy who would feel bad. That's a thing worth writing about."

"What do you mean?"

"I mean, if you write the story, you'll find out why you felt ashamed, and you'll find something else even more important: What you want to be, how you know you should be. You'll write yourself to a better place, and that's something you can keep. Far more lasting than the moment in the back of the school bus."

The current of his story was his alone-ness among a group of boys, his wanting to be noticed, heard, seen. It was his willingness to feel the immorality of his own actions and face his transgressions, to be transformed. There were stirrings in his heart that he revealed, with the implied trust that I could help him find a way to create something crucial and lasting. He was learning how to see. I was learning how to listen. To see, hear, and love them in their raw, awkward formations—this was teaching.

December was cold, frigid, dark. Not much snow had fallen, but the holidays were all around us. A giant wreath hung on the big front door. Ruby brought in her family's extra menorah. Katelyn brought ginger molasses cookies. Bennett and Nils ventured into the woods and cut down a small pine tree, jammed it into a maple syrup bucket filled with rocks, and dragged it into the big room where we decorated it with origami peace cranes and silver mylar stars of David.

Callum, however, couldn't get words flowing, could gather no words, could not give form to what was inside him. He was working on a story, about what, he was not sure. He was trying to find something in himself, some articulation to match feelings trapped inside him. He felt the weight of the world, but he did not know what to do with it. He came to me, his head hanging.

"Where's your story? Everyone's got something in but you."

He looked down at the floor.

"I can't start."

"You can't start?"

He began to cry and the tears dropped steadily from behind the screen of tangled brown hair.

"Callum, words flowing. That's what you said. You just have to start. Just the first word, the same as always. The first word won't be the whole feeling, but it's a step toward it. You can't reach the top of the mountain so easily. Just take the first step."

"I can't. I don't know." He clenched and unclenched his

fists. From the sleeves of his ragged T-shirt, his veins pulsed and rose.

"I believe you can. Just the first feeling. Like now. What are you feeling now? Can you name it?"

He stood, rocking on his feet. He shook his head, but I couldn't see his face.

"Do you remember the first day of school—that feeling?" I implored. "Or the day we were in the swamp—you were laughing and shouting? Or when we walked near the river and you asked me about Buddhism? All of those were places where you were feeling and thinking and seeing the world. It has to be in you. I can't make it come out, but I can tell you it's in you."

The next day he didn't come to school, nor the following day. I called his mother's house, where he was currently living.

"He doesn't want to come in because he thinks you'll be disappointed," she said.

"I won't be disappointed in *him*. I'm disappointed that he's not at school! He needs to come to school."

"He's a warrior,"x she said, as if that settled everything.

"I know he's a warrior, he's a fighter. But he has to come to school and do the fighting."

When Callum came into school the next day, he had a single, typed paragraph, a short editorial about the destruction of nature by man. His shoulders were slumped as he handed it to me, and he did not look at me. I took the paper and read it.

"Callum, I can see you struggling. But I'm going to go out on a limb and say a short essay about environmental destruction is not the same as a feeling that's sacred to you. This isn't it. This," I said, as I held the paper up, "is running away. It's a diversion. This is not what we're hunting. This is not the great wooly mammoth."

He looked up. His face was red, his eyes were wet.

"We're hunting the wooly mammoth. You're circling, but not getting to it."

"My mother said that it was good."

"She's wrong. It's not good. The words sound like her words. It doesn't have *you* in it. There's no risk in saying that we're destroying the earth."

His elbows were on his knees and he was crying still.

"I tried so many times."

"Callum," I said, "do you feel like a failure?"

His head rose and sagged down.

"Well, you're *not*, dammit. If you quit, and didn't try, that's a failure. You just haven't found the right door yet. You're good, you're better than good. But you haven't found your words yet. *Your* words. It's okay."

He nodded without looking up.

That afternoon in class I decided to get them writing. But really I wanted them writing and for Callum to be dragged along. If everyone was writing, he'd have to write.

"Has everyone got a writing utensil and a piece of parchment?"

They scuffled around the room, tearing sheets from notebooks and taking pencils out of the jar on the shelf.

"I'm giving you twenty minutes. When I say 'go,' you start writing. And you don't stop, and you don't look up. It's a sprint, and you keep moving your legs. Even if you have to write the same damn word ten times in a row. I don't care if you write the stupidest and most ridiculous sentences in history. Voices, dreams, things that disgust you, recipes, the phone book, I don't care." My voice was rising. In me was a desire to break through a wall, to make the room hot, to have them write so much that the room filled to overflowing. "But you do *not* have permission to stop. Go!"

They bent to their papers. I watched Callum. His head was down, and his hand wasn't moving. The paper sat before him on a hardcover book. Then he lifted his hand to the top of the paper. He began, slowly, his hand moving awkwardly, stopping, then moving again.

When the twenty minutes were up, I told them to count their words. They counted.

"Tell me how many words you wrote."

They called out numbers as they tallied.

"476."

"298."

"Callum?" I asked.

"425."

"Read the words to us. And then I'm going to say whatever you wrote, whatever the 423 words are, they are perfect words because they came from you.'"

He began to read.

Heart. What is it? It is simply to give, for nothing. To draw goodness from your soul, to use energy, simply, just for goodness. Goodness. What does it look like? It looks like me in the Big Room, in the gloom, probably having failed to get work done, having failed to write. To me the dust isn't glittering like the stars, I'm not breathing in the remnants of past North Branch. I feel rejected. But then I hear something: a car...doors open, close. Footsteps on dirt, stone, key chains jingling from a backpack.

It's Katy. She's goes by called Katelyn now, probably because she thought there was something wrong with "Katy." We're both from Rochester, and once we were in the same class in elementary school, even though she is a grade ahead of me. Now maybe she stops at the doorway, but I can't remember anything, other than her saying to me, "Good morning, Cal-Cal."

It was as if there was to her something to be good for, like she was charged with taking away my misery. Katy may have been like a sister to me. Bennett is like a brother to me, but Katy had no reason to care about me. We weren't even close. We did not spend much time together, but she cared for me anyway. I would do my best to return her gesture of goodness and love and reply, "Good morning, Katelyn."

Do we not all know what Goodness is? Metaphorically, it is light. To receive it is to have something lively and sustaining dropped into the ocean of your soul. We live on these gestures, most commonly, like with Katelyn, as gestures of brotherly and sisterly love. To live a good life, you must be able to accept, notice, and give these gestures.

This was not the only time for me when someone made me feel accepted, worthy, good, happy, maybe even loved. Would you understand if it was only a name, "Callu-mine?" There was no one setting—a rink locker room, a hay-loft, a Dodge truck, a dining room. My friend Will's ex-step dad used to call me this, Callu-mine, a name given to me when I lived in North Hollow, Rochester. He was not the only one, but when he said "Callu-mine" it was as if my ears perked up like those of a dog who hears the food bag. There was nothing ever dramatic or unique about it, his voice was as it always was, just a little jollier and louder.

It was remarkable: the force of a room full of scribbling adolescents, a measure of tension, my insistence, and one restriction—somehow these had conspired to momentarily unlock him. Four hundred and twenty-five words and a brief release from his own purgatory.

"That felt really good to hear, Callum," said Katelyn, leaning in to smile down the table at him "I'm really proud of you."

"*Jesus H. Christ*, Callum, look at what was in there!" I said.

He shrugged.

"That's called going after the wooly mammoth. I'm proud of you."

Now he smiled. He'd made Bennett shine, he'd made Katelyn shine. He was shining. On this day he'd tracked and caught a beast. Love lived in him. By his example, he showed them that they had souls the size of oceans, that they too had so much to give. He showed them how the simple gestures could sustain and keep us all in the light.

One day after the holiday break I played the class a recording of John Coltrane's "My Favorite Things." Then I asked them to write about *their* favorite things. Nadia mentioned the moon that had risen on Wednesday night, huge and golden over the tops of the Green Mountains.

"That was one of my favorite things!" said Haley, as though Nadia had stolen it from her.

"Me too," I said. "Last night I was watching the moon. And I thought, *I wish we didn't have to die.*"

"Last night I was laying with my mother," said Ariela. "She was sleeping. She looked like a little girl. She looked really peaceful. When she's like that, then I stop worrying for just a second."

The room was silent. Ariela's mother! We went through our days usually forgetting or unaware, but Ariela's mother was alone at home every day, and that fact lived inside of Ariela. I could feel tears at the edge of my eyes. The tears might come and I wouldn't hold them back. Why would I? To tell my students to live less feelingly?

"I wish we didn't have to die," I said again. I looked at Ariela. What did I want her to know and learn? I had no method or intention, except to say what came into my mind, to be as real and true as the world. We were talking about the full moon, our favorite things, and Ariela's mother, Ana, who was dying. We all knew it. And all of us went to sleep at night holding onto as much of life as we could.

"It's a sad and beautiful world," I said.

"Is it sad because it's beautiful," asked Nils, "or is it beautiful because it goes away, and that's sad?"

"All, both."

I looked across the table at Ariela again. She was looking down at her clasped hands in her lap. Nadia's hand was on her shoulder.

I asked them the same questions that consumed poets, philosophers, psychologists, and artists: What does time do? What is matter, and what is spirit? How do we hold onto the past and move into the future simultaneously? What are we made of? How close to life are we, and how do we get closer to life? How do we accept death and loss? What is *wholeness*? How do we fill the space of the world? What, even, did the life and death of a newborn, sightless mouse—once found at home and so briefly loved by one of my students—have to do with living a good life?

But they were adolescents, and they did not always live in the muscular currents of spiritual or philosophical questioning. In science, they'd recently watched a movie about the reproduction of snails. As the movie began, it inspired a few *awwwws* in reference to how cute the snails were. Then the two snails started to "kiss" and mate. This apparently was too much for the class, and the whole school reverberated with *OOOs* and *AAAHs* and *WOW, SNAILS GETTING FRESH!*

The freedom to swing between moments of profundity and absurdity was a source of great happiness for them.

Later, I handed back Brody's character sketch. It was about Rose.

"Why are you writing about your math teacher?"

"Well, I love Rose," he said.

"That's beautiful. But why?"

"Um, she's so calm under pressure."

"Really?" That seemed a strange inspiration for loving someone.

"I guess," he said.

"But I'm also wondering—what are you getting from Rose, besides her math corrections?"

He wasn't sure and didn't answer.

"It's partly your age that you're looking at attributes of people around and wanting those attributes. You're like a voracious largemouth bass that wants to catch and eat all the fish it can."

There was an awkward silence. "Sorry, that was a terrible analogy," I said, and he smiled.

"What I mean is: Do you feel like sometimes your feelings for Rose are like the feelings you don't lately have around your mom?"

"Yeah. Like I hardly ever do anything with her any more."

"So write about your mom, and figure out what you're feeling."

As long as we kept the questions active and living, we could come up with new answers.

One morning in meeting, Hannah raised her hand. She usually only listened in meeting, sketching ornate flower-shaped mandalas in her journal. But today there was a quiet urgency in the way she leaned forward, looking at me down the length of the table. Some kids were still piling in the room in their coats, faces bright red from the cold, with bags on their shoulders.

"Um, this doesn't have anything to do with school or us here, but I wanted to say it."

"Go ahead," I said.

"Well, I was working this past weekend with a woman who has cerebral palsy, helping her ski. I had her on a harness and I was skiing behind her. Her ski tips had a rope holding them together because she can't control her legs. And she was so happy. And I was watching her, the smile on her face. And she has a life where everything she never hoped for has come true, but she was so happy and, I don't know, it made me feel so good. I don't know."

Oh, but Hannah did know. Everything in the room slowed down, the bustling motion arrested. A different kind of listening attended the tremor in Hannah's voice. The jokes of the morning, the small anecdotes of homework and coming to school, these receded as she labored to tell us something vital and true.

"I didn't even know you worked with people skiing," Winn said.

"I don't know. It's just something I do on weekends." She blushed and pulled her hair back.

"You were giving that woman something she had never had," I said.

"Yeah," said Nils. "It was like you made her whole."

"You know that good feeling you felt, Hannah?" I said.

"Yeah?"

"Maybe that was the feeling of you making yourself complete. Or greater. Doing great things, becoming great, feels really good."

Haley raised her hand. She'd been in Boston at the hospital with her father, who was having his pacemaker replaced. While she was there, she'd met another man on the ward, and she'd spoken to him in the corridor, and he had told her he was afraid of an upcoming surgery.

"The next day when I came to see my dad, I found out the man had died the night before."

Now many tears came, big feelings, not yet coherent. I was stunned to suddenly have these two stories alive among us. How did they land in Yeb, whose mother was dead? In Ariela, whose mother was at home in a dark room, curled up like a small child, asleep? This sudden eruption of emotion was entirely unpredictable, and with it came discomfort and possibly more pain.

There was no way to avoid it. Perhaps the pain would lead us to something that could teach us.

Haley continued. "I want to write about it, but I don't know how," she said. "I don't know how to get the feeling across. I don't know, the feeling, it was like . . . "

"You know what it is. You feel it. You just don't have words yet."

She nodded.

"You'll write about it," I said. "Give it a little time. For now, just tell the story of the moment. If you can make a picture of what you saw, the power of it will arise out of you."

Nils, as if to protect her, shifted the conversation back to Hannah on the ski slopes. "What Hannah was talking about is what she was talking about earlier in the year. She's doing what she said she wanted when she said she wanted to be a domino—give to others and make something happen."

"Yeah, I remember that," said Ariela.

"That's exactly right," I said. "Amazing. Remember how intensely she stated what she wanted then, and look at how intensely she's sought it, and look at how she's trying to understand what it means, and now she's giving it to us."

The class was poised in an electric, quivering silence.

In their stories they lost their shadows and they gained themselves. There was nothing more important in our days than what was happening among us, and to us. We listened to words, we wrote our own. I asked them to write the truth of themselves, to find the root of the root, the opening below the deeps. Callum wrote of moving from Rochester and his memories of the river by his old house. Hannah wrote of her blushing, her extreme self-consciousness, and she titled her story, "Idiopathic Craniofacial Erythema," which she and I had once looked up on Wikipedia because she wanted to know why she blushed so much. Bennett wrote of his father, and how, before his parent's divorce, they would build radio-controlled planes in the barn in winter so when spring came they would have something to fly. The stories were about love and memory, rich with the learning and contours of young lives. Pages and pages, scene upon scene, all set in motion on the page, in the room, in the mind, causing creative stress and energy, mental transformation, sifting, digging, and ordering. Not fictions, but truths. Not external subjects, but internal struggles. Not impersonal, but the self at center. Not the outer surface, but rather, as Frost called it, the "inner weather."

Something fell from a white-gray sky. Winter, and white flakes of snow falling from white-gray skies. Our story ideas coming out of merely not nothing. The snows of winter piling up. White on white, gray on white, white on gray. Black lines on white pages, white pages piling up. *Our* woodpile made in our small school in the mountains. If we were lucky, out of many gray days came a day of clarity—like sun on a snow-glittering field. If we were lucky, we got a story like Haley's.

As all the stories were, it was a kind of invitation. *Come inside, and see what I have to tell.* Haley had an adventure to describe and counsel to offer. The mirror—and the adolescent gazing into the mirror—was the point around which her story turned. With a searching anguish all her own, she asked: *am I beautiful?*

When my students wrote about looking in the mirror as small children, the image staring back at them nearly always appeared completely perfect and free of judgment. Haley envisioned herself as a six year-old girl dressing up in her mother's clothes, and with perfect blissful innocence and knowing:

> I looked beautiful, pig-tails and all, glowing in my reflection. My eyes shone as an outburst of giggles leaped out of the mirror, and tears of laughter hit the floor. I saw myself as

a beautiful girl, whom time could not ever change, not in a million years. I saw myself there in the mirror just as I saw myself inside. I liked this person I saw; I loved her.

Haley and her image were an integrated whole, with no interfering self-consciousness—a self-accepting self. The world was simple and good. But later, when she was not ready, time, experience, and new thoughts impinged. The image was wounded, fractured, muddied.

I opened one of the empty stalls and closed the gate behind me; I walked out into the pasture and saw an old wash tub filled with water and sat down next to it. I could see the metal was beginning to rust through the ice cold, crystal clear water. I could see the dim reflection of some person, someone I didn't really recognize. She looked stupid, with big red puffy eyes, shaking hands, and a blotchy face. I could no longer see her eyes as denim blue, but now just gray and bloodshot….I looked at the girl…her ratty hair, her big belly, her chicken stick legs and her clammy hands. I began to cry again. I grabbed a small clump of mud and threw it as hard as I could, right into my reflection. The mud dispersed into clean water, and I could no longer see that ugly person.

Ugly. "Don't let it in," she cried. But there it was, filling her up, her own process of self-criticism and nullification, one that could be taken to dangerous extremes. She was caught in a drama she only dimly perceived, but her story gave her a chance to re-vision herself.

Later in the story she wrote about approaching her first day of North Branch, that strange cauldron of older kids and adolescent energy, an entirely new stage of life.

My stomach dropped to my feet as we drove in. I took deep breaths and looked into the visor mirror, which showed my new braces. The damn things had just been put on, and I wasn't used to eating or talking with them yet. So one night before the first day of school, I had video-taped myself eating and having a fake conversation, just to see how dorky and stupid I really did look. Imagine this: a spitting Tasmanian devil with hot oil all over his face, occasionally a scrunched nose who picked at his teeth. There was not one thing elegant about that video...As we drove into the driveway, I looked back at the visor mirror to make sure no breakfast was stuck in my braces...

Elegance. Against the image of herself as an ugly, spitting devil with food in her teeth, she sought the grace that could only come with confidence and a clear sense of inner worth. But self-consciousness exacted its own tribute. It caused her to look into the mirror and only see what she felt others believed, not what she knew to be true. The mirror confined, ensnared, and wouldn't let go.

As she worked on the story, she'd gotten stuck in that snare. "I don't know where to go," she had complained one day. "I don't know how to end my story."

"Go write a long list of everything you know to be beautiful," I had said.

She returned the next day with a four-page list, a manifest of her soul, from the voices of her friends to the sound of our pencils writing in school to the bountiful meals her mother cooked to the Jello her father burned. Like a once-empty basket filled with apples from a bough, her list was heavy and sweet.

I thought of Frost's poem, "The Pasture." Along with doing the mundane chore, he wrote, parenthetically, *wait to watch the water clear, I may.* He was not thinking of the raw drama of adolescence when he wrote his poem—and yet, it echoed now. Haley only needed to clear the grit to see herself anew, to discover her many selves, one growing from another, none of them fixed. Power lay in identifying the self that needed to be lifted up and cherished.

I liked to think my students would be the kind of children Frost would want as companions—that he'd be happy to have them with him in the pasture to watch the water clear or to marvel at a tottering newborn calf. I hoped he would see them as I did: as ones who dreamed to see more than what was on the surface, who believed that springs needed tending and that something moved deep below.

Haley wrote:

I learned that even in the most ideal scenarios there are imperfections that flood the picture. I learned that make-up doesn't make you beautiful, but makes you self-conscious. I learned that a mirror is just a window painted with lies. I have learned that I am beautiful, I am me. I know what real beauty is, and I know I can be it.

The class clapped loud and long after her story. Listening and responding, they became her mirror that told her she was not alone in the pasture.

"She's so brave. I mean, it's so raw and honest," said Ruby. "I don't know if I could do that."

"Because she talked about her seeing herself as ugly?" I asked.

"She admits to things she's most self-conscious about," said Katelyn. "Tells the embarrassing things, lets us see what is true to her, even if they're bad. She showed everything. Exactly what I'm terrible at."

"That's how I want to be," said Nadia, with a hint of determination.

They gave back to Haley what had filled them—not the reflection tinged with darker shadows, but the ones that were most lovely.

❧

One dark gray morning I came in thinking about the essential problem: *How to start from nothing?* Outside it was minus six degrees. The school driveway was an ice sheet. I clambered over a heap of snow that had recently avalanched off the back roof to get in. The door was frozen shut. Ice dams, icicles, windows, everything frosted over. Snow tracked into the school. The sky a blank gray, low clouds, the sun weak and barely visible.

What better day could there be to read them the most difficult, complicated poem I thought they could handle: Anna Akhmatova's poem fragment from *Requiem 1935-40*, "Instead of Preface." Could it possibly ignite them, this poem about the most terrible of years? Was there a bridge between our classroom—with its warm floors and Tibetan flag hanging from wooden beams—to the time of the Yezhov Terror, deep in Stalin's Soviet Union? I explained some of the background of the gulags, political oppression, the great purges and terror campaigns, and then I read the poem.

In the terrible years of the Yezhov terror, I spent
Seventeen months in the prison lines of Leningrad.
Once, someone "recognized" me. Then a woman with
Bluish lips standing behind me, who, of course, had
Never heard me called by name before, woke up from
The stupor to which every one had succumbed and
Whispered in my ear (everyone spoke in whispers there):
"Can you describe this?"
And I answered: "Yes, I can."
Then something that looked like a smile passed over
What had once been her face.

"What's the poet doing here?" I asked, looking around.

"Not much. It seems hopeless," said Henry. "I mean, the whole thing sounds really depressing."

"*Totally* hopeless?"

"No," said Callum. "It kind of seems to be trying to be something giving hope. Like she's telling people what's happening."

"So that's good?" I asked. "I mean, to try to tell people what's happening?"

"It's the only thing they have," said Ruby.

"It's sad *and* hopeful," said Henry.

"I don't really get it," said Nils. "How could the woman smile before she disappeared?"

"Well, she probably disappeared, literally," I said. "Maybe this is her last smile. What's in it? Relief? Happiness? There isn't a lot to be happy about. Everyone's disappeared. No one knows anything. No one even knows where their family members are."

"But the poet is giving the people something," said Nils. "She's seeing *them* and giving them life."

"So maybe it's about how important it is to know what's happening to us?" offered Hannah.

"But the truth is scary," said Nadia. "The truth is that people are disappearing and no one knows where they're going."

"But we can smile before we disappear," said Hannah. She was ever insistent, hopeful, believing.

"The face is fading, they're all disappearing," said Ariela. "But the poet is telling them that before they go, knowing they were alive, that makes the woman smile. To have existed."

"Knowing the truth is more important than life?" I asked.

"It *is* life," said Callum.

"So . . . what?" I asked.

"The poet has strength to stand in the cold for seventeen months waiting for news," he answered.

"The poet gives strength by believing there can be an answer," said Haley.

"She's bringing life back to pale faces," said Yeb.

"Or the poet tells us what survives," added Ariela. "It's like a story of how souls kept going."

Ariela left her mother every day at home. She walked into the dark room where her mother lay sleeping, with her tiny head peeking out from under the blankets, exhausted from chemotherapy treatments. And each morning before she left for school, Ariela walked in to kiss her mother good-bye, every day Ariela said, *Adios Mamita, te quiero mucho.*

In Ariela's life, smiles were infrequent. For her, a poem in which the smiles were disappearing was too true. In this most terrible of years, her mother was disappearing, yet she might be the one to understand and teach us the way souls could keep going.

Ruby wrote to ask me if I got the email about her wanting the whole school to go ice-skating on the Lemon Fair River, which had frozen solid after a week of subzero temperatures.

There was nothing I wanted to do more than take the whole school skating through the flooded, frozen fields and swamps and glide among the black winter trees. But I informed her that, alas, we did not have the time in our schedule to take a herd of adolescents skating over the flooded farm fields of Addison County.

Instead, we prepared for our annual winter cross-country ski trip. We would ski fifteen miles up into the Moosalamoo Wilderness, winding through Vermont snowmobile trails and the trails of Blueberry Hill, a local cross-country ski center. There we would spend the night on the floor of a barn, with a large antique wood stove to warm us, then ski back fifteen miles the next day.

The sky was a high blue, not one cloud. The snow was shadowed and purple, tree limbs laden with powder that fell, whispering, like soft flour spilling and puffing under the limbs of trees. Winter days like this were just as Frost had written—*You'd think the inner dome of heaven had fallen*—the dark woods crystalline and sparkling in the morning light.

We gathered at the trailhead, rainbow-hued in jackets, spandex and nylon pants, backpacks, water bottles that were already freezing solid, wool hats, and mittens. Excited chatter filled the woods as boots snapped into bindings and hands slipped into loops on poles. Some of them were at ease on skis. Many were not. Callum had already fallen and was half-buried in a heap of snow the plow had left. Bennett laughed and pulled him backwards onto the trail.

When we hiked or skied, there was only one rule: at some point in the day, each person had to be with and talk to each other person. We did the math: in one day we could make 256 different human combinations.

As we worked our way up the steep Catamount Trail, they broke out in clumps of two or three, little specks of color in the glaring white-lavender snow, clouded breaths rising above them. We moved slowly, a great, extended snail. Sometimes, in the classroom, I felt that my students were snails, moving glacially, imperceptibly, grudgingly. We could have tested, to see if there was progress, but we sought the kind of movement and change that was not testable. Sometimes they were stubborn, reticent to take risks. Sometimes they regressed, or went to a default fetal posture when life got hard. They could retreat, become invisible, afraid of their own feelings and inclinations. Sometimes they hid behind repetitions of half-truths. Sometimes they masked their real desires, spoke falsehoods diametrically opposed to the inner truths clawing inside them waiting to be born.

Outside, though, physical limits could be tested, and such tests brightened and lightened them. Callum had gone for a week without smiling, another week not saying a word in literature class. But on a day like this, he was at the front of the pack, flailing his arms, sweating in the single-digit morning, shouting for everyone to "man and woman up!"

"We are hardcore!" he shouted into the woods.

Ariela carried her own sadness and also the sadness of others—of her sister Martina, her aunts, her mother's friends. She worried about everything—whether the house was clean, packing lunches for school, if Martina was happy at her school. But on this brilliant day, below the long white back of Breadloaf Mountain, she skied with a cluster of friends who might have even believed that they could carry her through the cold for as long as we were out in it.

Their cheeks were bright, they shouted and kicked up their skis to flip snow onto each other. They tore into beef jerky and Snickers bars. When I looked at them all, piled together for a photograph in the snow, I could believe they were something more than snails or caterpillars inching toward adulthood. It was easy to see their loving compassion and wish to be good to one another as they bent to scrape ice off each other's bindings and passed water bottles back and forth.

We stopped for lunch at Frost's writing cabin and sat on the stone wall in the snow with the low southern sun warming us. Across the frozen pasture, a pair of apple trees still held a half dozen shriveled apples. Beyond the pasture, the view was all lines of trees, just like in Frost's poem. When the wind blew, curled beech leaves shivered on their limbs.

At the edge of the woods, Callum and Bennett dug a deep trench through the fourteen inches of snow in which, they claimed, we could all survive should darkness come. We made a pit and set a fire to warm freezing toes. Hot dogs on sticks jutted toward the coals like ragged spokes on a wheel. Ashes and smoke spilled upwards with cries of, "Smoke follows beauty!"

Before we started out again, Haley read the daily poem. It was by Rabindranath Tagore and contained the line: *It is the most distant course that comes nearest to thyself.* With those words ringing in us, we pushed out of the clearing onto an old logging road. Up and up, mittened and layered, skiing in lines or four abreast, the lines stringing out, chattering, slowing, zooming ahead, coming back, keeping the tail moving behind the head. Clambering up and plowing down dips and turns, we threw curses and laughter into the bright woods.

We skied into Blueberry Hill Ski Center. Adrenaline and hormone-charged rosy-cheeked teens piled around the pot-bellied stove, where they dumped wet gloves and coats. We ate dinner and skied in the full moonlight, then back into the *hibernaculum*, as Eric required them to call it. "That's the scientific word for a womb-like chamber for hibernating and nesting," he explained. Then to the hard floor amid a chaos of sleeping bags, the litter of candy wrappers and wet socks, and the smell of woodsmoke in the darkness.

Slow or fast, all of them were part of an intimate band. The most important test was that we made it back together.

We were writing our annual play. It was all they could talk about. They decided it should be about a high school class in which the students did not care about learning, but whose dormant minds would be transformed and come to life.

"It's about us!" Bennett shouted.

Of course it would have been easier to perform a conventional play—"Our Town" or "A Midsummer Night's Dream" or "Oliver"—classic, predictable, safe. But the idea of writing a play, of producing something, of truly playing and inventing, *that* inspired them. There was danger in it too—them alone, making something of their own. This awareness drove them to want to make a play that they would all be proud of—the shared responsibility to produce something of value.

I read about a theater troupe from Belgium comprised solely of adolescents, whose work was described as "the merry disorder of young consciousness." Embracing this disorder was the doorway to the power of their wisdom and wild-growing selves. The students in our school were autobiographical narrative writers, literary deconstructionists, astronomical observers, bread-oven builders, Utopian theorists, poem-intoners, geometers, swamp navigators, backwoods skiers, and mountain geologists. Why couldn't they also be dramatically and comically uninhibited playwrights?

When we began to write, all I said was, "It's all yours. Go for it." I pulled the string on the spinning top to release the initial motion. Where the merry top went—its blur of color, the frictions it might cause, how wildly it might spin or wobble—would be a function of the mass and makeup of these particular students. And there were ten thousand decisions to make, energies to direct, voices to moderate, ideas to bring forth, identities in formation. I told them: "Say anything." The class could then become its own full-spinning and tilting orb, a wild nebula of the Green Mountain Galaxy on its own luminous path. Everything we did in class—writing workshops, projects about Utopia or Freedom, poetry, literature class—might become part of the fabric of the play.

One morning Ruby announced in meeting: "Did everyone hear what happened at Frost's cabin?"

Everyone had heard. Unidentified teens had broken into the Homer Noble Farm, Robert Frost's summer home, and had a party. They had burned old furniture and left broken bottles and beer cans in the rooms. Someone had vomited in the kitchen. Frost's writing cabin was still standing. The estimate was $30,000 worth of damage.

Because they were familiar with some of Frost's words, and because we had visited his cabin, the students had affection and concern for what had happened. Frost's farm was their farm; they'd walked in his woods, sat in his writing chair. He was *their* poet.

"It makes me feel sick," said Ruby. "If anyone read his poems, or thought for half a second, they would never do that."

"So maybe they never read his poems," said Bennett.

They asked why things like this so commonly involved alcohol. I told them there would probably be future situations they would encounter, moments when something bad or wrong was happening, and that there would be an opportunity to stop it from happening or make a right thing happen—to help steer the ship to a better harbor. They would need to be ready.

Because we were looking at a real incident, they were listening.

"Why would anyone do this?" asked Yeb. "In Awassa no one even has anything. Why would people destroy the things they have?"

"They're spoiled, stupid, and blind at the same time," I said.

"It pisses me off," Yeb said. "When I first came to the elementary school everyone complained about school all the time. They shouldn't be complaining."

"Because . . .?"

"Because they *have* a school," he said. "It makes me, like, sick. We didn't have school in Ethiopia."

"Maybe the kids didn't have any connection to Frost. So it wasn't even a thing to them?" I suggested.

"Maybe it was a shout to be heard," said Ruby. "Even though it was destructive and stupid."

"What a bunch of morons," said Henry.

"Who did it?" asked Yebsera.

"I heard it was some kids from the high school," said Nolan.

"But really, what do we learn if we only think about who did it?" I asked. "Why are we not asking what is being said, or not said? What's the *meaning* of the thing that happened?"

I didn't expect an answer, but I wanted the seed planted in their minds.

Nolan compared it to an incident of vandalism that had happened in the Northeast Kingdom earlier in the fall. The sculptor Joel Fischer, whose work was in the Museum of Modern Art, had recently had thirty of his sculptures—valued at $1,000,000—stolen from his studio.

As work on the play continued, we had in our minds this sculptor in Danby, our poet, Frost, and a band of drunken teenage vandals. We had in our minds Anna Akhmatova and the beauty of the lives of the precious ones who vanished. I was thinking about creation and destruction; my students were not sculptors or poets, not yet anyway, but they had it in them to make something true and real from the stories around them. And I wanted more than anything for them to become creators who could make something out of what had happened.

The next day, to continue the dialogue, I showed them Meta Vaux Warrick Fuller's sculpture, "Talking Skull," a bronze of a boy kneeling in the dirt while gazing at a skull that also rested in the dirt.

"What's the meaning of this sculpture?" I asked them. "Why'd she make it? Is the sculpture the 'skull' she left behind to talk to us, just as Frost's poems were left by him to talk to us?"

In the darkened room, they wrote down ideas as they looked up at the illuminated whiteboard. Ruby raised her hand and offered to read.

"Is the boy meant to be us, looking at a reflection of his future self? Is he talking to the skull. Can it talk back? And if it can, what's inside of the skull? Wisdom, love, stories of endurance. Maybe that's all we are trying to do. Dig up important things."

The next day I showed them Michelangelo's image of "God Creating Man" from the Sistine Chapel. We looked at the painting as a picture not so much about what God did, but what an *artist* could do. We talked about that small distance between God's finger and Adam's.

"That distance is the space we're trying to comprehend," I said. "Everything we do is about how we cross that little space, about what happened before and what happens after. How we grow from what we are towards what we will be."

We looked at Michelangelo's "Awakening Slave" sculptures and saw a body trying to emerge from a stone. The chisel-marks remained visible. Had Michelangelo not finished the sculpture? Or did he leave it unfinished as a way to show how we eternally struggle to break free of the inert stones of our lives? What, we asked, drove humans to make images of their struggles and hardships?

"Maybe that's us," said Nils. "That's us trying to learn and become something."

We looked at Rodin's "The Thinker" and studied his face. The knit eyebrows, his fist jammed to his mouth, the twist of his body, the roughly worked bronze surface. We tried to imagine both what the thinker was thinking and why Rodin might have created it for us.

The range of expression in three-dimensional works let them see the actual contours of humans being: anguish, suffering, imprisonment, inner questioning, creating, seeking, love, despair, the human touch. These were the same contours they touched in their stories, or in the poems of Frost, the man whose voice called to us through these very woods.

Looking at Michelangelo's "David," our attention went to David's massive hand—the hand that could slay giants, but was also the hand of the maker. It was filled with blood, power, and potential.

Finally, we looked at Rodin's "The Kiss." Was this what we were trying to get to? To the place of open acceptance and tenderness? Was this not the pinnacle, the ultimate height, the star we steered by? The play they were trying to write was their attempt to make something filled with the potency of blood and true life. I hoped the play would be our own "David," with all the hand-work visible.

For playwriting, we spent afternoons divided into groups, four or five of them crowded into my office or in the basement, hunched around a computer, making up silly scenes, a hybrid of Monty Python crossed with Saturday Night Live crossed with the lunacy of adolescents. I sent Callum and Hannah down to the clay room to write a scene in which Hannah, playing "Hannah Mahkmatova," visited a moribund classroom in a place called Crapperstown where she was given the task of inspiring high school students into an appreciation of poetry—a task which, based on the characters they'd already created, would appear impossible.

HANNAH MAHKMATOVA: Does anyone have any other ideas about poetry? About what it is?

BENNETT: Words?

HANNAH: Yes?

EVAN: Put together?

RUBY: What about this: *(sad)* Seals are dying, seagulls are flying, icebergs are melting, and I am crying. *(happier)* OH MY GOD! I just made that up!

HANNAH: Alright, yes. *(points at Haley)*

HALEY: Poetry is like, feelings, expressing your heart. It's love and hate *(starts to break down)*. Poetry is . . . It's there for you! It's like, enveloping you in a realm of your imagination!

YEB: Oh yeah, isn't poetry, like, rhyming or rapping?

HANNAH: *(approaches Callum)* Well, sometimes it is. Okay, anyone else? How about you? *(points to Callum)*

CALLUM: Well, err, isn't poetry like the truth?

HANNAH: Alright, yes, that's a start. *(She starts walking around behind students.)* Now before we begin, let me tell you a little bit about myself. I grew up in Russia and started writing poetry when I was your age. I had to change my name because my father wasn't proud of me. And then in later years Russia became a communist state, my people were terrorized and used by our government.

BENNETT: Why didn't you leave?

HANNAH: I didn't leave because being a Russian meant living in my home country no matter what the circumstances were. In my town, we lived during Yezhov terror, and people disappeared with no warning and without reason and even if there was a chance they were still alive, you would be told of nothing. Citizens would wait outside of prisons for weeks on end, hoping for news of their lost family members. So I'm going to recite a poem of mine entitled "Instead of a Preface."

"In the terrible years of the Yezhov terror, I spent
Seventeen months in the prison lines of Leningrad.
Once, someone "recognized" me. Then a woman with
Bluish lips standing behind me, who, of course, had
Never heard me called by name before, woke up from
The stupor to which every one had succumbed and
Whispered in my ear (everyone spoke in whispers there):
"Can you describe this?"
And I answered: "Yes, I can."
Then something that looked like a smile passed over
What had once been her face."

MR. MALLOY (teacher): *(coming to center)* What can you learn from that, class? Did you have any noticing, observations, epiphanies, realizations, glimmerings of truth?
HALEY: It didn't really rhyme but it sounded like a story.
MR. MALLOY: What kind of story was it?
HALEY: Well, it was kind of a sad story. But it was true?
HANNAH: What is important about it being true, anyone?
HENRY: *(starts to talk, but isn't sure)* Well . . .
MR. MALLOY: If it wasn't true would it mean anything? Is it worth creating something that isn't true?
HALEY: Uh, well no, because then if it isn't true then it would have no real meaning.
YEB: If it has meaning then it makes you feel? Half the time I talk about feelings that have no meaning.
HANNAH: So isn't that saying that the truth makes you feel?
CALLUM: Yeah, like me, I've been asleep a long time, *(as though in pain, this is difficult)* and in the poem they all had succumbed to a stupor where they knew or felt hardly anything.

HANNAH: Is the poem just one of the many whispers among those who have succumbed?

YEB: No, like, there was still life there.

HALEY: The smile where her face had once been.

MR. MALLOY: Think, class, about what that line means, "Then something that looked like a smile passed over what had once been face."

BENNETT: Uhhhh, that doesn't make sense though, how can she smile if she doesn't have a face?

ARIELA: If you say to the blue-lipped woman that she can describe what's happening to them, that is so miraculous it can make a faceless person smile.

MR. MALLOY: So guys, like you said, if poems are meant to be meaningful, then they have to be true, and isn't this poem about the value of speaking truth?

CALLUM: Then wouldn't it be the poet's responsibility to describe the truth?

WINN: And if no one does, what are you left with?

We were left with their revisioning of what they had learned—echoes of their own conversations. Inhering in their lines was a belief in words and the power of the poet to lift us from the world of suffering. In the heart of their play, they'd made a home for a poet who was a shadow of themselves to show that poems could light the darkness.

We continued reading the morning poem, and the poets ranged widely: Allen Ginsberg, Emily Dickinson, Langston Hughes, Gwendolyn Brooks, Elizabeth Bishop, Pablo Neruda. Sometimes it was a sonnet by Shakespeare, other times it was a contemporary spoken word poet like Kate Tempest or Saul Williams. There were no standard procedures for the selection or the reading. It was a ritual of sounds that we awoke to—music, rhythm, and cadences of other times and places.

We heard miracles, flashes of insight, questions that resounded through time and space, living echoes—anguish, sadness, doubt, delight, joy, merriment—all of those feelings riding on words. Then, without any discussion or contemplation, we headed off to other corners of the school, or, in the case of science on some late winter days, into the frigid morning air to study the properties of snow.

Mary Oliver's poems came up again and again. We read her *New and Selected Poems* for literature class every few years. Her poems attracted the kids, perhaps because on first reading, the words held an inviting simplicity and the subjects taken up were understandable: herons, a black snake, irises, springtime. The language was neither ornate nor obscure. The poems were direct and luminous, earthy and mystical, natural and numinous, each one cloaked with an authority that demanded we evaluate how we lived. In "The Summer Day," for instance, she looked straight into our eyes while pointing to our hearts: *Tell me what is it you plan to do / with your one wild and precious life?*

One morning I read to the class her poem, "What I Have Learned So Far." I wanted them to consider the question in the first line: *Meditation is old and honorable, so why should I / not sit, every morning of my life, on the hillside, / looking into the shining world?*

When I finished reading, I asked them: "What have you learned so far in this day, this life?"

It was an enormous question with a massive door and a road going in all directions. At 8:39 on a Thursday morning, they had to ask themselves: *What have I committed to my marrow and memory?*

"Here's the assignment: during the next week, write your own poem about what you have learned."

"Can we put anything in it?"

"Anything from your whole life. Backwards to birth all the way to the edge of the unknown."

They set off to write their own poems about what they'd learned in their lives. The assignment, improvised in a moment, simply gave them free reign to lift their own self-created knowledge in a chalice to celebrate and cherish.

The poems came in the following week. Though based off Oliver's original, each was a unique creation about the power of seeing, feeling, and growing. Some contained beautiful lines and images; all of the poems were filled with vagueness and generalities. We worked on the generalities. How could this idea—*I have learned about love, I have learned that the trees are beautiful*—be transformed into something more precise and textured, alive and original.

The second drafts came in. The poems contained a variety of rhetorical structures, internal logic, and music. None of these I could have taught, nor would I have dared to, as the real learning happened when the students—mediating and transforming experience and understanding—created forms of their own invention. Each of the poems tentatively opened the pages to the limits and limitlessness of themselves.

We decided we would read one of their poems every morning in meeting. At the end of meeting, just before we tramped off to class, one student would volunteer. Winn started, and hers was exquisitely good. I was sure she and the other first readers would present the strongest poems, but each day the poem-reader called out a new lyric of learning to us. In poem after poem, the day's reader had not only perfected their poem, they had added numerous new details, facts, thoughts, and feelings after hearing the other poems. It was a living process of accretion and accumulation.

One slow, gray morning, Brody raised his hand to read his. The overhead lights were off still, and the only light in the room came reflected from the snow outside.

"I was thinking about Ariela's mom when I wrote this," he said. "And Yeb's mom. And also Haley's dad."

"Why?" I asked.

"Well, when I was little, I was afraid of dying. And I was always afraid of things like dying in a plane crash. But I'm thinking a lot more now that dying is something different than I thought it was. And I shouldn't be afraid."

"What do you mean?"

"I guess I should be more worried about how I'm living, or something."

"Can you read it to us?"

"Okay." His face was red, his lips barely moved, he sat before us in a wool hat and a scarf wrapped around his shoulders.

I once learned that I would live forever.
I had all the time in the world.
I wouldn't die.
I did not even know about death.

I later learned that I would die,
but that was fine.
When I died I could choose.
I could be another creature, or stay as a ghost.

When I was a ghost
I would remember more.
I would remember the first word I spoke,
I would see when I first learned.

I could also take the form of an animal.
I learned my mom wanted to be an ocean duck,
My dad and brother didn't believe in it.
I wanted to be everything.

I learned my uncle had died.
I didn't know him.
I learned that others were sad.
I was sad for the sad ones.

I learned that I did not want to die,

I didn't want to leave.
I learned that I didn't want to think about death.
If I didn't think, I would not learn.

I learned that when I died,
I would forget everything.
I knew so much.
I learned it would all be gone.

Death is unfair—
that is what I learned.
I learned I can cause death,
anyone can kill.

I learned how I want to die:
it is of old age
I do not want to leave until I have to.
I don't have to yet.

I learned I want to be made fragile,
not by a disease.
I want to become fragile by what I have done.
I will then die, and forget everything.

Polite clapping followed his reading, and then we all sat in silence in the dim, snow-lit room.

"Holy crap," I said. I could not come up with any other words. He'd taken us into the heart of how he was growing from a child into an adult. He'd stared death in the eye and told us: we are given but one chance to live long and beautifully. *To be made fragile by time.*

At that moment I wanted to take Brody's poem and blaze it across every standardized test ever printed. I wanted to mail it into every school-board meeting and every teacher advisory and simply say: *we must devise a way for students to discover and create this.*

The subject of our school was simple: the students, and their lives. Our textbook was the story we made together. Into such a wondrous text we sprinkled Martin Luther King's speeches and the cadences of Whitman's lines, land formation and the geometry of stained glass, the science of sound and the Sistine Chapel. But those particulars only leavened what we made—mere detail and ornament. A poem like Brody's was a new realm altogether. I knew Oliver was right—thought *did* bud toward a divine and radiant light.

As we gathered for meeting on a bright, cold morning, Ariela raised her hand. "I'm so happy," she said. "My aunt is coming to stay with us. She'll be able to help with getting us to school and keeping the house in order."

"Will that relieve some of the stress?" I asked.

"Yes, and I know Martina will be happy. It's such a relief. I've been keeping the kitchen clean, trying to make it so there are less germs in the house. And making Martina's lunch, and making sure she brushes her teeth. It's so freaking hard but now there'll be someone else. Plus I'll be so happy to see my Aunt Maria."

We felt her happiness, as if we could believe with her that her mother's cancer no longer existed. Aunt Maria was coming; the disease was defeated.

The swirl of school continued. We worked on the play in the basement. Haley presented a project about the United Nations High Commission on Refugees. Yebsera presented his project on Rosa Parks. Henry presented his project on the 1960s in which he posed two colliding ideas: idealism and nihilism. Callum's project was about Sufism. At my suggestion, Nils and Callum began reading *On the Road*. One morning, Callum read Gary Snyder's short poem, "Why Log Truck Drivers Rise Earlier Than Students of Zen."

In the high seat,
  before-dawn dark,

Polished hubs gleam
And the shiny diesel stack
Warms and flutters
Up the Tyler Road grade
To the logging on Poorman
      Creek.
Thirty miles of dust.

There is no other life.

Later, during the excited clamor of break, we bantered about the poem around the big table.

"So, compared to the log-truck drivers, are the students of Zen like total freaking candy-asses?" I asked.

"Yeah! Candy-asses!" came an excited response of philosophizing ninth graders.

"What do you mean? That poem is sha-WEET!" Bennett declared.

"Who needs these Zen poet wimps anyway?" I shouted. "Loggers are the REAL men."

"But Tal, you're the *poetry* teacher. You can't say that!" said Haley.

"You're right!" I shouted back. "Without the meditating Zen poets, we wouldn't even know the loggers are there telling us about the only life that matters. They're *both* telling us what matters!"

"Oh, snap!" said Nils, "That's like a Zen paradox."

"So what would you rather have?" I asked. "Zen poets or

the shining exhaust stacks coated in dust? Which is the poem, which is the life, and how do we separate them?"

On it went until we hustled off to the next task or activity. Thirty pages of *1984* to discuss, postulates to prove, Vermont's winter climate to study. In such a manner did we play at school and life.

The next week we took a field trip to the Green Mountain Dharma Center, a Buddhist Monastery in Hartland Four Corners. Part of me was anxious—no, nearly mortified—to bring a whole school of potentially unruly, skeptical teens to a holy sanctuary for a day of quiet, mindful contemplation. The potential for a humiliating clash between the desultory culture of American adolescents and the ancient traditions of peaceful, brown-robed monks was enough to keep me awake for nights. I had to trust, though, that being in the presence of the brothers and sisters would bring out the innate hunger of my students to become contemplatives themselves.

Before our visit, the sisters emailed me and told me that they hoped our visit would be a fruitful one. *At GMDC*, they wrote, *we are practicing living in the Pure Land, the Kingdom of God. From what I understand, your school aims for a similar goal.* The kids, however, were intrigued that Buddhist nuns used the Internet; they were further amused by the fact that the sisters had signed the email: *A Lotus flower for you.*

We arrived, piled out of our cars, and walked through the frigid air to the Hall of Contemplation. The building sat above a long, snow-covered hill looking over further fields and low mountains. The hall was filled with the scent of incense. Flanked by two novitiate monks, the abbot Brother Phap Dang spoke to us about the Pure Land. He explained that it was not an imagined idea of perfection, but a very real attempt to locate and cultivate such place inside of ourselves.

"The pure land is here." Then he pressed his palm firmly on his heart. This place, *this heart*, he explained, was not void of suffering, greed, illusion, cruelty, or anger. Rather, it was a place that we were always creating through mindful contemplation. He told us how at each sounding of the bell we could return to that place inside of us—the inviolate, compassionate part of ourselves from which we might mend a broken or fallen world.

After the talk, we set out on our Walking Meditation. We were supposed to be concentrating on our breathing, but I violated the instructions, staying in back so I could watch my students. When I wasn't teaching and only watched them, I thought of them as my flock. High up on the hill, I regarded them slowly moving through the snow-encrusted pasture. One foot in front of another, as they had been instructed, in absolute silence, with their heads bowed and their hands clasped behind their backs in imitation of the monks, they paused briefly at each step alongside the brothers and sisters, then gazed into the distant meadows and woods.

We passed the Aldrich Cemetery on a knoll at the top of the pasture where two gnarled apple trees grew up through lichen-spotted gravestones with the barely legible words: "*Died 1850.*" Under gray clouds, Brody closed his eyes. The only sounds were the wind in the trees, boots crunching the snow, a single cawing of a crow. Katelyn paused on the side of the path and simply stood, perhaps for ten minutes, looking to the southwest. She might have been approaching or creating the Pure Land—absent of self, or with the fullness of self—I couldn't know.

My students were not afraid of new experiences, though they were sometimes a little scared and sometimes their voices shook. They would attempt to play ice hockey for the first time, or ski fifteen miles, or close their eyes and feel the cold air in their throats. When I had counseled Nils to read *On the Road,* he actually did. He told me he had even awakened to read at 3:00 in the morning, "Just like the log truck drivers!" he said. In the morning at school, when he excitedly told us about where Dean Moriarty and Sal Paradise were on their pilgrimage across

America, he was dreaming himself into that time and place. And when my students heard about the poet listening to the thirty miles of dust, they wanted to talk about it, to taste it, hear it for themselves. They were, as Kerouac wrote, mad to live.

On the way home from the monastery, we drove in the winter twilight over the salted, snowy roads, past stone walls, maple trees, and farmhouses where blue smoke rose from chimneys. Along the back roads, trucks, excavators, and log skidders sat parked in front of garages or in the frozen mud at the edges of clearings. Heaps of harvested logs were stacked, waiting to be transported and split into cordwood or milled into lumber. I was thinking of that truck driver sitting high in the seat with his hand on the wheel, the Peterbilt Bodhisattva, the Llama of the Green Mountains.

I thought also of Hannah, who had recently read Billy Collins's poem "The Lanyard" in morning meeting. Her voice had been shaking as she read, because she had chosen the poem for her mother, an admission of her own gratitude, mediated through a poem about gratitude.

> *Here is a breathing body and a beating heart,*
> *strong legs, bones and teeth,*
> *and two clear eyes to read the world, she whispered,*
> *and here, I said, is the lanyard I made at camp.*

There were moments that were as silent as a lone hilltop in winter, mornings when we were awakening and really listening. Those breathing bodies and beating hearts were warm and fluttering. It was early, and the world was waiting to be read.

I asked them to each write a response about their experiences at the monastery. I was not concerned whether their writing fit a particular form. Nor was I concerned about structure, or organization, or any other measurable or quantifiable quality. I was interested in what they chose to express. I wanted to hear what they had to say, and they needed to hear what the others had experienced. Nadia wrote:

During the beginning, when were all in the big sanctuary, we were listening to the brothers and sisters explain and tell their stories. While that was going on, every so often I would look straight ahead. There was a door, and within that door's window I could see the top corner of another door of another building. And whenever I looked over at that door within a door it would be opening or closing. It was like the me behind myself, my true self, and my other self was being opened by this way of living and breathing.

Everything I could not understand before was now being given a chance to be exposed. I put my hands together in prayer, when you bring together body and mind. I loved every time I did that. It was a true feeling. It is exactly as they say it is, you bring together your two halves. It feels like all of myself is there in the present time, in the present self. It made me feel like past time and present time were all watching me and waiting patiently for me to keep going on thinking and talking like I used to.

It felt like just this one day didn't really count as living, but more like watching it all flow past. I felt like we were doing what god would do every Saturday. Like we were above the world and ourselves.

That trip made me question everything I was living and wanting. It made me rethink all that I was so sure about. I came home being clearer than I ever was before. I felt happier and more thoughtful when I got home.

Experience and life were teaching Nadia. Did there need to be a test if she figured out, on her own, what God would do every Saturday? We'd gotten to a place where she was creating her own questions and she had time to wonder about the answers. With a student like Nadia, it was not so hard.

My own great teachers, the ones that made me feel alive, they pushed me to the edge. They asked questions about who I was and who I could be, and they did so by creating the heat of discomfort and tension. They lit me up. I could either walk in the fire or run away.

In my freshman year in college, I had written a sloppy, thoughtless, and rushed analysis of Frost's "Acquainted with the Night." I had misread the entire tone and thrust of the poem, and I had done no research to give me any kind of basis of understanding. When my paper was returned, there was no grade on it—only one phrase: "See me in my office."

I made an appointment. I wasn't sure what to expect. Maybe a gentle offer of help, or some suggestions for rewriting. I half expected to be let off the hook.

I walked into Professor Cubeta's office and sat down. Passingly, I thought of Holden Caulfield going to see Mr. Spencer before he left Pencey Prep. Maybe he'd offer some wisdom and send me on my way.

There was nothing in Cubeta's office except empty shelves, two cushioned chairs, and a low coffee table in between. On the table sat one hulking book, *The Riverside Shakespeare*.

I had my paper in my hands. Professor Cubeta came in from another room and sat down. He wore pale blue slacks, a gray tweed jacket, and a thin black tie.

"So," he said. "Your paper. I think you misread the poem." He spoke quietly, his words clipped.

"I think I must have."

"You also appear to have not worked on this paper very much."

"No, I didn't. Not enough."

"Why?"

"I don't know."

"Why didn't you commit?"

"I'm not sure."

Then his voice rose. "What the hell is the matter with you?" He stared at me from behind heavy black glasses, his face now red.

I didn't answer.

"What's the matter with you? Do you not like poetry? This school? Do you not like my class? Do you not like me? What do you think this is?" Specks of spit flew from his lips as he leaned forward. "This is college. You are in a freshman poetry seminar. Are you just one of those party boys?"

I was caught, pinned, revealed. He was raging. Everything he believed was behind his words. He had known John Ciardi and Robert Frost. His life was about the poetic tradition. *Commitment*—to excellence, truth, poetry, learning, tradition— poured forth. I stood for nothing.

"I'm not sure. I do like the class. I like the school. I, uh, I didn't start my paper until too late." That truth was no more than a poor excuse. The truth was I really didn't care, not yet, and he knew it, and wasn't going to let it slide. Cubeta's method was simple: make me feel shame for not caring. I could not say he was wrong. He was kicking in a door so I could see what I was.

I left his office determined to be better. Our next paper was to explicate Donne's sonnet "Batter My Heart, Three-Personed God." I had been battered, and I knew what it felt like, so I had a way into the poem. I spent three nights in a cubicle in the study of my dorm, writing and rewriting, hacking away at the poem. I wanted to be a student, and even if I still lacked the skill and technical facility, I wanted to commit.

When the paper was handed back, I turned the pages quickly to find the grade. On the back of the fourth page, in the low corner, written lightly in pencil, was a "B+."

It wasn't so much that Cubeta believed that my life depended on understanding a seventeenth-century religious poem. Or maybe he did. He believed that there was something existing in me that I could not yet see. He took it as his job as my teacher to make me see myself, to direct me to becoming my better self.

Spring rolled around and I made an appointment to see him.

I walked into his office. On the table was *The Riverside Shakespeare*, open to *King Lear*.

"I was wondering if you would be my advisor," I said.

With his eyes squinting behind heavy black glasses, his mouth opened into a huge, laughing smile.

I hoped and trusted that my students were learning, that I was giving them something of value. But occasionally they revealed themselves in such a way as to change the terms. School was not about accruing facts or skills or virtues—school was about entering the temple of love.

Yes, at the North Branch School we talked about making love. We discussed the forms of love, how it happened or was created, what it could do, and what happened if we didn't have it, or didn't give voice to it when we felt it. We talked about the way love between two people created what the world needed most: tenderness, touch, comfort, compassion, the generations. We talked about the love of ideas, the love of learning, the place of love in a community, about how love was the force and the spark, a flowering source holding decay and annihilation at bay. We'd talked about love in terms of Ariela's mother, and Katelyn's mother, who was in prison; we talked about the love between

Boo Radley and Scout, and about Monet's love of light. We talked about Pascal's love for the mathematical order of the universe; about whether, by scientific definition, the feeling of love was a living thing, whether it had mass, whether it was constant in the universe.

It was late winter, full of bright cold days, the skies seeming to rise above the hemisphere to become an immeasurable blue. Footprints and ski tracks criss-crossed the field. We'd just finished reading *1984*. The major turning point in the book occurs when, one average day in the Ministry of Truth, Julia slips Winston a note. I said this in class, and I meant it: "This moment, when Winston opens the note and reads it for the first time—is my favorite moment in twentieth-century literature."

The note, from a woman he did not know, whom he had wanted to kill, reads: *I love you.*

Orwell writes: *At the sight of the words I love you, the desire to stay alive had welled up in him.* Against the force of a repressive, sadistic totalitarian regime, one human—risking her life—had the courage, as Shakespeare wrote, to heave her heart into her mouth.

Her action was audaciously beautiful, a brazen example of using "soul force" against physical force, as Martin Luther King counseled. For Winston and Julia, soul force was the greatest and only weapon they possessed. Her utterance, and his reciprocation, leads them to discover beauty and the Golden Country—first in Winston's paperweight containing the fragment of red coral, then to their love-making in their bower of bliss, then the liquid song of the thrush, to the beautiful voice of the washerwoman and the strength of her red arms and stout figure—all of them procreative, life-sustaining forces.

When we understood the way Julia and Winston loved each other, in their own secret cell apart from the world, we concluded that absolute power was not an abstract, commanding God; love, given freely between two humans, was the power of God.

Over the February break, Callum had an epiphany. Or perhaps, he felt a feeling and decided that the feeling only mattered if it was uttered aloud. He emailed me before we returned to school: *Tal, I left something I wrote on the big room table at school.*

I'd come into the gloomy building on Sunday night to do some work, and there I found what he'd written. On a sheet of Typar, approximately eight feet by twelve feet, draped across the big table, was Callum's "note." The sheet was white, and on it were spray-painted three-foot-tall black letters: "I love you," it read—his message to the school, and to the world.

Accompanying the note, Callum left a transcription of the passage from *1984*. At the end of the transcription, Callum wrote: *Now I know the difference between Big Brother and what Julia and Winston had in their room*, and he added words from Che Guevara, whom he had studied: *Let me say, at the risk of sounding ridiculous, that the true revolutionary is guided by a great feeling of love.*

Callum was becoming a true revolutionary. He had guided himself to make a gift, a bald, straightforward three-word statement that said everything.

On Monday morning he saw me in the entrance of school and asked if I had seen the note.

"Seen the note?" I said. "How could I miss it? The thing's as big as a mainsail!"

He was hyper with excitement. "I was thinking last night," he said. "I see how Che relates to Rumi. I see how Jack Kerouac relates to Whitman!" He drew diagrams on the board.

Other kids arrived and saw the note lying across the table. "Who made this?" they asked. "That's awesome. We have to hang it up."

At lunch, Callum and some others walked across the snowy field and suspended the banner high up between two trees. The first burst of wind ripped it straight down. The boys ran into the school to fetch stronger ropes, nails, and strapping for support, and suspended it again. In a school of infinite possibility, even in great winds, love would not be torn away.

For a few days, the note faced the field, the driveway, the school, and the world—a huge sheet of tattered notepaper. It was in blatant violation of the Vermont billboard law, legible from a quarter mile away. Reading it from the road made me smile.

At the end of the week we had a whole-class discussion about the meaning of the sign. Wasn't this what would defeat an un-feeling, unsentimental world that disregarded beauty? Wasn't this putting sentiment into action? The sign, we agreed, was like the red coral, reminding us what we should never forget. There were beautiful things worthy of our love, and our obligation was to seek, notice, make a stand, and call out.

When I first saw the note during the vacation, I had written Callum back. I told him what Van Gogh said: "The best way to know God is to love many things." I wanted for him to believe that loving many things was the right way to live, that we held and preserved the world by loving every earthly particle. We loved icicles and stone walls and the smell of the wet earth in spring. We loved the grass and red coral and the growing crystals we made in Petri dishes. We loved the worn brown spot on the stair railing where we rubbed our hands, the freedom of putting our feet up and reading our books, the sound of bells and the wind blowing across the field. We loved solitude and work and the sound of children playing, and we loved our parents. We loved each other, and always, this love might lead us to still more we could love.

Our reading of *1984*, and Callum's, said love would prevail. Nihilism could not exist, not forever, or not for long. The death count might get higher, but the students had something to give back, something beautiful and their own, given freely, speaking back to the darkness. Their answer was written in the trees and in the wind. It said: *I want to live, and I want to make the world live.*

Callum had spoken loudly, wildly, and freely. But for our class, as for all adolescents, the desire for true expression could outstrip their ability to achieve it.

"We're able to have meaningful conversations in class," I said, "but what happens outside of class? When you're in social situations? Is it just a lot of put downs and superficial chatting? Is there emotional meaning in your interactions? Are you able to say and hear real things or are you living your lives on the surface?"

There was a long pause. The more important the subject, sometimes the more tentatively they moved towards it. I reached for some way to make it clear.

"Rumi said that we live separated from the most intense truths about living by only the thinnest veil," I continued. "He said the veil can easily be lifted, but no one can lift the veil but ourselves."

There was a pause, and then Henry raised his hand.

"Sometimes it seems a lot of the time we're joking around teasing each other," Henry began. "But then it gets tiring."

"Like no one says anything real," Nils added. "I know I spent my whole lunch yesterday in the shop telling 'that's what she said' jokes."

Nils seemed to have arrived at an essential truth: precious moments were passing by. Something golden, something divine, was right before him: he could turn away or he could lift the veil.

Yeb raised his hand. "Sometimes I come into the room wishing there was a more philosophical discussion going on. Or people are arguing about poetic junk or something. I know I should start one, but I'm not sure if anyone wants to have one. A real conversation, I mean. Then I try to make jokes, but it doesn't feel good."

At the heart of it, Yeb was saying he felt alone and afraid of being alone. "Real conversations" meant belonging to others in a more authentic way.

"We have to be the ones to start those conversations," said Ruby. "No one is going to do it for us. That's what's hard about being a ninth grader. We can't rely on the older people to do the right things or do the work of talking."

Yebsera looked up at me. His voice was shaking, and he was almost crying. We had not gotten to what he wanted to say.

"I think I am not using my power," he said.

A few days later in morning meeting, I asked: "Does anyone have anything?" There were many of the usual comments: a glowing sunset seen the night before; going for a long walk with mom for the first time all winter; nuzzling a horse in the barn; watching a movie with a little brother, then jumping on his new bed.

Yebsera raised his hand discreetly, brushing it over his head, his fingers loosely waving.

"Yeb?" I called to him.

"Oh . . . me? I wasn't raising my hand. I was, um, just stretching."

"Just stretching? Come on, Yeb, what is it?"

"No, really. I was just stretching."

"Stretching? *Really?* Okay, Yebsera, whatever you say."

Later that day, he stopped across the table from me. "So, uh, I was going to read a poem, but I know no one will understand it." He looked down at his feet.

"You think people in our class can't understand a poem? Or do you mean that you were afraid to be the one who had a real poem that you really wanted to volunteer to read?"

He suppressed a smile and persisted. "No, like people don't like poems. They don't understand them."

"Oh, really? Interesting theory, considering we read and understand poems here every day. What were you thinking about reading?"

He pulled a book from behind his back, a collection of poems by David Budbill, Zen-like meditations on age, the mountains, chopping wood, and surviving the winters of Vermont.

"Oh yeah, I see what you mean. People will definitely not be able to understand these poems," I said.

He smiled tolerantly at my sarcasm.

I flipped through the pages. "Read this one," I said. The poem compared John Coltrane to Lao Tzu and the endless search for knowledge and answers. He took the book from my hands.

"I don't know, Tal. People won't understand it."

"Hey, Hannah, you're people. Read this poem and tell me if it's cool or you don't understand it or what." I tossed the book across the table.

Hannah read the poem quickly and looked up, smiling. "That's an awesome poem. Of course I can understand it. Of course you should read it!" she exclaimed, and she walked out of the room.

Again Yebsera smiled, shaking his head, holding his hands up as if to push back, muttering a series of artful and creative *buts*.

The Budbill book lay around the school for a week. I would see it in the entryway on the bench, on the floor, on the middle of the big table. The book, in its passive but persistent presence, was waiting for something to happen, waiting to be awakened. We were waiting for something to happen.

At the end of the week, I called out in morning meeting: "Anything else?"

I saw that hand discretely rise up again, grazing the top of Yebsera's head, the fingers loosely waving. He was standing in the doorway, neither in nor out of the room, but at the threshold.

"Um, I have a poem," he said.

"That's great, Yebsera."

He pulled out a folded sheet of paper.

"So, I was looking for a poem for like forty-five minutes last night. I wanted to find a poem about wanting to learn." The room was still. He looked down at his paper.

"Forty-five minutes you looked for a poem? About wanting to learn? You searched for a poem for forty-five minutes?" I asked.

"But I couldn't find anything," he mumbled. "So I picked out this poem by Mary Oliver."

"Did you find a poem about wanting to learn?"

"No," he said, "just this poem." He unfolded the paper and began, his voice shaking.

> *When death comes*
> *like the hungry bear in autumn;*
> *when death comes and takes all the bright coins from his purse*
>
> *to buy me, and snaps the purse shut;*
> *when death comes*
> *like the measle-pox*
>
> *when death comes*
> *like an iceberg between the shoulder blades,*
>
> *I want to step through the door full of curiosity, wondering:*
> *what is it going to be like, that cottage of darkness?*
>
> *And therefore I look upon everything*
> *as a brotherhood and a sisterhood,*
> *and I look upon time as no more than an idea,*
> *and I consider eternity as another possibility,*
>
> *and I think of each life as a flower, as common*
> *as a field daisy, and as singular,*
>
> *and each name a comfortable music in the mouth,*
> *tending, as all music does, toward silence,*

and each body a lion of courage, and something
precious to the earth.

When it's over, I want to say all my life
I was a bride married to amazement.
I was the bridegroom, taking the world into my arms.

When it's over, I don't want to wonder
if I have made of my life something particular, and real.

I don't want to find myself sighing and frightened,
or full of argument.

I don't want to end up simply having visited this world.

The words were not his, yet they were. The room was his. He possessed it; he filled it with himself. Death had come to him, we knew, and he had to figure out how strong death would be in life. He'd found a poem to say everything he needed to feel and know. *I don't want to find myself sighing and frightened, / or full of argument. / I don't want to end up simply having visited this world.*

As the class clapped, he looked up. Assent, pure assent was filling the room. When the clapping died down, there was a long silence.

"What do you guys think that poem was about?" I asked. "Was it about learning?"

"Yes!" came a cry from the class. I smiled at Yebsera and he shook his head.

"Oh my god, that's *all* it was about," said Katelyn.

"It was about learning to understand death," Henry said.

"It was about how to live beyond death," said Nadia.

"About death, questioning it. If it is powerful or not," said Haley. And though she did not mention him, I could feel her father—with his fighting, fading heart—in the room with us.

"It was all about you," said Nils, nodding to Yebsera, who still stood in the doorway. "It seemed like the poem was about you trying to do what the poem is talking about. Learning about what to do when death comes."

"It was about what's still alive when something great dies," said Nadia. "His mother died, and he has to live. It's saying that we shouldn't be here just visiting, but doing something great."

"What you gave us, Yeb," I said, "was your attempt, your *search*. Searching for a beautiful poem about wanting to learn *is* learning. You're being like that questioning poet, facing death like that lion. Your body is a lion of courage, and something precious to the earth."

"Yeb," said Nadia. She composed herself slowly, pausing, seeing each word in her mind before she spoke it. "We all come to love each other when we're here at this school, or I think that's what happens. But when I heard that, it made me *know* that I love you. Because you're a good person and you deserve love."

Yebsera had put his voice and his heart into the classroom. His classmates received it, and a new conversation was created. Poetry made something happen, at our school at least.

I don't want to argue with the world. / I want to be a bride married to amazement, Yebsera had read. I never wanted my students to argue or put up fences or defenses; I wanted them to leave dizzy and exhausted with the belief that there was more to get to than time would ever allow. I wanted them to be blown through with winds of feeling that said, *I lived in this world.*

Adolescents, my students, clamored for a class that was safe. And by this I do not mean a place devoid of bullying, but a place where students could be openhearted and emotionally vulnerable. My students, by turns unruly, jaded, disorganized, superficial, distractible—wanted to open up. When we heard their stories and poems and revelations in class, this became manifestly, undeniably evident.

Brody did not say a lot in class, but his writing was lyrically tender and true. When I read his stories, he became big; he filled the room, carried us through time, and we could grow with him.

As a child, he wrote, he had clung to his mother's leg when she left him at preschool. When he was eleven, he didn't need his mother. When he was thirteen, he needed her again, and he saw all that she did for him, and he understood something about her love for him, and his love for her. He'd learned something new about the constancy and depths of love.

"After hearing Brody's story, what do you know to be true? What's he given to you? Write it, and that will give you time to say something back."

I waited for the frantic scribbling to subside.

"Today," I said, "I don't want you to be shallow fishermen. I want you to be like the old man, Santiago. We want to go deep, into the sea. We want our lines to be deep, if you know what I mean."

And they did. Or they learned to. In these moments, my students—braces and acne and shaggy hair and awkward bodies and all—showed the selves waiting beneath the surface.

"That story is so beautiful," said Nadia, as she looked down at her paper. Her cheeks were bright and flushed as through she'd been running in the cold. On the top of the sheet was a flower she'd been drawing with a black pen. She fingered a corner of her paper. "His story makes me remember the thing I've been thinking about: how everyone grows up, and we just need to decide how, and it's up to us to figure it out."

From across the table, Haley raised her hand. She pushed her long brown hair behind her ears.

"I know there are things to know and things to learn," she read. "Everything in his story had order. I mean his feelings had order. All his feelings were in there, good feelings and bad feelings. But that's what made the story real."

Nolan raised his hand. "I know we often say the opposite of what we mean, and I know I want to live fully and not avoid the truth."

In return for what they'd heard, they were reflective, tentative, tender, careful. Brody's story demanded that they give something commensurate back.

I stood up to go to the bathroom. The conversation continued. When I returned, I stood in the open doorway, leaning against the frame. Hands floated up, and Callum, who was sitting in my chair, called on Yebsera. I was no longer necessary. The conversation has a life of its own. They were the caretakers of each other and the school; they were responsible for the life around the table. When the life around the table was *them*, there was little need for rules and restrictions. Liberation, possibility, and awareness of each other was the air they breathed.

Jasper wandered in, sniffing the floor for lunch crumbs, weaving among the children crowded around the table, stepping over legs and backpacks. Callum reached back to pet him as he passed. Jasper settled to the floor with a rubber chew toy between his paws, sighed audibly, and closed his eyes.

A few days later we're back in the usual routine. In math, the ninth graders were making architectural designs for cathedrals using geometric constructions. Rose and her class marked out a labyrinth behind the school by tramping in the snow. The design was based on the labyrinth at Chartres Cathedral. At the center of ours was a medium-sized maple tree—"An adolescent maple tree," Haley said.

"We should put poems in a jar and bury them under the tree!" she announced.

"That's a great idea, Haley," I said. "We'll put that on the agenda. When the ground thaws."

The next day I looked out the window to see her and Brody crawling on their hands and knees in the compacted snow.

"What in the sam hell were you doing out there?" I asked them when they burst back into the room.

"We were being like devoted religious people!" Brody said. "We were being all holy and stuff!"

"It was our grueling pilgrimage," Haley said.

In science, the seventh graders were making crystals from a concoction of sugar, food coloring, and vinegar, with strings soaking in the mixture. The eighth graders were outside, in snow boots and wool hats, with microscopes set up on a folding table, turning focus knobs with mittened hands, examining flakes of snow.

We heard the door open. There was Ariela's aunt, Maria, in her navy pea coat. Eric went to greet her.

Eric went to find Ariela. The kids from outside came in and stood silently in the open door. Snowflakes were on their shoulders.

Ariela walked into the entry. Maria spoke to her and wrapped her in her arms. Ariela picked up her backpack and walked out the door with her head bowed.

We gathered the kids in the big room. No one spoke. Some of the kids began to cry.

"Ana died this morning," Eric said. We sat silently in the room for a few minutes.

"Everybody is free to go and sit wherever they want to go," I said. "Sit for as long as you like. Write whatever feelings you want. We'll come back together in forty-five minutes."

They dispersed to hunch in corners or sit in the window sills, staring out at the tired snow in the field. Haley pulled a chair into the entryway, staring out the window at the driveway where it circled a clump of trees. Nolan sat at the big table, his jaw clenched, digging his pencil into a drawing pad. Some wrote furiously, some wrote letters, some wrote nothing at all. Nadia drew designs in pen in the margins of blank sheets of lined paper. What was there to say, really? In our school, Ariela was their sister. They knew Ariela's mother. Winn had been in the carpool not two weeks before when Ana had suddenly pulled over to vomit on the roadside. Nadia had seen her in the Co-op three days before, smiling, with her bright red scarf wrapped around her neck, her bald head proudly exposed.

Two hours later, just before lunch, the front door opened wide. There was Ariela with Maria.

"She said she wanted to be here at school for the rest of the day," Maria said. "This is where she wanted to be."

❦

The whole school attended Ana's funeral service. We sat together in Mead Chapel at Middlebury College listening to the service, much of it in Spanish.

Inescapably, all of this became part of what they learned, all of it a dimension beyond curriculum. Ariela's mother's death made them feel greater love for each other. They reflected on their own parents. In the morning, Bennett told the class he was realizing how much his mother did for him, driving him all over the state for basketball games. Haley added that she had gone for a run on a snowy morning with her mother.

"I realized how strong she is, and I know I get a lot of my strength from her."

"I sat with my mom and dad last night after I did my homework," said Nils. "And then we played cards, and that's something that I love to do with my family."

But for Ariela, what could we do? She came to school and received love from her friends and teachers. She kept up, barely, with her algebra assignments. She had a science project to do on snow compaction, but how, really, could snow compaction ever be important? I asked her to keep a journal in which she could record her feelings. She walked from class to class and room to room with friends on either side. The school was filled with her being held by her peers.

It became evident that our students knew exactly what to do. What they wanted most was to be themselves, which was to be loving and supportive. I held in our minds the quote by Mother Teresa that hung in the school basement: "We belong to each other." I knew the kids were endeavoring to hold Ariela. When they did, they became more, saw more, felt more.

I had once read a short essay, "Joyas Voladorus," by Brian Doyle. The title means "flying jewel," which is what the first European explorers called hummingbirds when they first saw hummingbirds in the Americas. The essay was about the heart—the heart of the hummingbird, the heart of the blue whale, and the human heart. Among the details, the humming-bird's heart, he wrote, beats ten times per second.

This was woven into the fabric of our days. The heart was a flying jewel, but it was also only a muscle, sometimes fiercely strong, sometimes under fierce assault, sometimes only a strug-gling mass of nerves, tissue, and valves. Our hearts were capable of becoming large, as large as Callum's, who left a love note as big as a truck on our table for us. When we walked in the great chambers of the heart, everything became clear because we beheld what was most dear.

In the presence of sadness and grief, my students became more aware, more conscious, more powerful in their ability to care about what happened to Ariela. Like Orwell's Winston, they cared about the small bits of life around them—a flower of coral, a fragrant memory, a mother's smile, her bright red scarf, the way she danced. They remembered these little fragments, and they lamented. Yes, the death of Ariela's mother brought us closer to each other, just as learning about Yebsera's mother had made them think about what mattered in the world. Knowing about the heart of Haley's father made them think about the power of any heart, and how it was, truly, a jewel. We learned of the richness that inhered to other lives, not just our own. All of us were moved by the sound of bells ringing in another's ears. One person's heart opened to us, and human majesty was revealed.

In class one afternoon, I asked Ariela how she was feeling. She shrugged her shoulders.

"Sometimes it's not terrible. I have nightmares. I guess they're called grief dreams. My thoughts are wild. I can't really control them."

"Let them go, let them do what they do," I said. "Your mind at night is a free thing. There's no road map or a way to go that is the *right* way. Just let what it is speak in you." These feeble words were all I had.

"Okay." She pursed her lips, her shoulders hunched in. She wore a large, puffy down jacket and had it pulled tight around her body.

"Let me just tell you one thing I know. Maybe it will help, maybe not. When you're alive, your heart and mind are always growing. The heart is a chamber, and it is either open or closed. When it's open, it's capable of adding rooms. It only gets bigger; it expands infinitely. If it loves, it can love more. If it loved before, it will love again. Don't let it close down."

She nodded as she looked at me.

"You'll feel love again. You'll feel her presence again. Right now you feel gutted and empty. But you're also filled with the love your mama gave you. She was beautiful and loving, and you have that beautiful love inside. Your work is to let what she gave you grow. You have two lives in you—hers and yours. In time, you'll feel that love and beauty coming through you into the world. Her life will live in your life. And then maybe you won't feel so much pain."

She sat straight upright at the table. On each side of her face a single tear tracked a clean line down her cheeks.

Some of the kids wrote her letters. The envelopes were decorated with ornate, colorful designs and carefully scripted. They left them in her cubby, little offerings for her to find. Every morning in meeting someone talked about a parent or sibling. For Ariela, they made drawings and cupcakes. They sent emails, they asked questions. Some of them rewrote their "What I have learned" poems. We could have prepared for a State-mandated test. We could have attended to the Core Standards. But we were about some other business.

One morning, Nadia raised her hand.

"I was thinking about Ariela last night. And then I thought, *All I want to do is hug my mom and dad.* And so I went into the living room where my mom was reading and drinking a glass of wine. And I just went up to her and said, 'Can I have a hug?' And then I hugged her. And that felt good."

That morning Ruby read a poem for Ariela: "Child," by Sylvia Plath. *Your clear eye is the one absolutely beautiful thing. / I want to fill it with color and ducks, / The zoo of the new.* Ruby, whose brother died before she was born, gave Ariela all the beauty that still remained in the world. It was good to have these words. They were not as powerful as life, they could not undo death, but they were something to hold.

There were days when the darkness was bigger than life, when darkness overwhelmed, even as sunlight filtered in through the high window.

"Does anyone have anything?" I began one morning.

Haley raised her hand, but spoke as she stared at the table. "I'm thinking about death all the time. I can't even say the word out loud. Sometimes I feel myself going away. Even though I love everybody in here."

No one said a word. I looked at Haley and thought about everything I might say. Sometimes I wished the kids would answer first. Sometimes I had to answer.

"It's like you're constantly living two lives," I said. "The life of your father, and your own."

I cast my gaze around the table, waiting. Huge spaces lay between what she had said and what might come.

"Sometimes I'm so wrapped up in my thoughts that I barely feel like I'm here," she said.

"You are here," said Katelyn, and she looked across the table at Haley.

"And we're here, and we aren't going anywhere," said Nolan.

"You're completely here," I added. "In the play. Your project was amazing. You're an incredible writer. When you sing at the piano, it's beautiful."

"I love looking at your hands going over the keys," said Nadia. "I was watching them the other day."

"Everyone here sees you," I said.

"But sometimes I feel like my body has left the room."

"I understand that feeling," said Ariela.

"Your life doesn't stop when you come into school," I said. "You're living your life, and when you come to school you don't stop being the person you are and feeling the things that happen in your life. You keep living here. So let your mind and heart do what they need to do."

"But like sometimes in science I don't feel what we're doing. There's no feeling about it."

"Haley, in science you're trying to understand the word *subnivean*. Of course you check out. But you're still in it. We feel you here. It's okay if you don't feel winter science terms in the same way you feel and think about your dad."

"I'm just worried that I'm missing things. Like when I have to go down to Boston. Or when I space out and don't have fun like everyone else."

"If you drift away, or you have to leave school to go to Boston, or if you're deep in your feelings, we're all still here," I said. "What we're doing is important, but not as important as what you have to do."

Haley sat very still, her face smooth and white, her ears barely protruding through her brown hair. She nodded, her hands in her lap.

The seventh graders were reading *Fahrenheit 451*. In the middle of the book, we had to take a detour into Matthew Arnold's "Dover Beach," the poem Montag reads to Millie and her friends in the "parlor." Arnold's poem was an anguished reckoning with what happens when all the things once believed falter or wash out beneath us. How will man respond to the force of time and tragedy and disillusionment? If the cliffs of Dover disintegrated, if the cities and books burned to ash, if God had left us—what could we hold onto to give us faith? It was a question for Ariela, and for all of us. How could we get on? How could we live in the valley of the shadow of death? Arnold gave us the desperately beautiful words: "Ah, love, let us be true to one another!" It was as though he were crying out to the last humans on earth.

Meanwhile, the eighth and ninth graders were reading *The Lord of the Flies*. We discovered that the boys on the island did not know how to be true to themselves with one another. They could not express tender feelings or their deepest fears, and these unacknowledged truths led them to sever the connections between them that could have saved them. My students felt immense tenderness for Piggy, who stood as an analogue to the parts of themselves that had been wounded or mocked.

"He tried to tell them the truth," Henry spit, red-faced and enraged. "He's the only one who could see. They blinded him, and he still stood in front of them all alone and he told them the freaking truth and they killed him! Why? How could they do that?"

Henry spoke as though Piggy were his best friend, his one true companion. To feel a book in this way, to apprehend empathically, was a rare and most soulful expression of intelligence. His fierce and personal identification with Piggy made the classroom come alive.

They admired and pulled for Ralph, who stood for their own efforts to inject order, civility, and clarity of thought into the classroom. And they loved Simon, the embryonic shaman, a Christ figure who was driven to walk into the darkness of the jungle. They desired his courage, the way he found his own inner sanctum in a clearing "lit" with the redolent perfume of white candle-flowers. They admired his determination to climb the mountain and face the beast. They empathized with the Littluns, who cried openly and freely, because the Littluns had not developed mechanisms to hide or suppress their tears. They despised the cruelty of Roger and Jack because they could see such cruelty in the world, even sometimes emanating from themselves.

"We also wear masks and do cruel things to each other," said Nolan.

"What do you think, Bennett?" I asked.

"I feel like they should be loving the Littluns. Somebody needs to love them, but no one does. Nobody seems to understand what they need, and they just ignore them. That's cruelty, I guess."

"That's worse than cruelty," said Nolan.

"Something is hurting in Jack, too," said Ruby. "He's only a little kid like all the rest; I mean, it says that Roger was wiggling his loose tooth. Jack wants to be a part of something. He wants to be a leader. He wants somebody to love him. He's just as afraid, but he doesn't know how to face being afraid except by hurting things. When the boys reject him, he said, 'Then I won't play with you,' and runs into the woods crying, because he's a small child. He's just like the Littluns but he hides it better."

"Aren't we all small children?" I asked. "Even adults. Adults are children too, just more practiced at hiding it. They have more layers, more violent or crafty defenses. These kids are learning to wear the mask, avoid their feelings, hiding, or blaming. The Littluns can't hide it."

"But they're going to learn to," said Nils, "or they won't survive."

Suppression of feeling is what most conventional classrooms required, manifested by the unceasing demand by teachers for students—who are trying to engage with books and themselves—to remove the personal pronoun "I" when writing. Such an approach leads to emotionally barren classrooms. If we asked them to remove themselves, then what were we teaching? How could we expect them to have an intimate connection with texts if we asked them to take themselves out of the interaction? Conversely, when they were touched or enraged by what they read, when they felt the books on a visceral level, the book had penetrated them. Simultaneously, they were entering the heart of the artist's creation.

Nolan wrote in one of his responses for class: *The only real beast—the only thing to be afraid of—is not being afraid. Because then they are all afraid of being afraid, and they turn into cruel, vicious savages who hurt each other for fun and start big fires that burn down the mountain. They don't or can't or won't do or see the important things, like building good shelters or keeping the fire going, because they are afraid to admit that they are afraid and want to go home. Someone needs to say, "I want to go home. I miss my mother. I want my father to come home from war."*

Facing themselves with honesty was one of the most difficult and important things adolescents could learn to do. It happened in a conference a few days later: Nolan had said in morning meeting that he'd had a good walk with his dad the evening before.

"It was nice," he said. "I hadn't walked with my dad for a long time." He'd said no more and we all scurried off to class. But as I thought about it over the rest of the morning, I felt we'd bypassed something important. Nolan's words scratched at a surface, but the intensity of feeling was missing.

Later in the afternoon I asked the class what kept us going. "What makes life worth living? What makes us feel most like we're living in a good world—as opposed to living on the island or in Montag's city?"

Bennett said, "When I'm skiing with my dad, I will sometimes stand at the top of the mountain and watch him go down."

Again, as always, tears began to fall down Bennett's face. He was a ninth grader, he was big and strong, loud and boisterous, happiest crashing down a mountainside on a bike or skis or whipping a lacrosse ball towards a goal—but he never hid his feelings, which made everyone love him deeply.

"I'll see him skiing away from me and going down, getting smaller, and I'll feel so happy, or lucky, or something." His words became hard to hear, but he was smiling, talking, and crying all at the same time. Yeb got up and returned with a roll of toilet paper and handed it to him.

"Do you know why you're crying?" I asked.

"I'm not sure," he said.

"How did you feel being with him?"

"I loved it. I love going skiing with him."

"You love being with him! It sounds like him skiing away hinted at another feeling in you. Or the same feeling, felt differently. Close your eyes."

With eyes open they could be relentlessly mind-centered and rational, distractible and evasively logical to the point of abject stupidity. So I told him to put his head down, close his eyes, and stop *thinking*, especially because he didn't know how he felt. With eyes shut, he went deeper—to confusion, or hurt, or love—to the heart of the matter which, always, was the heart of himself, and far more interesting and useful than reason, facts, or rationalization. With eyes closed, my students were more likely to cry. Those tears were prisms of light. Through them they saw wonderful things.

He nodded and closed his eyes, with his chin lowered to his chest.

"Sit with that feeling for a while and you'll know what it means and how full it is."

We waited. The room was silent and they looked at Bennett. Then he spoke without opening his eyes.

"When he's skiing down the hill and getting smaller, I mean, farther away and smaller, it's like he is getting old, or dying. Going away from me. But I feel happy because I am also with him."

He nodded and wiped his cheek.

"What about you guys? Look how fast those tears, and that love, came out. Those tears come from the well of love."

I thought about Nolan's comment from earlier that morning.

"Nolan, what about you?"

"I want to talk. I want to have feelings, like Bennett. He showed feelings," he said, nodding towards Bennett.

"What do you feel?" I asked.

"I feel—I don't know. I want to feel something. But I can't." He was on edge, verging on anger, grasping for expression.

"What about this morning? Was there a feeling behind what you said about your dad and going for a walk with him? Was there something in that? You said the facts. You said it was 'nice.' Can you give us the feeling?"

Something released in him and words began to pour out, mixed with flowing tears.

"I don't know. My dad, I mean, he tries to help me with my work and he wants me to do well but I get angry at him and sometimes we argue and then I think he's just an ass, but walking with him felt so good. We talked, you know. I know he loves me and he's a good dad and I felt bad for thinking he wasn't and being pissed at him all the time. I just miss him."

He paused for a moment. "God, I haven't cried in forever," he said, smiling through his tears.

"Nolan, you should cry more. It freed up a smile in you. Maybe you should tell him 'Thanks for the walk, dad.'"

"I did, I told him this morning." At this he smiled again.

"That's great, that's important. That's beautiful."

A class in which tears flowed was a place where feelings flowed, and more important, where children felt closer to themselves. Once, a Peruvian shaman had visited our nearby town of Lincoln, Vermont. When he saw Mount Abraham, our highest local mountain, standing bluish and purple in the distant haze, he gazed at it for a long time. Then he said: "There is a crystal palace inside that mountain."

From time to time my students realized that the same was true of themselves, that inside each of them were crystalline structures, histories of need and feeling, emptiness and fullness. When they understood this, they could see more clearly the beauty and complexity in history, in poems, in science, in the relations of numbers, in the complexity of the world. They could feel it when looking at Michelangelo's *David*, or in the sad life of Mrs. Phelps, or the inchoate cries of Percival Wymys Madison, or even in Jack, the rebel angel. Then maybe they could begin to respond to Arnold's plea: *Ah, love, let us be true to one another.*

I decided we would read Cormac McCarthy's *The Road.* I had described some of it to the class as I had been reading it, and they were interested. Some parents objected. *I've heard it's very heavy, depressing, they said in emails. I'm afraid it will be too much,* they said. There was desolation in the book, yes. But it was not only about death or an apocalypse: it was about the love between father and son, parent and child. Amid the gray ash and darkness there was the inextinguishable fire of love. I responded politely to the emails, but I did not care too much if the parents objected to cannibalism on the page. I was confident my students could understand the book's central truth: *We carry the fire.*

I told the class that, yes, despite some parental discomfort, we were going to read it. The kids were ecstatic; maybe because it was contemporary they felt it could be theirs. Or maybe the excitement of reading a marginally unacceptable book injected them with the thrill of doing something rebellious. But I was also thinking about Yebsera and Ariela and Haley.

"Ariela, do you feel like you can read it, or do you want to skip it? Either way it's fine."

"I think I need to read it," Ariela said. "I know it will make me think about my mama. But maybe that's okay. I'm thinking about her all the time anyway."

"Yebsera? You can skip it if you want. It might be too close."

"I don't know."

"It's harrowing. It's hardcore. It's about a dad who is dying and his child. You don't have to read it."

"I want to read it."

I wanted school to be unforgettable. And heaviness was more interesting than lightness. School should not skim over their hearts; I wanted them to feel it, to feel everything. I did not want them to read *Winesburg, Ohio*, go through the motions, and come away empty-handed.

"Okay, let's go."

The Road stunned them. In class there was reverence, silence, awe. A world without goodness? A broken world in which goodness survived? The seeds of humanity being carried in a grocery cart? Class felt like a holy place.

I knew what was happening. They were seeing their own lives with greater clarity. They were thinking about Ariela, Yebsera, Haley. They were thinking of childhood, how their parents devoted their lives to keeping them alive.

When I read about the man and the boy, wrote Haley, *and how the man loves the boy, it makes me want to live like that, to be so giving and strong. It makes me think about the love my parents have for me, and what I owe them. It makes me think of my father and how much he loves me, and what he has given me. My father is as strong as the Man.*

We came to the part where the Man remembers his wife, thinking about the life that was no more. The Man rips her pictures into bits and throws his wallet into a ditch. In class that day, Yebsera was leaning in his chair against the bookshelf. He was not at the table, and he was not going to talk. There was no point in going forward with class until we got to what was happening inside of him.

"Yebsera, what's going on?"

"Nothing."

"Really?"

"Yeah, I'm just tired."

"Come on, Yebsera. You might be tired, but that's not why you look sad and mad and are sitting alone in the corner. You're part of our class, man. We want you here. So get on up here."

There was a long silence. Everyone had their book in front of them, but no one was looking at the book.

"Sometimes I think it was my fault." His voice was failing, like he didn't have enough air to push the words out.

"Yebsera, can you say that again?"

"That my mom died."

"Your fault?"

"Did you start thinking that while you read the book?"

He nodded.

"Can you tell us that story and let us find out?"

"She was sick. I remember there were lots of people around. But I didn't know how sick. I was really worried. I wanted to go in the room and see her."

"Did you?"

"No, they wouldn't let me. I don't know why. Maybe so I wouldn't be scared. So I left and I went to play soccer. I ran around playing all day. I played soccer with my friends."

"And then what?"

"That night I went to sleep in our house. My mom was in another house where they were keeping her."

We waited. There was no rush, nowhere to get to, nothing else that mattered.

"The next morning I wanted to see her. Then they told me that she had died."

Tears fell from his chin onto his T-shirt. We waited again. As always, someone pushed the tissue box towards him. Yebsera took it and held it with both hands in his lap.

"So how was it your fault?"

"Because I left her. She was sick and I didn't do anything. I went and played soccer."

"You were a child, Yebsera. Children are supposed to play. You went to do what any child in the world would do. You didn't know about death."

"I left her," he said, shaking his head. "I didn't help her."

"You were seven. It's okay."

"I should have done something." His voice was barely audible.

"You wish you had been close to her when she died? And that you hadn't been having fun far away from her?"

With his head bowed, he nodded.

"Are you worried that that means you didn't love your mother?"

He nodded again.

"Yebsera, I am going to tell you something that you can be sure of for the rest of your life: You loved your mother."

Callum sat right beside Yebsera, and he looked at Yebsera's bowed head.

"You're loving her right now," Nolan said. "You're crying because you loved her. You're crying because you wished you could have saved her."

"She gave you something," I said. "She gave you love, and you're feeling that love. Without her you wouldn't feel anything. You'd be cold and empty. But feelings of love and missing are flowing in you."

"You are definitely not cold," said Nolan.

"I think you're one of the most loving people in our school," said Nils.

"Your mother died of a disease that no one could stop, not even all the great doctors or the loving-est boy in the world."

"She *did* love me," he said after a few seconds.

"How do you know?"

"I've said it before. Because of how she walked fifteen kilometers every day to sell the baskets she made so we could have food. She would make us bread and tea in the morning. That's what she gave us."

"That's a beautiful thing and it's good to keep remembering it. You haven't forgotten it. You won't. She gave you life. She would've wanted you to be kicking a ball out there with your friends. You loved her, and you learned about love from her, and that's why you still keep a picture of her on your dresser. It's all inside you."

He was looking at the tissue box, just staring. Callum still sat by him, with his hand on his friend's shoulder.

"Yebsera, here's what I would do," I said. "I would walk fifteen miles for someone I love. You can do that. And you will do that. And when you do, you'll be loving your mother with the love she gave you."

He looked up and wiped his hands across his cheeks. He bent down and reached into his backpack and pulled out his copy of *The Road*. He opened it, and he didn't look up again.

SPRING

There is only one question:

how to love this world.

—MARY OLIVER, "The Spring"

T
HE SUN ROSE HIGHER IN THE SKY OVER THE MOUNTAINS
and blazed in through the big window. Cold hung on,
but spring was coming. Our school days were packed
with emotion and activity, as though we were some kind of
giant, shambling truck loaded with the cargo of minds and
hearts, careening downhill ever faster. Projects and presentations, the building of a solar system in science, completion of
autobiographical stories, stained glass panels to be hung in the
hallway where the early spring light shone through casting jew-
el-colored patterns on the floors. Days were still a comedy of
adolescents, difficult pedagogical conundrums, conflicts between
students, and the crazy fury of making, building, creating.

After morning meeting, everyone stampeded out of the
room for a science class outside. They were turning our one-ki-
lometer nature trail, where old snow still sat in the shadows,
into a scaled universe with displays about planets and nebulae
hanging from the limbs of trees.

I went into the office to sign a letter. There was discussion with a board member over the difficulties of converting
the anecdotal, narrative evaluations we wrote into letter grades

for the departing ninth graders. The difficulty, the injustice of it, was that we had to decontextualize and reduce each student to a most minimal form. There was no way to do this with absolute fairness to the whole child. Every child's experience was a unique, multifaceted, and expanding story, not something reducible to a letter.

Yebsera was building a model of the Milky Way, but wasn't sure how to start.

"Describe it to me," I said. We looked at a picture and came up with an idea for a model that would use a wooden disk with copper-wire arms spiraling out covered with pulled-apart cotton balls. In order to cut the wooden disk, we went to the basement to set up the jigsaw. Henry was in the basement, trying to put on a vapor mask so he could spray-paint the inside of a box to make a model of a pulsar. I instructed him on how to attach the mask to his face so he would not breathe highly volatile organic compounds, and then I helped Yebsera cut his disk.

Upstairs, Hannah and I discussed *The Road*.

"How old do you think the boy is?" I asked.

"Maybe eight? But he still plays with that little yellow truck."

"What do you think the yellow truck symbolizes?" I asked, but before she could answer, the seventh graders spilled loudly into my room for study. They wanted to talk about their weekends, but I hushed them and they settled down to work.

Katelyn sat across from me at the big table. "I'm hopeless! I am *such* a loser," she said.

"Why, Katelyn, why? Why hopeless and a loser?" I asked.

"I lost my story. The computer quit and I lost it."

"Let me see your computer." We did an Auto-Recovery Save and found "Document 2" in its whole form.

"Thanks, Tal."

Bennett walked in, suddenly appearing to have grown an alarmingly large bosom. He was working on his "Dark Matter" science project, and he'd placed two full balloons inside his sweatshirt, giving him a distinctive feminine form.

"Bennett, what in the sam hell are you doing?" I asked.

"I just finished my math homework and I'm thinking about what to do next." He sounded pleased with himself, in no hurry at all.

"Maybe you should read your lit?"

"Well, perhaps, but at this moment I'm adjusting my assets," he said with a grin.

For the rest of study we examined the constellations in the Zodiac and tried to decide whether only twelve signs of the zodiac could accurately describe each of us, *all* the humans in the world. This segued into a discussion of Sesame Street. As they left the room, Bennett and Callum shouted, "We are all unique!"

Ruby entered the room at lunch. She dropped her belongings on the table. Computer, binder, math book, pencil pouch all thundered. Her hair was in a sloppy bun.

"What's the matter, Ruby?"

"My schedule! I'm a disaster. I have skating. My coach said if I want to make the next level I need to be skating *five* days per week. I don't like the girls. They're mean. I want to play hockey also. But I can't do it all."

She began to cry.

"Okay, slow down, take it easy," I said. "Let's make a schedule for just this week. A little at a time."

"Oh, oh, I can help make a schedule! I'll do it!" Winn shouted, and she began marking out the days on a grid and writing out responsibilities and after-school activities. Ruby wiped her tears away and they bent their heads to the sheet of paper before them, making a schedule that granted time for sleep, homework, chores, dinner, and skating practice.

"But that's not everything," she said.

"What else?" I asked.

"My story. About my mom. How can I write a story about a person I never see and who never sees me? Plus I'm pissed at her. She does not give *one* shit about my life."

"Well, you definitely don't want to write a story that's just a long rant and big F-you to someone who will never read it. It's got to do more."

"What do you mean?"

"I mean, are you writing your story to tell her something, or are you writing it to tell yourself something?"

"I don't know."

"Maybe you should write your story as a note to her," I suggested.

"What do you mean?"

"I don't know. A note to her about your life. What's happening to you. A story of how you became yourself. Who you are, as you know yourself. Something like that."

"Okay," she said. "I'll try."

Hannah was studying Taoism. One morning, instead of a poem, she read from the *Tao Te Ching*. The last line rang through the room: *How do I know the world? By what is within me.* I tried to keep the thought in my head all morning as the day's activity pulsed in the school.

Yebsera burst in: "Tal, I have an extra study period. You want to help me on my Milky Way some more?"

Later at break, Nils asked, "Tal, do you want me to set up the lights in the basement now, or wait until we get in the real theater?"

"Set them up. All we need is a couple of chicken heat lamps. And make it so we don't trip over all the damn cords."

After lunch we moved down to the basement for play practice. It was mind-bendingly difficult—a class of students creating something that accurately reflected important and personal truths while maintaining a general state of collaborative joy and assent. Our first intention was to achieve insight into ourselves, *for* ourselves—insight about our ways of working, who we were and who we were becoming. The second intention was to make something entertaining.

The dark was filled with the glow of laptop screens, the sound of stools scraping the floor, bodies shuffling around, voices shouting, "Where are the props?" Where's my microphone?" Henry was playing acoustic guitar: "Love is What I Got," by Sublime, our between-scene music. I typed changes in the script as the scenes were run, thinking about how we could weave at least one strain of true love into the script they had written.

When we left play practice, we went straight into our class on *The Road*.

"He reminds me of the man in *The Old Man and the Sea*," said Nils.

"Is he an old, dead turtle, or is he a turtle whose heart is still beating?" I asked.

"He's dying."

"What's keeping him alive?"

"He's driven by his love."

"How would you describe that love?"

"It's what he says: 'We carry the fire,'" offered Nadia. "They have nothing, but they have everything on the inside. The Man is exactly like the Old Man."

"It's like, the Man in *The Road* is the child of the Old Man," said Bennett.

The questions rolled out, they theorized, they drew connections between themselves and the book. They sought to articulate the source of the love between the Man and the Boy. What kept the embers alight as the Man dragged his carcass through the heart of the ashen world?

That afternoon after school, I thought about the big questions. What did the Old Man give *us*? And why should I have them read this book, or any book, or write and tell stories? In Hemingway's story, the boy and the Old Man made fictions between themselves, about coffee and cast nets and the great

Dimaggio—beautiful fictions that gave shimmering nobility to a hard life. It was all they had, and it was *all*. Making stories, or shaping stories out of life as it was lived, that was a way to survive, to live and love the world. But fictions were not truth. Truth was rare and beautiful, as beautiful as the love between the Boy and the Man in *The Road*, as rare as a great fish from the depths, so great that when it rose from the sea it was unending, and never to be forgotten. This was the heart of teaching: to make the learning so alive, so deeply felt, that it would be rising in their hearts and minds forever.

Another morning: turning on the lights, placing the trash cans in most useful places, cleaning papers off the big table. Then an early morning parent conference. *Is what is happening the right thing to be happening for my child?* As we talked, I thought how my students moved with their own particular, strange velocities, which brought them from the child's land into the adult world. We could guide and protect them from catastrophe, and help them land in a good place, but the force within them preceded and was greater than me or the school.

Brody and Nils were the "head technicians" for the play. They took great pride in setting up the lights, running the cables, placing tape marks on the floor, and setting the props. They had also made a bit of a clubhouse in a basement storage room, which they worked on assiduously during lunches. There they kept Sharpies, duct tape, wire, scissors, box cutters, extra scripts, hair ties for the girls, flashlights, and extra surge protectors so they could plug in their laptops during rehearsal. They rolled in a derelict office chair as well to create a kind of "tech headquarters." We called it the Rat's Nest, and they loved the honorific title.

I granted them the freedom to do this, knowing that the

building of such nests or "bases of operations" within the school was reflective of the larger need to have a sanctuary. It was no different than Winn's room in the broom closet. They were making homes within the home, knowing, or intuitively feeling, that the home of the school would accept and absorb another defined place within it.

One year, two students created a "Music Library" in the basement, where they displayed as many CDs as they could get their hands on, loaning them out according to a strict set of rules that they administered. This was utopian energy fostering a community of music lovers. It was adolescents at work and play. There *was* a kind of work going on, with creative impulses clicking and flowing. These students, like grown-up kindergartners, created micro-environments within the larger one. These kinds of constructions, which were dynamic social extensions of their inner emotional and social lives, were a necessary part of their growth.

The emotional architecture of my students' lives came through most assuredly and thrillingly when they found their way, through hard work and writing hundreds of pages, to their own truths. I had sent Ruby away to write about her mother she no longer heard from. She returned with a story, written in the form of a letter to her mother.

> *I want to be great, I want to have and give moments, give myself, and take in and learn everything that I can. This is what I have taught myself, mom, this is the person I have become.*
>
> *I think about life in this way with the utmost humbleness. I am simply a person passing through this crazy, tragic, beautiful, wonderful, terrible world. I am so fortunate to be*

able to behold this beautiful place, with incredible, complex, twisted, contradictory, strong human beings everywhere in my life, and I get to learn, just learn, about everything under the sun for the rest of my life. I am a Beholder of everything in this world, of all the knowledge and wisdom and all the incredible things that have been created, all the things that we can use, that we can then take for ourselves and learn truly, for ourselves! For the betterment of our own lives! We can improve! We can grow! We can change! We can be stronger!

And so, mom, I am so happy to be on this earth, to be a part of this immense and extravagant thing. I am truly blessed.

I am blessed to be able to truly touch others in their lives, and in return be touched, and mommy, even though you let that go with me, I will never let that go. I just thought you should know.

Most Sincerely, Your Daughter, Ruby

When I finished reading, we sat mesmerized. She had let us into her most complex and private realm, proffering enlightenment that could serve a lifetime.

The following morning, Brody read from Gandhi: "Love is the subtlest force in the world. We notice the love between father and son, between brother and sister, friend and friend. But we have to learn to use that force among all that lives, and in the use of it consists our knowledge of god. Where there is love there is life."

He had not chosen the words for Ruby. Or maybe he had. We knew Gandhi was not speaking about Ruby and her mother. Yet we also knew that somehow Ruby had found her way to knowledge that Gandhi possessed. She'd found her way to love—not with her mother, but to love of her life and the person she was becoming.

"Where there is love there is life," I repeated. That was something they could understand.

The process of making our play was a wonderful thing. They'd labored for weeks in the glow of the five poultry heat lamps we had clamped to the floor joists of the windowless basement. The play had emerged from the conversations around the table, the hard and difficult ones, the funny and delightful ones; from threads and questions we'd been weaving all year; from working for hours, offering suggestions for how to do it, then being brave enough to try it again, or do it differently; from making mistakes and living in those mistakes and trying to do better the next time.

We worked in a spectacular clutter of props and art supplies, crumpled science assignments, coats, and lunch remnants. In the dark between scenes, Hannah played cello and Ruby played the piano. Callum had a lead role as the boy who came to life, awakened by the power of poetry. Nils and Nadia shared a tender kiss under the lights, full of the perfect awkwardness of children in love for the first time. Through and around us currents passed, a kind of electricity of the active heart, at once visible and invisible, and the currents seemed to multiply. Every student contributed something. Each of them was a player, a writer, a prop-maker. Our play was imperfect. It was not Shakespeare or Tom Stoppard or Rodgers and Hammerstein or Pixar. But they were thrilled by their own creation. To quantify its educational value would have been like trying to catch the wind. They kept announcing: "I can't wait to get out of the basement and go to the Community House for the play!" Having been cooped up all winter, they wanted to emerge into the spring sunlight, and when they did, they would have something that they had made together.

The week before the play, in the first week of April, we came to school in a howling spring snowstorm. Ice pellets whipped horizontally across the fields, pelting the windows. The door blew open twice before class started. During morning meeting, Callum sat in the farthest corner of the room, not smiling, not wrestling with Bennett, not even seeming to listen, as if he'd short-circuited.

After math class, I wanted to check in with him. I asked Bennett to find Callum and bring him into the big room. Bennett came back a few minutes later.

"I can't find him."

"Go outside, look on the nature trail. Hurry. Nolan, go with him."

"I'll go look in the basement," said Ruby, and she disappeared.

The vibrations of worry and panic could already be felt from the kids who stood in the doorway.

We couldn't find Callum because Callum had run away. We called his home, we called his parents. They had not gotten a call or picked him up. Callum's father, Dan, was calm.

"I'll go look for him," he said. "If I don't find him around the school, I'll call the police. Do you remember what he was wearing?"

"I think he was wearing an orange hooded sweatshirt," I said.

For the rest of the day we limped through the motions of geometry and science and lit class. Outside, the wind was raging, picking up swirling snow and whipping it into the trees. Inside, I was terrified.

Ariela came into the room and sat across from me.

"Tal, I'm so worried about Callum."

"We'll find him. Don't worry."

At two o'clock, the phone rang. It was Dan.

"I found him. He was at my mom's house."

"In *Rochester*?" Rochester was over the Middlebury Gap and into the White River valley, sixteen miles away.

"Yep."

"How'd he get all the way over *there*?"

"He ran."

"The whole way?" I couldn't believe it. To run that far in high-top basketball shoes in a driving spring snowstorm was practically superhuman.

"Is he okay?"

"Yeah, I think so. He got to his grandparents' house and they were away. He knew where the key was. I found him in the laundry room sitting on the dryer, freezing and wet. I put him in a hot tub and made him some soup. I'll get him to school tomorrow."

Rochester was where Callum had grown up, but where he no longer lived. He still called it home, even though he lived in Ripton. Callum had run over a mountain, towards home and away from everything. Callum had run sixteen miles in a violent spring snowstorm in nothing but a hooded sweatshirt, and we had no idea why.

The next morning, Callum sat in the big room with the whole school. His head was hanging. He was exhausted and drained of life.

"Callum," I said. He lifted his head. "We love you. All of us love you. All that we care about is that you are here. We want you here."

He dropped his head again.

"But I guess I have to say, I'm a little pissed. Because you left us, and you scared the hell out of us, and what you did was dangerous. Hypothermia. Trucks and plows passing you on the side of the mountain. You walked off the field in the middle of the damn game. Holy hell, you can't do that, ever! You cannot leave us, you *cannot* walk out. Not yet. You're with us and you are a part of us. Like everyone here, you're the soul of the school. You're our heart. You can't abandon the people you are with who are loving you."

He nodded and the tears were streaming down his cheeks.

But I was done with being an angry teacher. "Why'd you leave? What's going on?"

He sat with his elbows on his knees, his head hanging— like once before, on the first day of school. The tears puddled between his ragged tennis shoes. A string of snot hung from his face, stretching towards the dusty floor.

"Callum, all you have to do is say what you're feeling. All good things will come from that. The truth will set you free. Remember: *freedom is words flowing.*"

The words came choking out. "I don't want to leave the school. I'm afraid to leave the school."

Ruby moved next to him so that her chair was touching his leg. She held the roll of toilet tissue out to him, a classroom transaction that was now automatic. He reached for it without looking up, his hands shaking and red. He slowly unwound a length of paper and wrapped it around his hand.

"But, Callum, you did leave the school."

"I know. I don't know what to do. I'm afraid about when the year ends. I don't want to leave. But it's going to end."

"Well, you can't stop time. It *is* going to end. You were running away, from what I don't know exactly. You ran towards Rochester. You ran towards home. You ran east, towards home. You ran towards your past."

He nodded.

"But you're here now. This is the place." I was grasping for anything to convince him that he was right where he needed to be. "What about the Rumi you read to us? 'Wherever you are, be the soul of that place.' The Frost quote, 'Earth's the right place for love.' You've done that. You're still doing that, here, now. In a few months you *are* going to have to leave. You can't stay here forever. If you did, you'd never grow."

"I want it to last forever. It was so hard to make."

"What was hard to make?"

"All this." He gestured with his arm, sweeping it around him.

"You mean the school year? All this?"

He nodded.

"We *did* make a school year together. But everything has to die. Everything has to end. That's the hardest part of living."

Silence filled the room. No one moved.

"We make it every year. We have to keep going. We can't stay in one place. We have to be Buddhist about it and let it go to the wind."

"I know. That's what I hate."

"Callum, you put everything in. You're going to be a great tree, a beautiful tree. And a great tree will die. But when it falls, it feeds the earth and everything around it. When you leave the school, you fall, and we will still be here. But we will be living off you, remembering you. And other kids will come after you. And in truth, in fact, you will keep living. But you can't live and grow if you go backwards or stay in one place. You have to keep moving. You can't grow if you stay here. You can't be a little tree any more. You have to be a big tree. You have to keep growing. You have to keep being great."

There was another long period of quiet in the room. All of Callum's classmates, who loved him dearly, who loved him like he loved Boxer the workhorse, waited, hoping for him that he could find his way. His breath slowly calmed, but his head still hung.

"We worked so hard," he said. "We did all this. We made everything. What's the purpose if it just ends? We'll all just leave and it'll be over."

"Callum, that's the way of life. All the things we do, the life we make, is precious because it ends."

He didn't respond. I wracked my brain for words that might carry him.

"Callum, there's a part in *King Lear*. At the end, his two rotten daughters have taken everything from him, his land, his power, his army, his horses, his dignity, and he is with his third daughter, Cordelia, who has never stopped loving him. He says to her, at the very end, *Come, let's away to prison. / We two alone will sing like birds i' th' cage. / When thou dost ask me blessing, I'll kneel down / And ask of thee forgiveness. So we'll live, / And pray, and sing, and tell old tales, and laugh / at gilded butterflies—*"

"This ragged old man and his beautiful young daughter— he says they will spend the rest of eternity going on with their business as though they were above the world, no matter if they are in a prison. He says, we have our love and the sacrifices we made for each other, and that is enough to allow us to ascend, and we will be free, even in our cage of death. He says the only way they could ever be parted is if God smoked them out of caves like foxes."

I was out on the edge, not really sure of what might happen, no longer knowing the right thing to say or do.

"We're in a cage called life. It ends, everything does, but we have to keep singing like birds right to the very end. You sing in your cage until the very end. That's the only way to play it. You have to be here until it's over."

Ruby spoke up. "We've been singing here. At school. Callum, you've been singing too. That's why it's meant so much."

"Where are you now?" I asked.

"I guess I'm back in the cage," he said. He lifted his head and smiled.

"Is it terrible?"

He shook his head.

"Being in the cage is the only thing. This is where it happens. It'll keep happening. You'll go into your next school or next life, and you'll know what singing was, and you'll have guts and some knowing of how to do it, of how to live freely and wildly no matter what comes."

"Callum," said Ariela. "We love you."

Callum didn't look up.

"Hey, um, Callum," said Nolan. "I've never thought about how important you are to me. But I know it now."

"You've helped me so much this year," Hannah said. "Like you've been my big brother. Like when you cheered for me when we were skiing. And helping me with clean-up jobs in science. So I've been grateful for you."

"Dude, you *are* my brother," said Bennett. "We can't finish the year right without you."

Callum nodded. Ruby's hand was touching his bare arm ever so lightly.

I had told them once that I wanted to be inside the vein of a leaf. In that room that day, we were in the veins of Callum. We were in his blood. Or he was our blood, and the heart of him was *our* heart.

"Callum?" I asked. "Anything? Do you have anything?"

"Uh," he said. "I want to sing with you like birds in the cage. All of you guys. I don't want to leave you. I want to stay with you."

When we left class that afternoon, it was gray outside, with a light glaze of icy slush from the day before. Everyone got up slowly. As Bennett walked out of the room, he grabbed Callum from behind and put him in a gentle headlock, shoving him through the door into the hall. The room was filled with a dark glow and the class began cleanup. Brooms and sweeping, trash cans being emptied, the dishes being washed.

The nights of our play came. Our theater was the Ripton Community House, built circa 1866, and our stage was a creaking plywood platform covered in frayed carpet remnants. We had no curtains, only flimsy, black fabric flats from which the actors could enter and exit. Chicken heat lamps clamped to metal chairs served for footlights.

There were no theater "types" in our school: every student was an actor, a set changer, a properties manager. Callum was back. Before the play, he was wrestling with Bennett behind the theater in the warm spring evening, as nervous and excited as any of them.

Three months before, I had put Callum and all of them in a room to write a play. They created characters that were, in truth, *them*. They played themselves. Callum had created a boy sleeping through school, maybe even his life, until he was awakened by a poem, like the clapper in a bell suddenly stunning him awake. Now onstage was our Callum, his hair ragged and greasy, the spit flying from his mouth, the words growling as he ground out his monologue. It was filled with fragments of Shakespeare, Kerouac, Rumi, and Martin Luther King, a mashup of the voices he'd taken into his heart and mind.

> CALLUM: I have seen heaven in a wild flower, viewed the world through a grain of sand. *(To Audience.)* Guess what rang from my lips like freedom upon waking this morning. *(Laughing.)* Shakespeare? Yeah, yeah, I see now. In the deserts of the heart let the healing fountain start. It's everywhere raining. Droplets of truth coat us like tender reminders that the skies are clouded and that we should not seek God in the heavens but in our hearts. You see. *(Points to chest.)* That is the point, you always must go further in but you will never see the heart, all you have is the knowledge of its existence, the knowledge, *(holds apple and talks to it,)* it is the forbidden fruit that cast us from the garden.

> NOLAN: Have you gone insane?

> CALLUM: No. I am sane because I am insane! You must repeatedly seek without finding. The conversations echo in my head. It is me, you and God. *(To Nolan.)* I look deep into your eyes in the silence that is only interrupted by absolute truth, I do this so I might know you better, so that I might love you. *(Comes forward to audience.)* "The

best way to know God is to love many things." (*Intense.*) Beloved, the great end we have been searching for is here. I LOVE YOU. "Under the spreading chestnut tree I sold you and you sold me." Not this time! This time the words flow. Once we choked and foamed at the mouth with inarticulate pain, but now I kneel before a smile of the purest revelations. (*To each person in front row.*) By the sweat of my brow, in the center of the thorns, I have seen heaven in a wild flower. (*Bites apple, walks off stage, stops, turns and says last line, smiling.*) Free at last, free at last, Thank God almighty, I'm free at last.

Boxer was in there too, with the fighter and the hunter, screaming and slamming the bars of the world that would cage him. The school and the stage were his, and it was for all of them. With Callum running and leading, he found the freedom to seek what he needed to find. He let us see the heart beating inside his ribs, where, miraculously, the words flowed.

In the days following the play, we talked about what we had made. I told them that I believed—I was sure—that all of them had immense power to create.

"Like God in Michelangelo's painting we looked at," I said. "Do you remember?"

They nodded assent.

"I'm not exaggerating. You guys made something out of nothing. Something of great meaning, a play that no one had ever seen, or will again."

"Tal, do you believe in God?" asked Nils.

"Not really. Though I also believe that if someone believes in God, then God exists."

Nils looked at me and nodded, but he waited for me to continue.

"I guess I think of God like he's described in *Night*, by Elie Wiesel. I pray to God that he gives me the power to ask the right questions."

"So you mean, God doesn't really do anything."

"Not directly. I guess I think of the god in me that makes me want to become pure of heart. To act in accordance to what I think God might be. To try to make myself come as close to that godly image as I can. Even though sometimes I fall short."

Nadia raised her hand. "I think that what God is is when you feel certain good feelings."

"What do you mean?" I asked.

"Well, when I was little I always imagined that I was wearing a dress made out of red poppies." She paused and searched for her next words.

"And whenever I would spin around, the red poppy dress would open and spin with me. That was one of the feelings." She showed a small, sly smile as she spoke.

"So when you twirled you felt like God?"

"Yeah." She nodded and closed her eyes at the same time.

"What's another one?"

"Well, I've been thinking about this year, and what I've learned. And I don't think it's exactly things I've learned. But I think I've learned, like, *God* knowledge."

"How do you define God knowledge?" Nils asked. His eyes were wide open and he nodded his head vigorously.

"I'm not sure. But I know the main thing I've been thinking about is I know something I never felt before."

"Can you explain what?" I asked.

"I'm excited to live."

Nils was staring at her.

"Excited to live?"

"Yes, that's the feeling. I think *that's* what God is. When you can feel everything, and you're excited to be alive. I have this life. And I'm excited about it."

For a few moments we sat in the room, just thinking about that idea.

Later that week I received an email from Nils.

Tal,

I've been thinking about what you said in class. I was just wondering, what could I do to become better, a better student mostly. What could I do to be a better person within North Branch? I have been thinking that for one day, or two, or however long it is. I want to be purely good. I know that this is not possible, but I want all of my actions to do no damage to others. This came into my mind when I thought of that discussion we had the other day. I don't want to be the one that, through my foolish and unmeaningful actions, I cause some kind of fear, hatred, disgust, or any other emotion that someone would not want to feel. I want to see if I can do it, if I can purify my intentions.

I don't know what pushed me into this epiphany. I was just outside cutting wood with my dad, and as I came inside, I felt at peace, and whenever I feel this feeling, I wish to have it multiply, to fill up my being and my actions until every touch of my finger transfers this feeling into the world. That's another thing that I have been thinking about. I was thinking about karma, or something like it. I was thinking about creating a space, or creating a feeling within that space, that makes everyone else feel this feeling. I was thinking of the Buddhist monastery, I was thinking of every time that I have felt at peace. I want to create this peace.

Thank you, and sorry for writing such a long . . . thing.
love—Nils

Nils remembered everything, and it had been percolating in him: our earlier discussion about Boxer, the questions about pure intentions, the monastery, cutting wood with his father on a cold, spring afternoon in Vermont. He was shifting, growing, and transforming. This was his living and his growth, a process at once magical and impossible to measure.

❦

We read *Siddhartha*. The students were mystified as to why a prince like Siddhartha, or anyone, would give up a life of ease, renouncing all material comforts, to become a Samana, or Hindu ascetic. Why would one choose a life of physical suffering? What could the spiritual gain possibly be? Why not just stay inside the walled garden with the sun gently warming one's shoulders, meditating and taking the daily ablutions? I tried to explain it.

"I suppose you'd have to experience it, or suffer like the Samanas did in order to understand or find out if there was anything redeeming in it. If you denied yourself comfort, fasted, slept outside, were cold, hot, hungry, then maybe you'd have a better sense of it."

Without really thinking, I added to the reading assignment an additional task: do a "Samana action" before the next class.

"You're on your own to figure out some form of suffering. Once you have the experience, you'll have a better understanding. We can talk about what you discovered on Thursday."

We speculated about possibilities: not speaking all day unless absolutely necessary; running naked through the woods; fasting; not bathing; eating a spoonful of ashes, as St. Francis reportedly often did.

So on a bright Thursday morning, with a few birds singing over the wet field, I waited outside before school for them to arrive and tell us about the ways they had become Samanas. Callum had slept out in the horse pasture in a too-small sleeping bag until one in the morning; Nils had laid in the grass in his yard in the clothes on his back in sub-freezing temperatures until he was counseled by his mystified father that he had "suffered enough." Katelyn went a whole day without gazing at her reflection in a mirror. Bennett ran eight miles, past the point when he wanted to stop. Yeb did not avert his eyes even as the sun set brightly over the Adirondacks. Nolan fasted for eighteen hours, he told us, and had sat through class with his body shaking. I gave him permission to break fast in order that they would have the energy to play Frisbee after school. Hannah took a scalding bath. Ruby walked around our entire labyrinth on her knees. Henry took an ice-cold shower, ate cold food, and stared at the noon sun.

"Why?" I asked him.

"I wanted to try to let the light into me. The real source of light."

"It was awesome," said Nils. "I could feel the cold, and I felt strong enduring it. In order to know something, you have to feel it."

"I definitely could feel the power of the sun," Yeb said. "It hurt, but it also felt good."

They were willing to suffer, even if only a little, to gain the insight of mystics. They were willing to suffer, even if only a little, in order to gain something like illumination. By such steps, they moved towards epiphany and inner seeing. For his response afterwards, Nils wrote a poem:

Siddhartha and the river, Vasudeva and the river:
The river itself is God, God is the river,
Not for everyone but to those who take the time
To sit by the bank
Hearing the swoosh and splashing of words
Coming deep within the cool water,
Out of the brown sand
Through the shells and small creatures,
Through the sparkling, pearly water
Into the ears of the listener

Where they settle deep within the man,
Where they stay for the rest of their lives
Teaching everything they know, teaching us
How to live life right.

Clearly, St. Francis was devoted. Martin Luther King was devoted. But we asked: did *we* have the power and willingness to test the limits of the comfort-seeking animal body? Yes, these adolescents were willing, in what ways they could, to crack the shells of normal day-to-day existence. St. Francis did not eat ashes to become a better person; he did it to have a taste of the infinite. I wanted for my students to have a hunger for the infinite. I wanted them to be modern day mystics, ones who, like Nadia, were excited to live.

Hannah had written a story about her struggle with what she called "The Worry Monster." It was, in truth, a story about her struggle with Obsessive Compulsive Disorder. She was scared to write about it because to do so would be to reveal so many truths about which she felt great embarrassment and discomfort: her cracked, reddened hands, which she repeatedly washed; staring terrified at her dirty boots, worrying about how fast germs replicated. But she wrote it and I read it in class.

The turning point in her story came when one day she waited, ashamedly, for someone to open the door to her elementary school. She was afraid to touch it, and so she waited. As she pretended to busy herself with her backpack straps, a teacher approached. The teacher was in a wheelchair, and it was clear that getting through the door without assistance would be impossible. Hannah's mind turned wildly, trying to decide whether to run away or to open the door for her teacher. She chose to open the door. The teacher maneuvered her chair inside and said, "Thank you, Hannah!"

Hannah wrote. "I had confronted my fear. And I had not died."

As a student at North Branch for seventh grade, it was clear to her that she was in a school that was decidedly more messy and chaotic than any other school she had known. Our tables were covered in food, papers, half-filled tea mugs, paint-clotted brushes, crusted tupperware. At the end of each day the kitchen sink was filled with greasy plates and bowls. She had no choice but to live in it, and as she did, she realized that she was going through entire days without remembering to wash her hands.

The story then flashed to a scene from a class meeting. She remembered how one morning Katelyn had spoken of her younger sister. "I found her in the bathroom crying," Katelyn had said. "Hot water was pouring out of the sink and her hands were bright red and she was biting her wrists. My mom is really worried." Katelyn had gone silent then, dropping her head as she told us.

Hannah wrote:

I knew then that Katelyn's sister might have OCD. And even if she didn't, I knew some things I could help her with. I decided to ask Katelyn if I could write her sister a letter, and she said yes, and so I did. I then realized that for the first time in my life my stupid worry brain might actually be able to help me do something. I could help someone else who was in the same position as me. I began writing. I told her about all the challenges that I had in fifth and sixth grade, and how I understood how painful it was to have all these horrible thoughts in your head. I told her about what I used to be afraid of, and how I had mostly overcome it. I finished off with telling her that no matter what, no matter how despairing she was, to never ever hurt herself. I signed my name and told her to write back if she wanted to. I didn't want her to feel like she wasn't a "normal" kid. I had a feeling that the smallest thing, like writing her a letter, could be vitally important. A few weeks later I got a letter back from her. Apparently I had helped her out, and she had a few more questions for me. Sometimes I wondered why God gave me OCD to deal with, but I also tried to trust that he'd never give me something that I couldn't handle. And in the end, maybe I had gone through all this to help one person, and I had come out in more control of my body, and my fears.

Like all of the stories they wrote, Hannah's story was a reckoning with who she was. Like one who had suffered Shaman sickness, she was able to turn her experience towards others with wisdom and empathy. She understood the strange beauty and complexity of another mind. And she gave us the chance to see how we might have a more empathetic understanding of those around us.

I asked the kids to write a response to her story. For ten minutes, they scribbled on scraps of paper. Then I asked them to read their responses to Hannah's story.

Ruby read:

Dear Hannah,

I feel very empathetic to your story. I think I told you this, but over the past few days, last year, and as your story was being read, I've been thinking a lot about anorexia. I think about that a lot because it is something I fear in myself. It is hard for me to think or say that word because it is scary and painful, and worst of all maybe true, like it was for you to say you had OCD. So many things in your story made me strongly flash back to what I have felt. I know the amount of calories in every single thing I eat. I remember one morning I cried because I had eaten a bowl of cornflakes, and when I looked up "are cornflakes healthy?" it said no. They were not. I never told anyone, but I used to chew food, and then spit it out compulsively so I wouldn't get the calories. It was so bad that some days I would chew up three pieces of bread, a whole bowl of ice cream, any chocolate chips, or candy we had, and then spit it all out. Whenever people would confront me, or tell me to eat something that I deemed "bad" my heart would start to beat really hard, and I would be terrified. I hated that I sometimes can't stop, and I lie about it all the time. The other night I went out for dinner with my mom. We decided to share stuff. We shared nachos, a salad, and some French fries. I ate whatever I wanted and didn't feel bad at all. I was thinking a lot about this. Last year I would never have been able to do this.

As Ruby read, her voice and hands were shaking. I watched as she held the paper close to her face. Some of the kids were looking at her, but others were not. I wanted them to see how Hannah's self-revelation had opened another revelation inside of Ruby.

"What did you hear or see when Ruby was reading that response?" I asked.

"Her voice was shaking," said Nolan.

"Her hands were shaking too," added Bennett.

"What's it mean?

"She took a risk to show us something," said Nils.

"She's out on the edge, between who she is and who she's becoming. Hannah gave her permission. It's a scary place to be. So we have to tread tenderly when she's out on that limb. You can't shake the tree, you can't throw things, you have to be gentle. Hannah told us something rare and true and difficult. Ruby is telling us something rare and true, too. The shaking is a sign you must decipher. The shaking tells us what's important, like in the poem we read last year. *The shaking keeps me steady.* This is the stuff that lets us know who each of us is and what life truly is and where we stand."

Ruby was looking down at her paper. Then she looked up at Hannah, who smiled, as if she understood everything.

I proposed to the ninth graders that we head out on a back-packing trip to close their three years. The seventh and eighth graders would stay back at the school and have "step-up days," and we would trek for three days on the Long Trail in the Breadloaf Wilderness. We would climb seven peaks, from Mt. Abe to the Middlebury Gap, south down the spine of Vermont on the oldest mountains in the world. We would end only three miles from school. We would be far away, and we would be close to home.

"Do we want to do a short, easy trip?" I asked.

"No, we want something hardcore!" they exclaimed.

I told them it would be grueling. I told them we would only be listening to our hearts beating and the wind in the trees. The truth was, I had no idea how hard it might be, and I had no idea how they would respond.

The morning of our departure in early May was cold, just above freezing at the Lincoln Gap trailhead.

"To be hardcore or not to be, that is the question!" shouted Ruby as we divided up food, fuel, and gear.

"I'll never be able to carry this pack!" said Nadia. She tee-tered backwards as she tried to clip her hip belt. Her brow was furrowed with worry.

"You've got to woman up," I said. "You're going to find out how strong you really are."

"Tal," said Bennett as he stared into my eyes with a ferocity verging on violence. "We are going to kick this mountain's ass."

"And we are going to kick the ass of some moose, too," shouted Nils.

"Nils, we are going into the wilderness to commune with nature!" I said. "You must respect the mountain and the moose."

"I am going to commune with the moose whose ass I kick!" he cried.

"Oh, my god!" said Ruby.

Each of us read a poem before we began. Hannah read part of a Chinook psalter:

Ice mountain melted
ages ago and made this ridge,
this place of changes . . .
Bless us, dark earth as we give back
That which we have received,
As we make a forest of blessing, a ridge of blessing
For the future to grow upon.

And so we went up, straight up, on the ridges, tipping under the new weight of our packs, breathing hard, sweating, and wondering what we'd gotten ourselves into. Along the trail, the first spring flowers bloomed: Jack in the Pulpits pushing up through the leaf litter, spring beauties, trillium, false cabbage, and the first unfurling beech leaves. At Sunset Rock we looked over the Champlain Valley, across the lake to the Adirondacks, north to Montreal. Sitting on the bare rock, we gazed down through interstices of spring's first green, clearings alternating with gray wood lots, the thin back roads bending into and out of sight.

Only a few steps onward, we found our first patches of old snow, crystal filigrees of melting ice holding pine needles and wet leaves, ledges of ice in the shadows under the balsam firs, snowmelt dripping from root masses and moss banks. Piles of moose droppings in the ice, water, and mud marked the trail. Who needed blazes on trees?

A few more miles on the trail and then a bank of clouds rolled right over the tops of the trees, occluding the sun. Wind was blowing up the mountain from the west, and I could hear my own heart pounding and heavy breathing as we slipped and struggled upwards as the snow deepened. We flung curses to the Breadloaf Wilderness and the mist and cold rain began pelting down as we made our way through sodden glades and straight through ankle-deep puddles. Freshets of spring melt rushed down rocky trails and under icy snow-bridges that arched over frigid streams. Winter's windfall trees blocked our way. Suddenly we were knee-deep, post-holing to our waists, breaking through layers of rasping snow, ice raking our shins, our packs sopping and dripping and heavy, ponchos flapping in the wind, sweat mixed with blood mixed with rainwater dripping down our shins.

Ahead of me I heard Bennett shouting, referencing Huck Finn. "It's all up with the North Branch School now!" and Nils shouting back, "Dern the dern snow!"

As they hiked, they reminisced, telling stories of their three years at North Branch, remembering themselves as scared seventh graders, not sure what to say, listening to the older students. They talked of the past while moving forwards. I lingered behind, just out of sight, and listened to their disembodied voices rising and falling as they shouted through the woods, above or below on switchbacks as they trudged step by step. I walked in their footsteps as they made their way up a trail they'd never walked before and might not ever walk again.

At top of Mt. Grant we rested on wet rocks looking towards Breadloaf Mountain as it extended broadly in the mist. The mountains we still had to summit lay before us, but we couldn't see them as the clouds blew over. Dark skies, then briefly brightening skies, then clouds again, the ghostly firs below us rising up like gray shadows in the white-gray mist. We ate, we laughed, we shouted, we scared off all the wildlife. Ruby exclaimed with glee: "We're hardcore! We're not summer soldiers or sunshine patriots! We're doing it! We're hardcore! Out of this rabble rose a group who could conquer the mountains!" And they did.

From the summit, we descended to Cooley Glen and found our shelter, a three-sided Adirondack lean-to, the cedar shingle roof covered with thick patches of red-tipped British Soldier moss. The trees dripped, and the ground around the shelter was deep with snow, mud, and melt-water. We lay boughs of pine at the opening of the shelter, collected wet firewood, and made a small fire. Smoke billowed into our faces. The boys hung their socks on sticks and the insides of their boots steamed.

In the evening, all nine of them snuggled down in their sleeping bags, laughing and teasing each other, recalling embarrassing times, remembering seventh grade, recollecting. In the dark, headlamps flashed across the low ceiling. The dying fire smoldered in the night's drizzle, steaming and flaring, then fading to a faint glow. I had brought *The Road*, and sitting at their feet at the edge of the shelter, I reread to them the last pages when the Boy and the Man have their last conversations.

In the dark, they listened. These were some of my last conversations with them. The wind was in the trees, and they became quiet, and the words sounded big as I leaned against a post with a headlamp shining on the pages.

. . . You need to find the good guys but you cant take any chances.
No chances. Do you hear?
I want to be with you.
You cant.
Please.
You cant. You have to carry the fire.
I dont know how to.
Yes you do.
Is it real? The fire?
Yes it is.
Where is it? I dont know where it is.
Yes you do. It's inside you. It was always there. I can see it.

The next morning, we woke to the call of a white-throated sparrow, a silver-sharp needle stitching the day into wakefulness. We circled around the sodden ashes of the previous night's fire. We stood in our plastic bags and ponchos with water dripping over our brows. Wisps of mist and cloud swirled over the steep mountainside and around us. I held out their poems for each of them, like a priest passing out some kind of alpine eucharist. They held their damp scraps of paper with their chosen words to read at our setting out. Nils read last.

"This is a prayer by Thomas Merton," he said. "I don't know who he is. But I'm down with what the man is saying." Then he read.

What a thing it is to sit absolutely alone,
In a forest, at night, cherished by this
Wonderful, unintelligible,
Perfectly innocent speech,
The most comforting speech in the world,
The talk that rain makes by itself all over the ridges,
And the talk of the watercourses everywhere in the hollows!
Nobody started it, nobody is going to stop it.
It will talk as long as it wants, this rain.
As long as it talks, I am going to listen.

We could not retain all the words from the poems they read, but we listened and they were in us, a fortifying elixir soaking into our minds. To hear these words spoken in the rain did seem to be the most comforting speech in the world. These were truths I hoped they would carry with them.

We made great time, crossing over Mt. Cleveland, Little Hans Peak, Mt. Roosevelt. But climbing up Mt. Wilson, we hit steep rocks. The climb kept rising, snow heaped and crunching, icy rock faces, clawing onto branches and roots and each other, climbing over criss-crossing barriers of trees. Nadia began to hyperventilate, and then she began to cry. Nils and I stopped with her. She bent over and the weight of her pack threw her forward into the snow. She kneeled there, her chest heaving.

"I can't go any more. I don't think I can make it." She began to sob.

"Hey, just breathe easy, Nadia. You're doing great. Just calm your breathing down."

She got to her feet and took a drink of water. "I can't go any further." She shook her head. Sweat and rainwater dripped down her face and pine needles stuck to her cheeks.

"Here's the deal, Nadia. It's the same distance either way. You can go backwards, or you can go forwards. But you can't stay here. All you have to do is put one foot in front of another. Every step you get is a little closer. This is the way of the world. You have strength in you that you didn't know existed. And now it's going to come out and you're not going to believe how freaking strong you are. This is how you do it."

"What he said, Nadia," said Nils. "Come on, I'm gonna tell you jokes until we get to the top." Nadia wiped her hand across her cheek, then turned to the trail, shrugging her shoulders and snugging her straps. As they walked ahead of me, I heard Nils launching into a George Carlin monologue with Nadia at his side. Nils's voice and Nadia's laughing filtered quietly through the trees, and then I could no longer hear them. When I got to the top, there was Nadia, sitting at the edge of the rock cliff, gazing into the distant view of mist and the tips of fir trees rising from the clouds a hundred feet below us.

And then we plunged down into a steep valley to the Emily Proctor shelter. The white blazes of the Long Trail were impossible to see as they blended into the lichen-spotted trees. We got lost and turned around and could only find the trail when we found piles of moose scat.

"Why are we doing this?" cried Haley.

"GOD ONLY KNOWS!" screamed Ruby.

I thought of Wendell Berry's words: *So, friends, every day do something / that won't compute . . . Give your approval to all that you cannot / understand.* Taking young adolescents into the wilderness did not quite compute, and yet it was joyous. I could hear Hannah up ahead cackling. Winn sang songs from "O Brother, Where Art Thou?" with Haley singing harmony, such an angelic sound as we slid down into muddy trails, then pushed our way up again, giving each other our hands over the winter's snow. More of Berry's words echoed in my mind. *Through the weeks of deep snow / we walked above the ground / on fallen sky.*

Going down, it was steep and then steeper as we careened into snow-filled gullies. We dropped down the south side of Breadloaf. They did not know it, but Skylight Pond shelter was one of the most beautiful shelters on the Long Trail, a log cabin with four walls, windows, a door, a sleeping loft, and a porch that overlooked a beaver pond filled with spring peepers. Beyond the pond, the sky opened up and the valley stretched toward New Hampshire.

As the cabin came into sight, the woods filled with shouts of joy and thanks to God.

"It's a good island!" called Nils, referencing *The Lord of the Flies.*

"This is friggin' Nirvana!" shouted Nolan. He had taken off his shirt and only had the white tatters of a trash bag sticking to his torso.

We changed into dry clothes, ate our meal, and climbed into our bags. Arguments over card games and laughter filled the cabin until exhaustion took over. As we fell asleep, out of the silence Nils's voice sounded in the darkened cabin.

"I love the world."

The words hovered for a moment. No sound, except the door swinging slowly closed on its hinges. Then it swung open wide again and the moon showed through the breaks in night clouds. That was a kind of love, to feel joy in the hardest of places.

The hissing of the camp stove woke them slowly.

"Hey, Tal," called Nils. His voice was muffled, still buried in the warmth of a down sleeping bag. "You know what?"

"What?"

"The three days of this hike are like the three years of the school. The first day was the easiest. That was seventh grade. Then yesterday was eighth grade. That was the hardest. And today is the easiest, and it's the end. That's ninth grade. Did you plan that?"

"Maybe," I said. "Now who wants some delicious instant oatmeal?"

After packing, we gathered to read the final poems. We gathered in a circle and faced ourselves. Behind us to the east was the mist-covered pond. They could look backwards at themselves three years before, and they could look forward to the unknown shape of things to come.

The morning sun was on us. Each of them stood with their packs on, holding their soaked sheets of poems. Hannah read from "Forgetfulness," by Billy Collins: *Long ago you kissed the nine Muses goodbye / and watched the quadratic equation pack its bag, / and even now as you memorize the order of planets, / something else is slipping away, a state flower perhaps, / the address of an uncle, the capital of Paraguay.* Ruby read "Spring Pools" by Robert Frost—those pools we had seen on our hikes, the last of winter snow seeping into the bogs, moss, and wild, dark roots:

> *These pools that, though in forests, still reflect*
> *The total sky almost without defect,*
> *And like the flowers beside them, chill and shiver,*
> *Will like the flowers beside them soon be gone,*
> *And yet not out by any brook or river,*
> *But up by roots to bring dark foliage on.*
> *The trees that have it in their pent-up buds*
>
> *To darken nature and be summer woods---*
> *Let them think twice before they use their powers*
> *To blot out and drink up and sweep away*
> *These flowery waters and these watery flowers*
> *From snow that melted only yesterday.*

And finally, Bennett closed the circle with a benediction by Meister Eckhart:

> *If I were alone in the desert and feeling afraid*
> *I would want a child to be with me.*
> *For then my fear would disappear*
> *and I would be made strong.*
> *This is what life in itself can do*
> *because it is so noble,*
> *so full of pleasure and so powerful.*

Here they had touched the nobility and pleasure of life. Like the spring pools, it was also true that my students would soon be gone. They would forget dates, procedures, capitals, equations. They were, in their schooling, like the snow, full of themselves and residues, winters of leaves and bits of pine needles and old stones and rivulets of spring waters. They had something in their pent-up buds that needed to flower. And that flowering would happen somewhere away from North Branch. I hoped with all that I was that they would think twice as they became summer woods.

As we passed down the back side of Burnt Mountain, we left the cold and snow and found ourselves on a dry trail under the emerging leaf canopy. We hiked down the last mile in complete silence, with large gaps between us. A faint green was on the trees, swathed in sun and the scent of flowers. It was all in them now, as much as blood or memory: the mosses and encrustations of lichen, the gnarled limbs, the small flowers coming up through dead leaves, a clump of coarse moose hair on the trail in a patch of sun. They'd seen white quartz and woodsmoke and the distant mountains and black limbs. They'd heard wind whipping down the tree-rain and the one single white throated-sparrow piercing the morning mist. They'd even put fine silt humus on their tongues.

Now they hugged and high-fived each other as they stepped

off the trail into the gravel parking lot. They might forget every-thing they ever learned, but they would not forget this.

On a hot morning in May, as we gathered for meeting, Ariela came running into the room.

"There's a moose! There's a moose in the field!"

Everyone scrambled out of the room, tipping chairs and crashing through the doors. We ran across to the stone wall.

In our neighbor's pasture, a young, long-legged male moose was running along the fence line near the dusty road, galloping skittishly, frantic for a way out. Our neighbor was in the pasture trying to get behind the moose to guide him towards an open gate. It wasn't hard to feel the moose's panic and fear. We watched his struggling search for a way out and none of us said a thing. Jasper barked wildly, leaping and bounding with his hackles up. We could hear the moose's hooves pounding the wet grass as, like a bird seeking an open window, he sought escape. He ran to the corner, found an opening, then turned up the paved road, galloping towards the Ripton village. We watched him until he went over the rise of the hill and out of sight.

All day we mentioned it, as though we had all been part of some strange dream. I kept thinking of my adolescent students who, like that moose, in the wild motions of growing up, sought openings through which they could find their release. Soon my students would be gone, headed down the road, ambling away with eyes forward while we stood and watched them go.

Each of the students was busy completing their last major works of the year. Yeb completed his Nebulae project: a spiral of cotton, spray painted four colors, held onto a rickety framework of copper wire and hot glue. He raised it proudly above his head when he entered the room for meeting, trophy of his hand-to-hand combat with the stars.

Later Winn handed in her story. "Tal, here it is," she announced. "The ending is terrible, but I'm going to work on it. Then when I bring it to you at 8:30 on Monday it will be a work of art. It will be so holy and beautiful that it will shine with sunlight from angels' wings. It will be so perfect that you will not even have to correct it."

I held out my hand and she lay the story softly there. They wanted their last works to reflect their best selves: no final exams were necessary.

Haley was working, for the second straight day, on her phases of the moon project. She had approximately six hundred separate pieces of paper all the size of a Mongolian pea, each of which she was endeavoring to glue in perfect proximity to the others.

"Haley," I said, "you've put more time into making your phases of the moon project than it took for the *actual* moon to be made."

She leaned over and banged her head on the table. "I KNOW, Tal. You don't usually see this process because I do it at home."

I read Haley's story about the end of childhood. In it she remembered collecting monarch butterfly cocoons in the fields of milkweed in fall with her mother when she was little. The story ended with this:

In the spring when the weather is getting warmer a shiny, spotted, green gem shakes and quivers and cracks open. Black legs as thin as a spider's web drag out a small mass of crinkled orange wings as weak and delicate as wet tissue paper. And there the butterfly stands in the cool morning shade, unfold- ing its wings. In a matter of time the wings are unfolded and brilliant in the sunlight and the butterfly flaps them and lifts off. It floats up and down in the breeze and then floats back and lands on a flower. It flaps its wings in the sun for a moment as if it is still trying to understand what it has done. And then in the indecision of an instant it lifts off and flies away. Then it is gone and all that's left is what was there before—the still trees, the breeze and the sharp sunlight. And a memory of this birth into the green, orange, red and purple rainbow of a sea of flowers blooming in springtime.

Our springtime was coming on. Dandelions filled the field, ferns greened against the stone wall, the blackberry brambles sent out green tears of unfurling leaves. Haley's story was another kind of spring beauty, only heard by those of us who were there for its making.

Ruby presented her project on Women's Suffrage. "And it's not about suffering, exactly," she said. "It's about the fight for equality, for the right to vote, for rights to property ownership. For women." She taught the class about Elizabeth Cady Stanton, who wanted the word "obey" out of marriage vows, and Abigail Adams, Lucretia Mott, and the words of Susan B. Anthony: *Organize, agitate, educate, must be our war cry.* She read portions of Adams's letter to the delegates at the 1787 Constitutional Convention: *Include the rights of the ladies you have left at home... remember the wives you have left home on the farms, who raise the children. . . .* She taught us about Victoria Woodhull, the first woman to run for president, in 1872, and who was also the first woman millionaire; about Emily Wilding Davison, who threw herself under the king's racehorse in a derby to gain attention for women's suffrage. She told us about Madam C.J. Walker, the first self-made black woman millionaire, and Elizabeth Blackwell, first woman to graduate from medical school and first woman doctor. It came as a surprise to most of the kids in the class that the Fourteenth Amendment of 1867 gave black men the right to vote, but women, all women, did not get the right to vote until 1920. They were fairly shocked that women did not have rights to property ownership, and disturbed by the idea that in marriage the woman became the property of the man.

"That's insane!" shouted Ruby. "I'm a person! You can't own me!"

"Damn straight!" I replied. "Nobody can own you. But back then a man could."

"That's bullshit, man!" said Nils. "We need a revolution against . . . against history."

"Yeah, what kind of country is this?" shouted Yebsera. "I thought it was supposed to be all about freedom!"

"It *was* supposed to be all about freedom. What happened in history is your inheritance," I said. "It's your job to go out and raise hell about it. Now go do it!"

In the little time time we had, I could not explain it. I just had to hope that their rage would carry them on to further studies.

At the end of her presentation, Ruby wanted to play "Respect," by Aretha Franklin

"Tal, do I have enough time to play it?"

"Are you kidding? Of course, we have to . . . it's Aretha Franklin!"

Before she pressed play, she told us that of all the first women who were key in the Suffrage movement in the 1800s, none were alive in 1920 when the right to vote was granted. The class agreed that it was true, as Sir Isaac Newton had said, that we were all standing on the shoulders of giants, and so we did, as we listened to the Queen of Soul.

The day after Ruby's project, Nils asked: "If it's in the bible that sin began with a woman and thanks to her we must die, and it

has been that men have been the dominant gender throughout history, how did it come to be? I mean, why did it even start?"

"That's a question worth a lifetime of study," I said. "And I can't answer it."

They speculated about prehistoric times, evolutionary biology, cultural factors, physical differences between the genders, who the authors of the Bible were, and the disparity in pay between women and men. It didn't matter so much that we couldn't get an answer, so long as they were asking questions.

It was May, and they were still asking questions, still learning from each other. Nobody was marking time. Yes, they loved coming to their school, because it was a place that thrilled them and helped them grow in the ways they needed to grow. But, like Callum, they were also afraid to leave, afraid of the future. Summer loomed, and what we had made would end.

I received an email from Ruby. *I was thinking about what Callum said during after he ran away, when he was talking about how everything will end. And I was thinking about what Nadia said about how she was excited to live. I'm afraid of what I'll do when I leave. Or what I will become. Who will love me? Will I know any of my teachers? I can learn about stuff, but that isn't really the most important to me. I am excited to live, but I am afraid to go. Can we talk about that in class?*

I had my lesson plan for the next day. What could have been more important than these children, on the cusp of going out into the wide world, talking about how they wanted to live their future lives, deciding what they would take with them when they left?

The next day, I read the class Ruby's note. "*Are* you afraid to leave?" I asked her.

"I guess I'm not afraid to leave, but I don't *want* to leave," she said.

"Why not afraid?"

"Because I know I can do it at the high school. But it seems like high school is about things that aren't the most important thing."

"Plenty of things at high school are important things," I said. "What's the most important thing?"

"I don't know. Everything we do here. People, feelings. We care about each other."

"But you can't stay here. You have to learn chemistry and French and take the SATs." There was a long pause in the room. "And people will care about you, but you'll have to seek those people out."

Nolan raised his hand. "What was that thing Hannah read to us in her project?"

During Hannah's project on Taoism, in her quiet voice, she had described to us the Ten Virtues. She had explained the meaning of the yin-yang so comprehensively that it became more than a symbol to be scribbled on the covers of notebooks.

"You mean, the passage from the *Tao Te Ching*?"

"Yeah, that one about the darkness."

From her notebook, Hannah pulled a sheet of paper, which she read.

*Yet mystery and manifestations
arise from the same source.
This source is called darkness.
Darkness within darkness.
The gateway to all understanding.*

"Why are you asking about that, Nolan?" I asked.

"The part about the darkness. That's how it feels now. But the darkness is a gateway. You have to go through it. You can understand this, but you have to go through this to get to the next place, which will be something you won't understand. That's how you'll be completing your life."

"What do you mean?" asked Bennett.

"Life isn't only here, I guess. Part of life is also when something ends," said Nolan.

"All of our learning, or a lot of it, has come from the hard parts of the year," said Winn. "That's the balance."

"So death and life are one thing," said Nils. "That's the yin-yang."

"Or you could say, life includes death," said Bennett. "I see that."

The conversation was completely their own. The classroom *was* a gateway, a threshold. What happened in the school came from them, and then it went away. Something else would happen the next year, and we could not know what it would be. That was the darkness, and we would embrace it again in the following year. And for the kids who were graduating? They would have to take with them the most important lessons, and try to live them on out.

"There's not much sunlight in what she's feeling," I said.

"But she's sad because it was good," said Nils. "I mean, the year was good. That's what life is, light *and* dark."

"You're sad, Ruby, yes?" I asked.

She nodded.

"So let that sadness be part of you. Make it be such a force living inside of you that you're driven to recreate another version of this thing you've loved. Let it inspire you and make you *great*."

My answer came from her question, and her question had come from our trying to go after everything.

On a morning in the last week of school, Yebsera read "Directive." Frost's poem walks us through geological time, and then through the history of Vermont's hill farmers, and now we walked back through it. We had read the poem in October, and as we read it now—when the trees were greening and the windows were filled with light—his words breathed anew.

For the whole year, for their three years, I taught them to believe that school was where destiny could unfold. This room, with these people, had been their waters and their watering place. Hearing the poem again was a reminder that the school had been a source and a home.

Weep for what little things could make them glad, Frost wrote. I thought I knew why they grieved so intensely for the end of a year, or three years. They were not so old to have become strangers to their feelings. And they had not lived so long that their defenses were impenetrable. The source of tears was still locatable.

"Remember when we read that poem in the beginning of the year?" I asked.

"Yes, Tal."

"It's still great, isn't it?"

"Yes, Tal."

I looked at them and sighed and looked down at my coffee cup.

"Who else has something?" I asked. Ruby raised her hand.

"I was going over my lit homework this morning, and I couldn't stop thinking about the Old Man and the end of the book, when there is nothing left of his fish but the skeleton. And I'm not sure why, but I felt . . . like I had lost him, even though I didn't know him." She paused again, and then continued. "He's just a character, a character in a story, but I felt for him. I guess it was the feeling of love for him."

Yes, Santiago was a fictional man alone at sea with his soul, but Ruby wept for all the things that made her glad, a man and a boy and fish and the sea, yes, but for all else that had happened in a year that would soon be ending. No matter where she or they went, they'd have to negotiate the deeps as solitary souls, soon-to-be adults, in the boats of themselves. Their strength would be found in rowing out far and on their own, but they had stores in them to take when they launched.

So they wept for the strange, joyous, unplanned alchemy that occurred in a school where they saw themselves and which saw and loved them. They wept because they felt a sense of belonging and mastery, because they knew they were part of a story, because they had a voice, and now it was ending. They wept because they believed they were going to lose everything they had made and become. Their bodies were still soft and delicate, and they feared that what they made could not be made again.

"And you have to go," I said. "Not because we'd get sick of you, but because you'd stop growing if you didn't. And the world needs you. The world needs people who love the world and want to make something good in it."

They just looked at me, waiting for more.

"Soon enough, you'll see the world outside as the right place to be," I continued. "The school will one day seem very small to you. It will shrink as you grow bigger and older. Your time here in the school is a beginning, not an end."

I repeated to them Yeats's formulation: "Education is not the filling of a pail, but the lighting of a fire." If they could believe *that* was true, then they could take the school with them.

"Wherever you go, the school goes too," I said.

They tentatively, shakily trusted all this, even as they sensed that the memory of a place was not the same as being in it. Leaving looked to them like staring into the cavernous black of the bear's mouth. But as Simon asked in *The Lord of the Flies*: "What else is there to do?" Nothing, we decided, but walk down the long path ahead. One foot forward, then another, and no going back.

I thought back to the beginning of the year, I remembered the wide-open door, the excitement of the first days, the tentative beginnings, the first tears and laughter. I recalled the adventures in the woods and snow, the long days of being cooped up in winter, the messes, the projects, the play, the stories, the crazy laughter, the speed of flying through May, the intensity of our last days of June. If I concentrated, I could see the beginning in the end.

We were a school that liked walking in the sun, yes. But we had walked equally in darkness. We'd learned, to paraphrase Robert Frost, that we had to go behind our father's sayings— beyond platitudes, the easy answer, the multiple choice, the filled-in oval, the glib reply, the complacent *whatever*. We had to go behind the masks, behind the well-made wall, to tip over stones and rake the muddy earth to see what was really there. There were worms and grubs and tangled undergrowth, and that was part of the whole of it, and that was what we wanted, because the whole of it was the truth, the whole of it was life.

One day in the last week of the year I played for them a recording of Tom Waits reciting a poem by Charles Bukowski called "The Laughing Heart."

your life is your life.
don't let it be clubbed into dank submission.

be on the watch.
there are ways out.
there is a light somewhere.
it may not be much light but
it beats the darkness.
be on the watch.
the gods will offer you chances.

know them, take them
you can't beat death but
you can beat death in life, sometimes.

and the more often you learn to do it,

the more light there will be.

your life is your life.
know it while you have it.

you are marvelous
the gods wait to delight
in you.

I read it again after we listened to it. Tears pooled up in the corners of my eyes. I looked at Ariela, and I wanted her to know it and believe it.

"The world is still out there," I told her.

It wasn't *the* solution to loss and sadness, but it was an answer, a prescription for how to counter, how to hope, how to get on. There was always another move. Against all odds, we said, *you are marvelous.*

The end of the year resolved into a kind of song, one they hummed together without ever being told to. They kept at their final projects, stories, self-evaluations. The doors were wide open, black flies coming in, the piano tuned, Nolan and Henry playing "While my Guitar Gently Weeps" at lunchtime. A shouting from outside, voices together calling, "Say you want a revolution!"

In Nolan's project we listened to Malcolm X give a speech in a ballroom in Harlem, and we imagined what it would be like to be present at the beginning of a historical movement. I asked them to imagine sitting above a public house in Stratford-upon-Avon, writing the first words of *Romeo and Juliet*. Wislawa

Szymborska wrote, *I don't see the crabbed and blotted draft / that hides behind the Song of Songs.* Even if we didn't see it, we tried to feel it with all that we were.

It was hot, and they wore shorts and sandals, holding their battered, torn notebooks and binders. We sat in the big room as it filled with heat and brightness, dust motes rising with the movement and excitement. The table was littered with papers and food wrappers and dishes and pencils. Once, we had read Szymborska's "Miracle Fair," a poem that catalogued the simple magnificence of our life on earth, reminding us that we lived in a temple of infinite beauty. That was something I didn't want them to forget. Szymborska's poem opened with the phrase, *The commonplace miracle: / That so many commonplace miracles happen.* The truth was, most of my students would spend their lives in the commonplace. Whether they grew to be happy, or whether they lived good lives—much would depend on whether they could see the miraculous in the commonplace.

"I know you've got a lot of stuff to finish," I said, "but I want to do a little final writing exercise to wrap things up. So, what are the miracles you know, or remember? You guys get to make the list. Together we'll be the reincarnation of the Nobel-Prize-winning poet."

They wrote, and when they were done, we read their composite list.

A miracle is our beautiful wooden table, given to us from tiny seeds. Another miracle: My mother's life and her being here. A miracle: this community I learn in. Love that is shared. The innocence of our thoughts and minds; a miracle—the rose that blossoms in spring, crafted with some sun and rain. A miracle: that I have loved my parents for 12.5 years; that my father is still alive. If he was having these difficulties twenty years ago both us would not be alive. An ordinary miracle: that we are still here and that we have made so many small things. Miracles: the mountains; a baby opening its eyes; that my great grandmother was so brave; that the leaves come back everywhere; that we can love animals, that we cry when they die; that frog embryos are protected by clear slime; that ducks can float, dive, swim, fly, and walk; that the water beads into little diamonds on their feathered backs; the mountains which are illuminated by the light from behind by the setting sun; my five year-old sister running around in her underpants.

Then I read Ruby's list.

Yesterday I sat at in the field watching everyone play. And I noticed a leaf with a hole in it in the exact shape of an arrow. I noticed a lot of things. Rocks are cold. I noticed we take a lot for granted, everything, it seems: laughing, the ability to love, grass, tractors, fingernails, clothing, the blue sky, enzymes inside us, water, hills, wind, color, people, familiar things, fresh air. I truly could go on forever and name everything in the world.

For one of the last morning meetings of the year, we gathered on the picnic table in front of the school. The sky was crystalline blue, the field wet, the sun just rising over the tree line. The kids smiled and jostled each other, telling silly stories, continuing inside jokes, talking and laughing.

Rose's ninth-grade math class, using its knowledge of the cardinal directions, mapping, and geometry, had marked out a twenty-foot circle in the grass, and had inscribed it with arcs and a center point using string and small stones, making it a compass rose.

Callum, who was a few minutes late, walked up the driveway.

"Rose! Rose!" he implored. "God did not make me to do algebra! God made me to plow the fields!"

"Callum!" Rose called. "We're not doing algebra problems! We're doing an all-school activity!"

Contained in the circle were borders and divisions so each student had possession of some part of the marked space. The instructions were simple: Go to the woods alone and find what you can, take a portion of the circle as your own, work in silence, alone, or together, and fill in the circle. They had a responsibility to the whole, but each of them was free from the dictates of others. They each had freedom to express an individual vision. In microcosm, it was what our school aimed to achieve.

In silence they scattered and collected handfuls of dandelions, birch leaves, fiddlehead ferns, ashes from the fire pit, balsam or fir sprigs, a pile of mossy rocks brought from the woods, a bucket of pebbles. Others returned with armÔfuls of sticks, goose-foot maple leaves, a bucket of apple blossoms, a wheelbarrow of stones. Each portion of the circle began to take on texture and color.

As it came closer to completion, they wanted to climb the ladder and see. They teetered on the top step as I put my fingers to my lips to remind them not to talk. When Bennett saw what they had made, he gave me a thumbs up as, silently, we stood by our beautiful, multi-hued composition, a mandala of the North Branch School. Our location and our direction was before us.

Then we ended the period of silence.

They burst out, "This is so cool!" They loved what they'd made. Inside the school I asked them to write about it.

"Write anything, a poem, feelings," I instructed.

We read aloud when they were done. I gave the scraps of paper to Hannah. "Take it home, pull the best lines from each one, and reassemble it into one poem that you feel says something about us."

The next morning she brought the poem in.

"Okay, let's hear what we got."

And she read.

Here. This is us. All of us. We're all here,
learning, feeling, speaking,
being one big thing, made of ourselves.

We create our own melody.
We live out what we have learned.

Here is where a small group of people work together
to create something beautiful.
We put all our values together
to make something beautiful.

What we learn here
is not how to live the rest of our lives,
but how to live now.

When a hole says, "whole," we fill it with ourselves.

We are together because of
love, compassion, hope, faith, and belief.
These feelings weave us together,
along with our arms and our legs.

We are mighty good at making things,
and we work hard.

Here, where the leaves have returned,
every direction is as beautiful as another.

We had been reading *The Old Man and The Sea* for our last book of the year. One morning, Bennett asked about the modern ways of marlin fishing and we looked at pictures on the Internet. We then discussed the way the Old Man braced himself in the boat and how the rope was over his shoulder and the reasons why he wanted the fish to rise and jump.

"That is the most tremendous pain he was in," I said, "with the rope over his shoulder."

"How did he do it? How was he so strong?" asked Haley. More important than the question was her belief; the strength of the Old Man deserved to be fathomed; The book was real.

"The Old Man and the Sea is so awesome," said Bennett.

"Hey, Tal, this was my favorite line," said Nolan. He was wearing his San Francisco Giants hat, which he'd worn every day of the year. "Can I read it?"

"Go for it."

Nolan flipped the pages of his tattered paperback. "Here it is. 'Now I have no time to think of baseball, he thought. Now is the time to think of only one thing. That which I was born for.' That is so cool."

"So what are we after?" I asked.

"That which we were born for." Nolan nodded knowingly and with the pride that came from discovering his own truth.

When I thought of them leaving the school, I thought of Hemingway's Old Man, Santiago, who had given them a picture of Man alone, or nearly alone, in the boat of himself.

"In the end, why is he dreaming about the lions on the beach?" I asked. "Where is he going, so far out to the depths?"

"Because you have to go all the way," said Brody. The boy who was afraid to tell us his middle name on the first day of school was telling us about what it meant to risk one's life.

We came to the part where the Old Man is drawing-in the great, exhausted fish. Brody asked to read the passage. *I must get him close, close, close, he thought. I mustn't try for the head. I must get the heart.*

I had taught the book at least nine times, but we'd never spent time discussing this particular passage.

"I thought this was the most important part," Brody said, confidence in him rising with what he knew. "I was thinking it was saying be sure, be *complete*. In the final moment, after all the work, don't take the common way. Or the first way. Take the pure way."

"Going all the way out is the pure way?" I asked.

"On the surface it applies to the work of killing the fish," Nolan said. "But he's also telling us how to live. This is the pure way."

"He could be talking about writing," I said. "Or loving. Or working. Or giving. Don't go for the idea of the thing, go to the richest, truest part. The heart. And do it fully."

"He and the fish are the same," said Nolan. "They are both hooked, connected to the same line. They're both strange, both old, both strong, both wounded, both hungry, both trying not to die, both intelligent, and they're both suffering."

"The Old Man is the greatest man ever to live!" shouted Winn gleefully.

"Say more," I said.

"It reminds me of when we read 'Do not go gentle into that good night.'" She read the two lines, which she had included in her written response. *Good men, the last wave by, crying how bright / Their frail deeds might have danced in a green bay.*

Brody raised his hand again. "When he says 'I must get the heart,' he's making it so those things will last forever. Because his heart and the fish's heart are the same heart. Because they are brothers."

These last conversations were the distillation, the pure song, like the mockingbird's, beautiful and true, the good heart with which they had returned. From my students I learned, as they did, that rowing out too far was at the core of living a godly life. *If we are going to become anything great*, they said, *at the very least we have to be willing to row out too far.* With that devotion, they came closer to themselves in their time on earth, which, after all, was the right place for love. They discovered all was lovely and unending, like the great fish as it surfaced majestically from the depths. *He came out unendingly and water poured from his sides*, Hemingway wrote. The word "unendingly" was not literally true, because the fish *did* end. The Old Man would end, the book would end, the school year would end, but the image of it all could remain in their minds and in the pages of their lives unendingly.

Ariela finished her last story, which was based on her "What I Have Learned So Far" poem. She'd needed a vehicle for the feelings that weighed in her, and the free form of the poem had opened her up and given her a way to say it all. Everything important was alive in her words. The only thing that mattered *was* life.

> *Look, the little girl opens her mouth to catch the snow. She smiles at the cold, and spins in circles. She makes a snow angel for the sky to look at. Her small footprints trailing all over the yard. In school, she learns math and spelling and science. She studies hard to remember how to spell two, too and to. She loses her first tooth, and goes home to brush it clean for the tooth fairy. She calls grandma and grandpa to tell them about it.*
>
> *Mommies and daddies were once little girls and boys. They played medieval lords and ladies and cowboys. The little girl tries to picture her mommy as a little girl. She*

laughs because she can't. The little girl hides, in a deep hole inside herself. She cries only when she can't hold it in any-more. Her tears flow over her face, and her grey eyes shine with sadness. She hides in a tree, where the sun can't see her.

Sometimes medicine makes the girl's mommy sick. She doesn't know why, shouldn't medicine make you better? The girl feels lost, she cries almost every night now. Her curly hair gets wet from the tears, but she doesn't tell anyone what's wrong. The girl has learned that she gets to choose how to be in her world. She knows that sometimes people do bad things, without a reason. She hears stories of children who die, without ever having done something wrong. She cries for those childrens' mommies and daddies.

She hugs her own mommy, because she's scared. Sometimes the girl runs out of the thing called patience, even though she's been told that she mustn't. She gets angry with her family, and she wants to get away. She closes her door, and hugs her stuffed raccoon to feel better.

People tell the girl, that she is old for her age. An old soul, an empath, a heart of gold, a wise one. She doesn't know what these mean, or if they are even true. She doesn't even know for herself what she is.

But the girl knows that she can choose how to be in this world. She knows that she has her own individual power to make a mark in history. To leave behind whatever she wants. Her words and thoughts and art can be preserved.

The girl knows that her mommy and daddy are not going to stop loving her just because they don't love each other any more. She knows that even though people do bad things around her, it doesn't mean she will do them as well. She can protect her integrity, because it is hers and hers alone

The girl is me, and I am growing. I am constantly having feelings and thoughts cycle through me. Some unknown thing disturbs the pond of my mind and causes ripples to flow out, in a particular pattern. Then new thoughts evolve from the motion.

I don't know why some things happen, Why a man would shoot children, why parents are grieving now for their loss. I don't know why my mom is sick, or why her sickness exists on this earth at all. I don't know why, I suddenly have to change all of the things I say about my mama, to be in the past tense instead. For some reason, that I do not comprehend, there are bad things here on earth.

I have heard explanations, Pandora's box, Adam and Eve and the tree of knowledge, and evolution. They all have some sort of story, and I can choose what to believe and what not to believe. I get to choose what to bring into myself.

I have learned in two days, what it's like to be in shock. I have learned what it's like to lose a parent. I have learned that the worst week of my life, will probably be the one when I lost my beautiful mother.

And yet, throughout all of these explanations, I still do not know why. My small existence on this big planet, and in the incomprehensibly constant passing of time, my mind is simply not large enough to understand. And I know now that I can keep on trying to. Maybe in the subconscious parts of me, I will begin to really know because I can know many things, and I will continue to learn more but in the whole complete circle which makes up everything I do know, I will never know the why for some things. And that is just fine with me.

At least that is what I thought, but there are those moments in life that nobody ever expects. Those moments when everything stops because something broke. And someone's life turns totally up-side down. Like my life, and even if I know that I can't always know the why, I still have the right to ask.

Death is that one incomprehensible thing. Nobody can understand it or decipher what it means. It goes about taking people and changing lives forever, without seemingly a second thought. Something that at a far distance can seem so simple, is infinitely more complex, like a rock under a microscope.

Or maybe its the other way around. Maybe we see things as more complicated than they are, and we take the simple puffy white cloud shape of something and make it into something more difficult. Maybe we don't always have to understand things, and a puffy white cloud can remain that way. We don't have to label it cumulus, or cirrus, or stratus, we don't have to make it into a shape. Some clouds just have to stay in their pure white forms to be really understood.

Winn had not forgotten the maple tree in the labyrinth, nor the idea that we should bury poems in a jar under it.

"You promised!" she said, her arms on her hips. She was making her last stand.

Rose told them to collect a favorite poem. We read them to each other in morning meeting. Henry had written his own poem.

Tell me what's in your mind,
Because I can't see it.
Don't move the obstacles out of my way,
They are there for me to accept.
Let me take my path,
Even though yours is worn soft.
Drop me in the sea,
Don't give me a rope.
Let me swim through this raging world.
I am not the same as I was, so let me grow.

What harvest could come? Poems? More poem trees? Children who grew up and planted poems under trees? We simply trusted that our tree, standing at the edge of the woods, would yield another kind of harvest. Saplings would grow into great trees. Good lives would grow from that.

Graduation was our one last chance to show what we'd been up to, what we'd found and discovered. The Ripton Community house, with its twelve-foot-high windows, was filled with afternoon light and a crowd of parents, siblings, grandparents, former students, friends of the school, neighbors, and former teachers. Vases of flowers surrounded the table where we read. Jasper slept on the podium, just under the table. Each of the students held a speech they'd written in the last week of school, each one containing one important moment from the school year, a vignette, revelation, or singular moment. Every student had something important to read. With their speeches, and our speeches about each of them, the ceremony was four hours long. Callum was the last to read. He stood at the lectern, his face flushed, sweating. Others in the school had dressed up—in wild hats, lace dresses, and new shirts, but Callum wore an old T-shirt torn at the collar. His hair was as long and tangled as ever. He held his speech with both hands, gripping the sides of it like a root he held onto to keep from being swept away.

He could barely speak. He had so much to say, so much flowing in and from him. *In the deserts of the heart, let the healing fountain start.* I spoke the words to myself, willing him to begin, to let the beauty welling in him come out in his most true and beautiful way.

Terrified, his voice clotted in his throat. Then the words began to come, mixed with some tears, but louder and louder, imploring, insistent, vital, incandescent. He was speaking to his classmates and teachers, yes. But beyond that, he was speaking to himself, the only conversation that would ever truly matter.

I want you to know I have gone so far that I thought I could wester no more. It is possible to go far at North Branch and you should go that far. I came to an ocean of tears, deep with depression, with restless, frustrated waves all ruled by a three-year tyrannical storm of expectations. I became a glorified addict to learning. There was nothing wrong with it except maybe you might have thought I was upset with you, the school, but it is not so.

I stayed till the end, for every moment till and even for the end, for "in my end is my beginning." And I want to start again and come back. It will be different but I will never have stopped loving.

At North Branch you will get back what you put in. It is like in the Old Man and the Sea. The further you sail and the more your hands become like mush, the more magnificent a fish you will become. But I think like I have done before. I died and I was reborn, I sailed myself to death and now I am more real than ever, perhaps just like the velveteen rabbit. I feel as if in my ecstatic ferocity I drove my love to the bottom of my once self-nullifying ocean and saw the pain of my past that has now since gone. In its place is left its beauty, my grail. This last weight that kept me down was the confinement of having to go further. I found my grail, and the grail is the quest that is also the answer for you. I want to teach everyone to see heaven in a wild flower through loving them. And then I see that I am mad with life and, yes, I do want to be god.

I answer the question of how I did this at North Branch: I took as much as I could and in that mountain I found some gold, treasure worth keeping deep down inside. But why did I do it? Ever since the first day North Branch loved me, like a parent who gave you life. I was set free, becoming truly alive. All this North Branch will give you. But why do I want to be god? To breathe life into others, make them truly alive, make them see heaven in a wild flower, make them shout for more. Why have I become content, yet so intent, in the poise of water? Why do I write poetry, why do I want to be tender? Why do I think tears precious? Why is my heart in love with wild perfection? Why to me are you a song so much I cannot sing you overlong? Why do my words flow? Why am I free? Why? It is because I can say, I LOVE YOU.

Callum went back to his folding metal chair. The room was throbbing with cheers and clapping. He lowered his head, his elbows on his bare knees. His hair hung down and he rocked slightly, nodding his head. His crumpled speech hung loosely in his hands. Then he looked up. He turned his head and raised it towards the high windows, where the last rays of June's red evening sun came through, lighting up his face.

It was summer again. But I still thought of my students, who were now out in the world. They were near to and in me as much as I hoped that their learning was in them, enmeshed with their hearts. I remembered the last day of school, when I had read to them Donald Hall's story *The Ox-Cart Man*. In the heat of our final morning, the room was absolutely still, the doors wide open. Outside the rooster was crowing through the greening trees. My students crowded close together around the table, some of them holding hands, some with their heads down, some with their eyes closed. This reading, to a roomful of teenagers, was my last offering.

I read each page slowly and held up the pictures, showing them a story about planting and harvesting, getting and spending—a life of bare necessities and bounty, of life made by a patient hand, a life of honest meaning, every gesture one of love or creation or survival. And then the hill farmer from New Hampshire sold it all: the goose-down feathers he had collected in spring, the candles and potatoes, the carved yoke, the syrup from the sap his family boiled and boiled, and the beautiful white ox who pulled the great weight. He sold the ox, his help-mate, and kissed him on the nose. Then he turned around to head home to the warmth of his family, and began all over again.

My voice quavered as I read, and tears rolled down my cheeks. Tears rolled down their cheeks, too. My students, they were as lovely to me, and as loved, as the ox was to the "Ox-Cart Man." We gave everything, we went as far as we could go, and then we parted. I loved their wild, untamed animal hearts, so dazzling and tremendous. I loved watching them grow, struggle, create, stumble. We walked alongside each other for a year or three, and then I kissed them goodbye.

EPILOGUE

These wonderful things
Were planted on the surface of a round mind that was
to become our present
                                time

—JOHN ASHBERY, "A Last World"

W HEN WINN CAME INTO THE SCHOOL SHE WAS excited—to be in middle school, about boys, about friendship, about the world. She loved science and she loved to build stone sculptures by the North Branch River. She loved to speculate about poetry and symbols. In seventh grade, she made a fractal design for math class, then grew obsessed by the idea that the world might replicate itself endlessly, that there was no smooth edge, that there was no end. Contemplating infinity, she hopped and danced in front of the whiteboard in science class, exclaiming: "Don't you see how amazing this is?" She boldly strode into the world ideas and the search for meaning.

She was fascinated with the idea that every creature in the biotic universe had a niche. "And shouldn't it be true that the meaning of our lives is about trying to find our niche, however large or small, our place where we fit and do the most good?" she wrote in her speech. She illustrated a cartoon for science called the "Spark of Life," which explained the origin of everything. She heard a poem at a Winter Solstice performance, "In the Sweetness of Spring," by Guillaume de Portiers IX, and she'd read the poem to the class. When we could not find any information about it, she found a volume that contained it, Robert Bly's *The Soul is Here for Its Own Joy*. She wrote to Coleman

Barks, the world's preeminent translator of Jelaluddin Rumi, to ask him about de Portiers, and Barks wrote us back. On the day she received the letter from Barks, she ran screaming through the school. "He wrote us back! He wrote us a letter!"

She was falling in love with ideas. She was finding her niche.

One day I asked the class to write for ten minutes: "What is the purpose of your existence? Why do you live? Why do you breathe?"

They all began to write. When the ten minutes were up, Winn still had her head down, writing in her minute script, so packed with anylytical and poetic musings.

In lit class the next morning, I asked again: "What is the purpose of your existence? Why do you live? Why do you breathe?"

Winn raised her hand. "I wrote my lit response about those questions."

"Do you want to read it?" I asked.

"Okay." And she began to read. Her life, she wrote, was developing like a fractal. She spoke of the poem she'd heard and of the sweetness of spring. She wrote about finding her niche, her perfect-sized place in the universe. And then she told us about working at Zeno Mountain Farm, a summer camp for disabled adults and teenagers. There, in the summer, she had worked with a disabled boy named David. She had been afraid of him because he was older than her, and he lacked all of the capacities she had believed were normal.

> *And he couldn't really talk. And I didn't know how to talk to him. I didn't know how to move to him, or with him. I was afraid of him. But I shouldn't have been. But I didn't know that. And one day I walked across the yard. He was sitting on a stone wall in the shadow of the barn. He was holding his arms out towards me but I wasn't sure if he was gesturing to me or not. I wasn't sure if I should go to him. But I did. And when I got to him he held out his arms to me and I was pretty sure he wanted me to hug him so I did. And he hugged me. And I just held him there for a long time. It was a real hug. There was real love in it and even though I did not really know him, I could feel that I had love for him.*

After Winn graduated, I did not see her again until the Fourth of July at the town parade in Bristol. On the noisy small streets, in the steaming morning heat, there was the Lincoln Volunteer Fire Department, and the Cub Scout Troop 497 in the back of a truck, waving cheerily to the Bristol citizens who lined the streets in their lawn chairs. There was Miss Teen Vermont in a convertible, there was the Filipino Canadian Marching band, and the New Haven Five-Town champions baseball team riding in the back of a hay-wagon.

And then came the Zeno Mountain Farm. They'd come down from their summer retreat in Starksboro for the parade, and now rode the float they had built with help from volunteers from the community. They were all dressed in white, all of them carrying giant sunflowers like great sweeping wands. There were children, aides, and helpers carrying banners and flags. And then there were the Zeno campers, in wheelchairs mostly, or riding in the backs of pickups, all moving forward with pride and gusto, dressed up as dogs and cats and cows and sheep, smiling huge smiles as they threw candy to the townfolk seated along the parade route. Children scrambled from the curbs as the parade spectators clapped and cheered to the clashing sounds of bass drums and penny whistles, country music, and the intermittent musket-fire of Ethan Allen's Green Mountain Boys. Drums and tambourines banged and rattled, men and women and children danced and twirled in the streets.

And then there was Winn, pushing David in his chair in the middle of the hot street. I remembered her at school, in her backwards John Deere cap, eagerly writing down every important word she heard. I remembered her smearing clay on her cheeks as war paint and diagramming her epiphanies about the secrets of the universe on the whiteboard. Now, like all of her cohort from Zeno Mountain, she was dressed in white. She wore a white taffeta dress fringed with lace, long and billowing in the hot morning sun. A strand of white flowers was woven into her hair, her face lifted up as she walked behind her David. He was beaming, looking from one side of the street to the other, basking, a part of the great celebration. I knew the great reaches she had attained in her years at our school. Her willingness to grapple with any idea, to explore any mental struggle that life offered. As she walked by, I saw her as a poet, a philospher, a mathematician, a suffragette, and no longer quite a child. Winn was smiling too, head turned to the bright day, white petals in her hair, like the bride of the world coming down the aisle.

BRODY QUIT PLAYING HOCKEY in high school. He had a chance to do a semester at sea, and he took it.

"At first, high school was exciting," he wrote me, "with all the people and lockers and regular classes. But then it wasn't exciting at all. I felt like it was grinding my soul to dust. It's hard to find a place like North Branch out in the world."

RUBY CONTINUED HIKING ADIRONDACK PEAKS and spending her summers at a canoeing camp in Northern Ontario. Each summer she was allowed to bring two books ("not enough," she said). She and the other campers portaged all their food and gear and canvas-skin canoes themselves. First it was twenty days out at a time. By the time she was a senior, she was leading fifty-day trips.

"I loved it because it was the closest thing to North Branch I could experience. I knew how to be, how to help, how to be strong. By the end of the summer my Carhartts were in dirty tatters, and that was something I was proud of."

KATELYN GOT A SCHOLARSHIP to the Westover School for Girls. She attended Lehigh University where she majored in marketing. She returned to Vermont, where she became a credit analyst at the National Bank of Middlebury. When I think of her, this girl from Ripton who had been raised by her grandmother, I feel a wonderful wave of joy and astonishment.

After graduating high school, Yebsera had stints in school at Hamilton College and Clark University. "But I wasn't ready," he said.

Instead, he journeyed back to Ethiopia to visit his family. He also spent time in Addis Ababa working in an orphanage.

"I was helping the kids with schoolwork, walking them to their school and church, hanging out with them, teaching them English, and helping around the orphanage with minor tasks. It was a great experience and I think somewhat necessary for my well-being."

But when he first got there, it wasn't easy.

"I was definitely nervous in the beginning, but that quickly turned into confidence and joy," he wrote. "It just felt great to be part of something that helped me so much."

It was not an orphanage set up for international adoptions. Rather, it was to give children the education, care, and support needed to stay in Ethiopia and eventually return to their communities. "These kids are being cared for in ways that, if every kid in the country was also given the same attention, support, and consistency, then I imagine the country wouldn't be the way it is now."

Yebsera later spent a summer on Martha's Vineyard, met a great girl, and is working on his degree in political science at the Harvard Extension School.

Nils took many different roads after graduating from high school. He moved to Brooklyn, seeking to find his way into the electronic music scene, but found the city and living alone for the first time overwhelming. He traveled across the country three times, visiting Yosemite and Burning Man, trying to come into contact with spiritual truth.

"Then I heard about Vipassana meditation from my traveling companions, went to sit that winter, and cemented that path of freedom as one I will follow; throughout many changes and experiences, that has never wavered."

He too then met a girl, yet does not feel any inconsistencies between that and his explorations in identity in eighth grade. Regarding sexual identity: it was "not a fork in the road . . . that aspect of identity was not fundamental. The safety to decide and reveal within the community of NBS (anything about identity no matter what) was and is the important thing."

Nils continues to go deeper into Vipassana and is completing his degree in biology at the University of Vermont.

CALLUM DID INDEED BECOME A FARMER. After he graduated high school, he traveled to Scotland to study cattle farming. When he returned, he worked on a dairy farm in Rochester. He visited the school every six months or so, usually at the end of a day when the students were cleaning up. He'd pull up in his rusty Chevy truck, wearing barn boots and a shredded work coat. He smelled of manure and silage, and I thought of him again, as always, as our Boxer. He'd ask me about how the school was, and he would laugh bemusedly and shake his head at the adolescents shouting around him, swinging their brooms and chasing each other in and out of doors. Occasionally, he would ask me for advice.

"How do you know if what you're doing is the right thing?" he asked once. And I would rush an answer for him, something to encourage, a little thought for him to take with him.

One Friday afternoon, I sat with him at the big-room table to chat, watching the students loudly pack up their bags at the end of the day.

"You told us that the world would be full of love," he said. "But sometimes it's not like that at all. And it seems everyone in the world is living separately, and no one knows anyone, and it's hard to know what the purpose of living is." His lips were quivering.

And I remembered him as a fourteen year old, asking questions, pushing himself to the edge of what he could understand. But he was nearly an adult. He wasn't shouting about geometry problems or running through the woods, or talking about pursuing the wooly mammoth, but he *was* still asking what in the world God made him for.

HALEY'S FATHER DIED THE YEAR AFTER SHE GRADUATED. Everyone in the school had heard about it. The new kids in the class, who had not shared the school with Haley, wanted to know about it. The older kids explained about Haley's years of worry and hope that her father would one day get a new heart. He did finally get a new heart, they explained, but the new heart had given out.

A few months later, Haley wrote me and asked if she could come to visit school.

"To visit, like a lunch?" I asked.

"No, for a day. For the whole afternoon."

"You want to talk about your dad?"

"Yes. I need to spend some time there. At the school I mean."

"Sure, we can do that," I told her.

Of course this did not fit into any normal course of learning, to have a graduated student come back to school to share her feelings about the death of her father. I asked myself the one essential question: *could we learn something vital?* I knew unequivocally the answer was *yes*.

She came on a Friday at lunch. It was a cold day, the sun bright, shining as it did through the glass orbs hanging in the windows. The trees were mostly bare, but when the wind blew, the amber beech leaves shivered in the woods.

The same messes were on the big, honey-colored table where we gathered. Computers covered in stickers. Orange peels and tea-mugs, scraps of paper covered in doodles, a glue-stick missing its top, pencil shavings. The students knew something was different, and they settled more quietly than usual.

I asked her why she wanted to come to the school on this day.

"This is the place where I feel safest," she said. "It's a healing place."

"Tell us about it."

She told everything that had happened since she left the school. She gave background information to the new kids. The summer after ninth grade. Beginning high school in tenth grade. Her father's heart transplant. The failure of that heart, and Bud's body. She cried several times. She told stories about Bud, laughing about how he stubbornly refused to stop lugging stones around his garden when his heart was weak, about his insistence that he get a place on Lake Bomoseen, about his wanting to build new gardens there when he barely had the strength to climb a flight of stairs. I told the class how Bud had always come up to the school on parent workdays and always spent hours weeding the flower beds.

"And he was always smiling and laughing and so happy to be outside with a shovel in his hand," I told them.

"Gardens were his happy place," Haley explained, wiping her tears as she sat at the table in the center of the school, surrounded by twenty-seven kids, some who knew her, some who didn't, but who were all trying their best to understand.

She wrote me a letter later, describing what that afternoon had meant:

> *That afternoon I didn't know one-third of the students, and they didn't know me. But it did not matter. We had more in common than perhaps any other group of thirty people sitting in a room together. We had a place called The North Branch School, which over the course of time built its messy, hallowed structure around each of our amorphous, growing hearts, not to shield or shelter us, but to help us learn to call a place in ourselves "Home."*

WORKS CITED OR REFERENECED

Animal Farm, 1984, George Orwell
*Lord of the Flie*s, William Golding
Siddhartha, Herman Hesse
The Letters of Alfred Steiglitz and Georgia O'Keefe, Vol. I
The Social Contract, "Discourses" Jean-Jacques Rousseau
Romeo and Juliet, King Lear, Julius Caesar William Shakespeare
Sonnet 65, William Shakespeare
"The Last World," John Ashbery
"Ode on a Grecian Urn," John Keats
"Dover Beach," Matthew Arnold
Letters of Keats,
Martin Luther King: speech in Detroit, 1954
"Among School Children," W.B. Yeats
The Red Pony, John Steinbeck
The Old Man and the Sea, Ernest Hemingway
The Road, Cormac McCarthy
The Soul is Here for Its Own Joy, ed. Robert Bly
Che Guevara, "Socialism and Man in Cuba" Letter to Carlos
Quijano, 1965
Emerson: "Essays" "Circles"
James Dickey: "Them, Crying"

Wallace Stevens: "Prologues to what is Possible"
  "Things of August"
The Ox-Cart Man, Donald Hall
Tao Te Ching, Lao Tze
Billy Collins, "The Lanyard"
Stephen Dunn, "Homage to the Divers"
"Down By Law" (film by Jim Jarmusch)
Charles Bukowski, "The Laughing Heart"
Phillip Larkin: "Here"
"Do Not Go Gently Into that Good Night", "Fern Hill,"
  Dylan Thomas
Vincent van Gogh- *The Letters of Vincent van Gogh*
To Kill a Mockingbird, Harper Lee
The Sense of Wonder, Rachel Carson
The Lives of Children, George Dennison
To the Lighthouse, Virginia Woolf
The Power of Myth, Joseph Campbell
Stanley Kunitz, quoted in *A Wild Perfection: The Letters of James*
  Wright
Leaves of Grass, Walt Whitman
Robert Frost, excerpts from "West-Running Brook," "A Late
  Walk," "The Pasture," "The Road Not Taken," "Directive,"
  "Birches," "Mending Wall," "Spring Pools"
Wendell Berry "Manifesto:The Mad Farmer's Liberation Front,"
  "Another Descent"
Richard Wilbur, "The Writer"
Mary Oliver: "When Death Comes," "A Letter From Home"
  "What I have Learned So Far," "The Summer Day," "Starlings
  in Winter," "White Flowers," "Fall Song"
Theodore Roethke, "The Waking"
Gary Snyder—"Why Log-Truck Drivers Wake Earlier Than
  Students of Zen"
Anna Ahkmahtova, "Instead of Preface,"
Wislawa Szymborska, "Miracle Fair," "The Century's Decline,"
  "Landscape,"
Emily Dickinson "The Butterfly Upon the Sky,"
Rabindranath Tagore-Gitanjali 35, *Sadhana*
George Sylvester Morris, quoted in *Dewey: A Life*

Thomas Merton, "Prayer"
Chinook Psalter, from *Earth Prayers*
Sylvia Plath, "Child"
Octavio Paz, *Selected Poems*, "Hymn Among the Ruins"
W.H. Auden, "In Memory of W.B. Yeats"
The Upanishad
The Monkey-Wrench Gang, Edward Abbey,
Ralph Ellison, *The Invisible Man*
Archimedes*: famous sayings*
Rumi, *Kulliyat-e Shams*, 1304 taken from *Essential Rumi* p.63

PERMISSIONS

The author is grateful to the following publishers for permissions to quote lines from poetry throughout the book.

Anna Akhmatova, "Instead of a Preface," from Selected Poems of Anna Akhmatova © 2000 translation by Judith Hemschemeyer. Reprinted with the permission of Zephyr Press.

John Ashbery, "A Last World" from The Tennis Court Oath: A Book of Poems © 1977 by John Ashbery. Reprinted with permission of Wesleyan University Press.

Wendell Berry, "Manifesto: The Mad Farmer Liberation Front" from The Mad Farmer Poems © 2014 by Wendell Berry. Reprinted with permission of Counterpoint Press.

Wendell Berry, "Another Descent" from Roots to the Earth: Poems and a Story © 2016 by Wendell Berry. Reprinted with permission of Counterpoint Press.

Charles Bukowski, "The Laughing Heart" from Essential Bukowski: Poetry © 2016 by Charles Bukowski. Reprinted with permission of HarperCollins/Ecco.

ACKNOWLEDGMENTS

THIS BOOK WAS SOME TIME IN THE MAKING. First I want to thank Green Writers Press, which continues to do great work. Dede Cummings has been a tireless and enthusiastic supporter while shepherding this book to completion. Rose Alexandre-Leach disciplined me and drove me to write with greater clarity and focus. Along the way, a host of wonderful assistants read the book closely and made improvements. I am grateful to Grania Power, Ferne Johansson, Cameron Hope, Tyler Esparza, Chaya Holch, Alicia Tebeau-Sherry, and Kylie Gellatly for their generous contributions.

This book could not have existed without the extraordinary community that is the North Branch School, most especially and the generations of students, past and present. Any teacher worth his or her salt knows that the deepest teaching comes from what the students themselves teach and show. I have been blessed to have students who come to school ready to learn, are happy to be there, and with encouragement, are willing to take a leap. Over and over again, the largeness spirit of my students has been a inspiration.

The parents of our students over the years have exhibited great patience, faith, and humor. Each of these is attributes is vital to a healthy school. Patience and faith, because the process of learning is actually the process of growing, some times slow and difficult; and humor, in order to bear joyfully the turmoil and swings of adolescent children.

The board of the school, past, and present, has supported my teaching and the vision of the school. They have put the school on a firm foundation, creating a place where teachers can teach while seeding into the school trust, love, and appreciation for the sometimes messy process that schools can be. Mia Allen, Cindy and Michael Seligmann, Donna Rutherford, Kim Callahan, Michael Hussey, Bruce Catlin, Francisca Drexel, Sue Halpern, Meg Wyatt, Anza Armstrong, Marcia Croll, Carl Crawford, and Joanna Doria.

I have been lucky to have a number of friends and colleagues whose examples have been guiding lights; Bill McKibben, Jim Ellefson, Tom Verner, Deborah Lubar, Marianne Lust, Steve Holmes, and Eric Warren have all given much.

Finally, I want to thank my wife and colleague, Rose McVay, a devoted and gifted teacher in her own right, and my eternal Camerado.

Allons! the road is before us!

CPSIA information can be obtained
at www.ICGtesting.com
Printed in the USA
BVHW080141221021
619227BV00002B/8